PSYCHOANALYSIS AND ARCHITECTURE

PSYCHOANALYSIS AND ARCHITECTURE
The Inside and the Outside

Cosimo Schinaia

Translated by Giuseppe Lo Dico

Routledge
Taylor & Francis Group
LONDON AND NEW YORK

Originally published in 2014 in Italian as *Il dentro e il fuori. Psicoanalisi e architettura*

First published 2016 by Karnac Books Ltd.

Published 2018 by Routledge
2 Park Square, Milton Park, Abingdon, Oxon OX14 4RN
711 Third Avenue, New York, NY 10017, USA

Routledge is an imprint of the Taylor & Francis Group, an informa business

British Library Cataloguing in Publication Data

A C.I.P. for this book is available from the British Library

ISBN-13: 9781782204114 (pbk)

Typeset by Medlar Publishing Solutions Pvt Ltd, India

Dedicated to Antoinette,
my travelling companion

Author's note

Some texts do not exist in English translation; thus many of the quotes have been translated for this edition.

CONTENTS

ACKNOWLEDGMENTS

I am particularly grateful to Fausto Petrella and Lorena Preta: their intuitions and important reflections have ideally inspired me in this attempt to develop a significant integration between psychoanalysis and architecture. These disciplines seem to be quite far apart, but I believe they are inextricably interconnected. I am also grateful to the architects Riccardo Agnello, Alessandro Baldassarri, Guglielmo Bilancioni, Stefano Boeri, Maurizio Carta, Sara Marini, Enrico Pinna, and Massimo Prontera, and the psychoanalysts Marta Capuano, Matteo De Simone, Giuseppe Pellizzari, Giuseppe Ruggieri, Daniela Scotto di Fasano, and Matilde Vigneri, and the psychiatrists Antonio Maria Ferro e Giovanni Giusto: I had the pleasure of publicly discussing with them the arguments of this book in various Italian cities. The architect Enrico Pinna wrote the Preface to the Italian edition of this book: I am very grateful for his support in this editorial project. I want to thank my old friend Antonino Ferro, the current President of SPI (Italian Psychoanalytical Society), who wanted to pay homage to this book with an endorsement.

Furthermore, I would like to thank the photographers who have allowed me to illustrate some of my reflections on architecture. In particular, I would like to thank Claudia Guderian: she has permitted me the use of her photographic series on consulting rooms and analysts previously published in the magazine, *International Psychoanalysis*. I am also grateful to the architect Esther Sperber and the psychoanalyst Stephen Sonnenberg for their wonderful Foreword and Afterword to this book: I believe they instil optimism for a fruitful collaboration between architects and psychoanalysts. Last but not least, I would like to thank the translator Giuseppe Lo Dico for his patience and competence.

Finally, I want to point out that *Psychoanalysis and Architecture: The Inside and the Outside* had been conceived long before the 2015 encyclical letter *Laudato Si'* of the Holy Father Francis on care for our common home. Beyond my personal point of view about religion, I was deeply impressed by the smartness, the wisdom, the ethical rigor, the competence, and the respect for sciences with which Jorge Bergoglio had dealt with the issue of care for our planet. I appreciated that he did not separate this issue from the cultural, social, economic, and political determinants. Thus, I want to conclude by saying that I am sincerely and deeply grateful to Francis.

ABOUT THE AUTHOR

Cosimo Schinaia is a psychiatrist who has worked as Director of the Mental Health Centre of Central Genoa for many years. He trains and supervises psychoanalysts of the SPI (Italian Psychoanalytical Society), is a full member of the IPA (International Psychoanalytical Association), and works in private practice in Genoa. He has published many scientific papers for Italian and international journals, and his books include *Dal Manicomio alla Città* (From the psychiatric hospital to the city), 1997; *Il Cantiere delle Idee* (The place in which ideas are built), 1998; and *On Paedophilia*, 2010.

FOREWORD TO THE ENGLISH EDITION

Entering and exiting

Esther Sperber

Like a journey, a book begins with the hope of seeing new places, experiencing strange cultures, and discovering hidden aspects of oneself.

Books, like journeys, have many different styles. Some books take us on a business-like trip—efficient, productive, and quick. Others resemble long vacations, meandering in and out of adventures, letting the landscape suggest the next steps on the travel path. Some books follow a direct road from the place of departure to the final destination while others happen upon encounters in an accidental manner. And like a voyage, a book also must bring us back home. We return carrying our new experiences; a photograph of a sunset, the flavour of an exotic dish, and the email address of a fellow traveller with whom we shared a long train ride. Of these memories, some will be cherished and passed on as heirlooms to the next generation. Other experiences will fade over time, adding just a slight tint to the colour of the trip.

Dr. Schinaia's book takes us on his own personal journey through places, academic fields, and ideas that shape the way he sees the world. We are invited to join him, to travel in and out of his memories and to encounter a personal, rich, and colourful new world. It is a complex world that resists the separation into the intellectual disciplines that usually subdivide our world.

There is always a risk when beginning a new book or traveling through new territories and Schinaia reminds us that the only truth the traveller can reference is his place of origin. Our departure point becomes our anchor so that we can dare to meet new encounters and deepen our understanding of worlds around and within us. We embark on this journey accompanied by our past and present, our mother tongue and our professional discourse.

Schinaia tells us how the profound experience of immigrating informed his ability to venture from his original field of psychiatry into architecture, philosophy, literature, art, and poetry. Like Schinaia, I too am living on a continent far from my birthplace and speak an acquired language. And similarly, I have also ventured from my professional home of architecture into the world of psychoanalytic theory.

It was my wish to understand better the creative process in art and architecture that first brought me to the field of psychoanalysis. While traditional views of creativity focus on the artist as an individual, and his conscious and unconscious mental capacities, I was drawn to the understanding of the self as described in relational psychoanalysis, which sees the self as always constituted in an intersubjective, co-created field, between self and other. Given the many participants in the design and construction process even of a simple building, this emphasis on the collaborative nature of innovation resonated with my experience as an architect (Sperber, 2013).

From this personal entry point I followed Schinaia on his exploration of "inside and outside". The book studies the phenomenological experience of architecture, language, and psychoanalysis. It positions them as processes that investigate the complexity of the psychical and physical boundaries between self and other, our mind and the world, the exterior and interior. It reflects on a variety of transitional topics, such as immigration, interdisciplinary studies, languages and their translations, and therapeutic encounters.

Schinaia values the position of the traveller who is always a stranger wherever he may be: "Those who immigrate to another country become foreigners for life." Harnessing his position of otherness, he observes that which is invisible to the natives who comfortably inhabit their unquestioned culture and take their language for granted. With his cultural and professional baggage he sets out to contaminate the existing fields of discourses: "Through a continuous process of crossbreeding, the contributions from different disciplines … can lead to fertile connections and fruitful contaminations" (Chapter Two). It is in the borderline areas of each field that we find nomadic ideas that destabilise and open us up to new understanding.

When architecture and psychoanalysis are brought into conversation, one notes some fundamental differences: "the architect transforms emotions into form, whereas the analyst transforms emotions into languages" (Chapter Three). But as Schinaia continues to demonstrate, forms and language are not entirely different categories. When comparing architecture and psychoanalysis he suggests that psychoanalysis relies on spatial forms such as "the city, the house, room, windows …" (Chapter Three). And just as building elements occupy the imagery of psychoanalysis, syntactic and linguistic structures operate at the base of the architecture-creating cultural statement.

This book, which fosters a conversation between distinct languages, is also quintessentially Italian and European in its intellectual discourse. As a reader immersed in a North American, New York-centred, psychoanalytic conversation, I found myself constantly translating a slightly foreign culture when reading this book. The book reveals a rich discourse, situated in a dense continent of intellectual openness. It moves with ease between fields, quoting freely from philosophy, linguistics, literature, art, architecture, and psychiatry. I was disoriented at first by the many unfamiliar references, finding momentary rest in the familiar voices of Freud, Winnicott, or Bion. But this discomfort is accompanied by the joy of hearing the orchestra of voices that Schinaia brings in each chapter.

In her book *Architecture from the Outside, Essays on Virtual and Real Spaces*, the philosopher Elizabeth Grosz also chooses to study architecture from her own outside position as a philosopher. She posits that outsiderness is both paradoxical and perverse. "It is paradoxical," she writes "insofar as it can only ever make sense, have a place, in reference to what it is not and can never be—an inside, a within, an interior" (p. xv). And it is perverse because while it is defined relative to an inside it does not need to be faithful to the consistency of this inside place (Grosz, 2001). A relationship based on paradox and perversity points to a conflict while also suggesting a relational dependence. Inside and outside can only exist together.

Grosz proposes a new way of exploring philosophy with architecture, as well as other interdisciplinary studies, which is also fruitful for the study of architecture and psychoanalysis. She suggests:

> My central argument throughout is that architecture, geography, and urban planning have tended to neglect or ignore temporality or to reduce it to the measurable and calculable, that is, to space. It is central to the future of architecture that the question of time, change, and emergence become more integral to the processes of design and construction. (Grosz, 2001. p. xviii)

Grosz makes a profound claim that architecture has always avoided, perhaps repressed, the aspect of time that is inherent to any object or being in this world. She therefore turns to the study of temporality in architecture using her philosophical tools "reversing the usual specialisation of time with a temporalisation of space" (p. xx). Through temporality and embodiment, the human situation can become a central actor in the experience of architecture.

If time and bodies become part of the theorising of architecture, replacing style, form, and the modernist idea of space, the particularities of each culture, race, and gender can no longer be ignored by architectural theory. It is the human body, which is always sexed and raced, inscribed with personal and social memory, that inhabits and creates architecture. And it is this body that has always been the centre of the psychoanalytic exploration.

As Grosz has shown, temporality and transformation are central to the relationship of inside and outside. They expose time as an actor in interdisciplinary studies and architecture. A building is not a fixed edifice but is an event of becoming; it enables human experiences to come into being.

Deleuze points to this temporal quality of a building when he writes: "An event does not just mean that 'a man has been run over'. The Great Pyramid is an event …" (Deleuze, 1988, p. 76) A pyramid is an event insofar as an event is a position of form and matter in time. The pyramid, which stands erect in the desert for thousands of years, is a very static event. Nevertheless, this pyramid is not outside of time and it too will slowly transform under the sun, moon, and wind. By juxtaposing architecture and psychoanalysis Schinaia, brings time and memory into our understanding of this ancient culture of building.

Although this book is subtitled *Inside and Outside*, it might have been called *On Entering and Exiting*. While the inside and the outside are nouns, suggesting a pair of interdependent yet separate locations, the terms entering and exiting are gerund forms of verbs that describe a process. Entering and exiting reveal the constant physical and mental motion involved on both the inside and outside and convey the temporal aspect that Grosz suggests. Of course, the prepositions inside and outside are also not fixed. They contain an essential interdependence, as there is no here without a there. We take our own "here" wherever we go, creating "otherness" around us, as we learn in this book.

The words entering and exiting might also create a mistaken impression that there are clearly defined borders between the disciplines that Schinaia is visiting. But the human mind and thought processes tend to exceed the academic and professional disciplines we have come to accept, and recent research supports the claim that innovation flourishes precisely in the borderline zones in between these boundaries. Despite the somewhat arbitrary delineation of disciplines, these categories also have merit. Professional disciplines, like languages, have a heritage and a personality. They are expressions of culture and participate in shaping that culture (Chapter Two). While language is capable of translation, and it is also embedded with that which is unique and cannot be said in a different context.

The desire therefore to explore the intersection of different fields must also acknowledge the places where these fields lack a shared terminology that is needed in order to foster a mutual dialogue; it must notice the moments of inevitable misunderstanding.

Anthony Vidler discusses another interdisciplinary relationship, that of architecture and film. Vidler suggests that "we might treat these field relations as discursive, as conversations among previous and present specificities, as structured in fact on their several resistances, rather than ignoring and collapsing them" (Vidler, 2007, p. xii). For Vidler, interdisciplinary work is best framed as a conversation. This conversation accepts the unique, non-translatable sensibilities of each discussant while also striving to foster a valuable dialogue of links and affinities. Nevertheless, as Vidler notes, an honest dialogic process must respect the inevitable gaps that will emerge when each field encounters the professional language of the other. The conversation must not erase the limitations of a shared vocabulary.

From Grosz and Vidler I take two ideas that are central to the understanding of interdisciplinary work, especially in relation to architecture. Grosz has emphasized the centrality of time and temporality to the field of architecture and Vidler has shown the merit of studying the dialogue between different fields without ignoring the gap in the interaction of two languages. Interdisciplinary work is therefore always a temporal event that unfolds like a journey and a conversation, transcending the simple boundaries of time and place.

Psychoanalysis has developed a theory and methodology for engaging in long and complex conversations. It courageously explores intimacy, empathy, and understanding but also invites the full spectrum of human emotions; desire and aggression play out in the arena of transferences and mutual enactments. Psychoanalysis also resists the simplistic notion of time and place. The analyst respects the multiplicity of enacted transference as indicating both a here-and-now and the projections from then-and-there; the analysis is both a personal intrapsychic event and a mutually co-constructed shared dream. The psychoanalyst acquires a unique set of tools through her ongoing attentive listening to the words of others, noticing the stories that resonate and those that conflict with her own experiences. Psychoanalysis is also unique in its attention to a wide range of human thinking. It respects dreams and fantasy as no less real than rational, scientific modes of thinking.

We are therefore fortunate to join Schinaia in this book journey. His psychoanalytic expertise in the understanding of conversations, and the analytic appreciations for the vast terrain of human experiences both rational and fantasised, make Schinaia a trusted guide on this interdisciplinary voyage. We join him in a journey rooted in the human sense of time, and the intimacy of multi-vocal conversation.

An attempt to study the boundaries of two fields—architecture and psychoanalysis—would have been a sufficient task, but this book's attentive dialogue that fosters a fluid process of entering, exiting and re-entering the many fields and voices it explores. It is an invitation to follow a journey-conversation, unfolding over time, meandering in and out of times and places and gathering insights, dreams, and memories along the way. It takes us along a road full of colours, smells, shadows, and water, revealing the complexity of what it means to be inside and outside.

Esther Sperber
Architect, founder of Studio ST Architects (www.studio-st.com) in New York, and writer on architecture and psychoanalysis

PREFACE TO THE ITALIAN EDITION

Enrico Pinna

Cosimo Schinaia takes us into the deep depths of architecture. In this book, architecture is often characterised as a discipline pervaded by the idea of lightness and dealing with the places of our fantasy. For this reason, it has psychoanalysis as a sort of important friend with which it can deal with the world of human relationships.

Throughout its history, architecture has tried to transfer some relationships from the world of nature to the world of construction, first in an allegoric and mythical way and then in an evocative and suggestive manner. In this sense, it has used and consumed an endless list of icons and symbols. In spite of this, Schinaia's reflections mainly refer to human nature. In this view, architecture seems to be characterised by an excess of metaphorical images. In the understanding of these images, psychoanalysis can provide support to architecture. This is because psychoanalysis aims at helping people to establish a contact with emotions.

Thanks to the presence of emotions, the variety of forms and materials that can be used in construction finds a less narcissistic and more affective synthesis. Every day the architect has to manage much information by using his "grey slate"[1] and only in the evening he can find some rest and, as a consequence, the sensation of feeling good in a place and loving this place. Such a sensation can be defined as empathy for those who will live in the places he is designing and planning: it is the concept of *Heimlich,* that is to say, of a comfortable place, as the architect Anthony Vidler (1992) has clearly described it.

Although it is true that the connections with other disciplines and forms of knowledge have made architecture's framework quite varied and extraordinarily complex, in the case of this book the aim is very clear: discussing the relevance of the human condition for architecture.

The multi-disciplinarity in research is a common feature in the training and formation in many areas of knowledge. We can say that, if we think of Vitruvio or Leon Battista Alberti, it is something intrinsic in the architect's practice. However, if we think of later architects, the view of Adolf Loos is relevant, who in 1924 (p. 77) wrote: "An architect is a builder who has learnt Latin. However, modern architects appear to be more at home with Esperanto." Loos aims at exhorting his colleagues to be aware that their roots are in the ancient world. Thus, it is not by chance that, when Cosimo Schinaia writes about the relationship between Sigmund Freud and archaeology, he refers to a certain classical world (I mean, to a peculiar way in which the classical world was conceived in the same years of life and in the same city, Vienna, of Loos and Freud). I think that the part of Freud's paper in which the citizens are able to find their identities thanks to the excavation works, and to the *talking stones,* is really important:

> The fragments of columns can be filled out into a temple; the numerous inscriptions, which, by good luck, may be bilingual, reveal an alphabet and a language, and, when they have been deciphered and translated, yield undreamed-of information about the events of the remote past, to commemorate which the monuments were built. *Saxa loquuntur!* (1896, p. 189)

It is surprising how Freud conceives the history of architecture in two ways: on the one hand, it is a cornerstone of his analytic theory and, on the other, it can be the possibility for having some simple fun, for example when he admires "the third, Italian, Rome: hopeful and likeable".

I believe this Central European world represents another part of the "big territory" discussed in the book: let's think about *Das Rote Buch* (the red book) that more or less one hundred years ago Carl Gustav Jung started to write. The curator and contemporary art critic Massimilano Gioni put it at the centre of the 2013 art exhibition at the Biennale of

Venice by showing an infinite number of archetypical images aiming at understanding both the individual and the collective unconscious.

If in these years architecture has been able to represent our collective imagination, now it is time to assess whether it is able to represent our collective unconscious. This aim leads architectural research to focus upon the irregular and multi-layered character of mind and thus to propose irregular and multi-layered architectural solutions too.

This book promotes a deep dialogue between disciplines. It is true that the relations between them are often difficult and can result in something shallow. Every time we try to deal with a kind of knowledge different from the one we are expert at, we can either be prone to naivety and misrepresentation or, paraphrasing the writer Foster Wallace, we can swim quite well without knowing what water is. Thus, it is important to visit disciplines other than the one we are part of in a convincing way: this is because commenting and intervening on the environment and on the architecture in which we live is fundamental for both the single user and the community.

I think that what *Psychoanalysis and Architecture: The Inside and the Outside* clearly shows us is how some new discoveries and the recovery of certain visions lost in time or completely novel ones can be really fruitful. The target is to find the identity of our outlook, I mean, the way in which we as individuals conceive the relationships between architecture and life.

It is time to look again at our basic assumptions (always strengthened in our everyday practice): it is certainly fascinating to conceive architecture as analogous to nature, but I believe it is too restrictive. Actually, architecture is analogous to nothing but itself and is a sort of archetype of the space in which people live. Although the many similarities and comparisons with a great variety of organisms can give an idea of architecture as a soft and perhaps evanescent discipline, architecture is actually extremely physical and concrete. It is so also when it uses light materials: for example, in most of the lighting conditions in which it can be found, a flat glass is a nearly impenetrable barrier. Rather, steel is a sort of inescapable cage even in those cases in which it is made thin. I believe architecture is its opposite: what makes it truly light is its possibility to open itself to the world through a simple window.

Enrico Pinna
Architect in Genoa and teacher of interior design at the Scuola Politecnica di Design (Polytechnic School of Design) and the Domus Academy in Milan

We have never prided ourselves on the completeness and finality of our knowledge and capacity. We are just as ready now as we were earlier to admit the imperfections of our understanding, to learn new things and to alter our methods in any way that can improve them.

(Sigmund Freud, 1919a, p. 159)

INTRODUCTION

> There is an age at which we teach what we know. Then comes another age at which we teach what we do not know; this is called research. Now perhaps comes the age of another experience: that of unlearning, of yielding to the unforeseeable change which forgetting imposes on the sedimentation of the knowledges, cultures, and beliefs we have traversed.
>
> (Roland Barthes, 1977, p. 16)

Why is a psychoanalyst interested in architecture? And why would he write a book of reflections on the subject? I can answer these questions in two ways: By referring, first, to the many intersecting pulls of my biography (see Chapter One) and, second, to my continuous need to connect the inside with the outside, psychical reality with physical reality, and vice versa. Such a need has characterised all of my professional life.

The osmosis between the inside and the outside—I mean, the continuous and changeable redefinition of the relations between these areas through their changes and transformations—is a very awkward issue both at the interpersonal and the intra-psychic level. We live inside architectural structures, for instance our homes, but at the same time they live inside our minds: in dreams, for example, we can build architectural structures, modify them, or destroy them.

I did not want to write an essay on the psychoanalysis of architecture because it would have been an excessively biased and, therefore, unfruitful approach. Rather, I have attempted to make a comparison between the language of psychoanalysis and the language of architecture and between the aims of the two fields and their ambition towards the improvement of human wellbeing. In such an attempt I always respected the epistemological statutes and the peculiarities of both psychoanalysis and architecture and maintained the irreducibility of their languages.

Psychoanalysis and architecture are certainly very different fields. In fact, architecture creates private homes and public buildings. It is a process of design and construction that involves many other disciplines and competences. It must consider aesthetical, functional, technological, financial, and legal factors. In comparison to architecture, psychoanalysis is a strictly private affair. In fact, the psychoanalytic relationship takes place in the privacy of the analyst's room and filters the external world only through free associations and interpretations (Sperber, 2014b).

The search for points of convergence aims at allowing fruitful possibilities for the enrichment of both these languages. In this sense, I have not limited the book to a mere co-existence between psychoanalysis and architecture. Rather, I have tried to provide an integration between these apparently distant disciplines (but, as I will try to show throughout the book, they are actually strictly embedded). I believe this attempt at integration has inevitably influenced the style of the book.

I have opted for a tense and unusual writing style. I have let the various authors speak directly as much as possible and I am indebted to all of them. I have built ties between sentences, concepts, disciplines, places, and periods; and, by emphasising the many connections, differences, and difficulties, I have let my personal point of view emerge.

I have deliberately chosen to use many quotations and references. Such a choice is neither pretentiousness nor the need to bolster my arguments and point of view with citations from influential figures. Rather, it is an attempt to propose a debate—I mean, a sort of meshing of harmonies and contrasts beyond time and space.

I believe that my relative lack of knowledge of architecture could have been overcome only through the quoting of architects and architectural historians. Further, as I indicated above, in the name of integrating disciplines I have cited psychoanalysts and architects as well as writers, poets, philosophers, sociologists, and journalists.

I hope that, by the end of the book, the reader will have gained a recognition and an understanding of its leitmotifs and an appreciation of my personal considerations as part of a rich framework of theories, observations, and reflections. I am aware that this framework is wide and varied and not easy to understand: nonetheless, it is also rewarding and stimulating.

The psychoanalyst Donald Meltzer (1992, p. 67) defines psychoanalysis as an autonomous kind of art, no matter whether there are good or even great artisans practising it: "It is a method which is rich enough in its potentialities to allow for the possibility of inspiration and great beauty to emerge."

In his 1978 Paris seminar, Wilfred Bion goes beyond Meltzer's considerations when he makes a comparison between psychoanalysts and artists and encourages psychoanalysts to imagine their consulting rooms as ateliers and to consider what type of atelier they are to work in: "What sort of artist are you? Are you a potter? A painter? A musician? A writer? ... In my experience many analysts don't really know what sort of artists they are ..." (p. 186)

After this encouragement, Salomon Resnik asks Bion: "What if they are not artists?" Bion promptly replies: "Then they are in the wrong job. I don't know what job is any good because even if they are not psychoanalysts they need to be artists in life itself."[1] (p. 186)

I would like to add another sort of artist to the list proposed by Bion. I would ask the analyst: Are you an architect? This is because I want to stress the integrative function of the analysis between the intra-psychic and the interpersonal—I mean, between the internal and the external space. Such a function is crucial and mandatory for analysis since it aims at being an experience inside life and not parallel to it.

It is worth noting that the architect Le Corbusier wrote *homme de lettres* (literary man) as profession in his French identity card. He wanted to indicate the versatile and intellectual character of his professional identity. Laurent Beaudouin writes: "The words of architecture do not explain everything: they translate some images that maintain something inexpressible. In this sense, they can never be a substitute for a drawing line or a drawing. Nonetheless, they are travel companions that can lead us through the dark side of soul" (2007, p. 8).

In Chapter One—The origins of a meeting, I will write about my personal history as an immigrant. Although I was certainly a privileged immigrant, I had to manage a dynamic equilibrium between different polarities: certainty versus uncertainty, the known versus the unknown, familiarity versus confusion, and identification with my origins versus identification with the foreign. I oscillated between extremities: the fear of adapting too quickly and, at the same time, of not integrating enough—the possible risk of not assimilating can foster freedom but also provoke insecurity and instability. I believe that insecurity and instability on the one hand and open-mindedness and readiness on the other are the main feelings that have always accompanied my professional double identity: that of a psychiatrist and that of a psychoanalyst. The continuous exchange between these two identities has allowed and constrained me to empathise with the determinants of people's mental pain. The result of this situation was an anti-conformist flexibility and an intellectual curiosity that has nothing to do with eclecticism. In fact, I have always wanted to maintain a rigorous respect for the scientific status of each discipline I have dealt with. However, through my flexibility and curiosity, I have been able to have an outlook not limited by the boundaries and "orthodoxy" of each discipline. The homes of the psychiatric patients I was treating and the residences in which they often spent most of their lives were in continuous interaction with their internal homes, with the thickness of these walls, and with their possible or impossible accessibility. In the same sense, there was also a continuous flow between the concreteness of the consulting room, the analysands' internal worlds, and the rooms of their dreams.

In this chapter I will also point out that the conversation between different scientific and cultural languages can foster the emergence of new and original forms of language and experience. These forms cannot be conceived as the sum of the languages and experiences of each single discipline, but they assume an unpredictable and autonomous life.

In Chapter Two—Fruitful contaminations, I will deal with the concept of the border and its two functions, that is to say, that of translation among different socio-cultural dimensions and that of identity separation and preservation. The border is phenomenologically ambivalent: in fact, it simultaneously permits relations and conflicts, and tradition and innovation. The method of comparing different disciplines can make use of processes like metaphorisation, analogy,[2] and correspondence. These three processes must be intended as having the function of transferring a certain structure into another field. It is clear that the degree of similarity increases from metaphor to correspondence. Further, the relation among theories can be based upon juxtaposition rather than direct comparison; that is to say, upon the possibility of taking advantage of the co-presence of the various hypotheses available. Such comparative processes (that, as I have just shown, have different and increasing degrees of similarity) are necessary to test whether the various theories or points of view are different and incommensurable, or comparable, or can be partially integrated.

In Chapter Three—The metaphorical architecture of mind, I will underline how significant the archaeological metaphor is to psychoanalytic thinking, specifically in Jung and Freud. I will argue that, in Freud especially, such a metaphor deals not only with historical and scientific knowledge, but also with emotions, affects, feelings, and their figures. However, unlike the archaeological work, the analytical work is not only a matter of simple digging because it calls into question passions that break up the order of the representation and confuse it. Freud's passion for archaeology and his admiration for Schliemann (1881) (a pioneer of archaeology who discovered the site presumed to be Troy) are signs of how the archaeological metaphor is crucial in his own thinking and work. The further reflections of Bion developed and completed the ways in which Freud used the archaeological metaphor. Bion stressed that, in the analytic work, the situation is never static, that it is subject to an easy scrutiny. This is because, unlike archaeological work, analytical work takes place when the conflict is present and thus not in a state of rest or sleep. Finally, the psychoanalyst Christopher Bollas compares creation and destruction as fundamental and intrinsic elements of the human existence and condition. In this sense, he argues that in our minds there will always be two types of construction: the destroyed one and the existing one.

In Chapter Four—Space, I will describe space in its phenomenological aspects. In this sense, I will distinguish between the geometrical space (an object of study of the natural sciences and mathematics) and the anthropological space. I will then consider space according to the thinkers of Gestalt psychology who argue that the leitmotif of every life is the relation, or rather the continuous oscillation, between the inclusion and exclusion of our psychological space from the environment. Freud conceived space as having a fictional value. In other words, he always considered it an invented space that can be represented only through a metaphor for the construction of the first and the second topic of psychic apparatus. The psychoanalytic inquiry on space as a mental process begins with Winnicott's research on the starting organisation of the self and his description of the transitional space. The transitional space takes place between the subjective and omnipotent space of the child and the objective and physical space of the external reality experienced through the mother-infant relation. I believe that, finally, almost all the psychoanalytic models of mental functioning focus on the complex relations between internal and external space, between intra-psychic and inter-personal reality. I think that all these relations are also the main focus of the reflections of many architects.

In Chapter Five—The architecture between past, present, and future, I will deal with one of the fundamental problems both of architecture and psychoanalysis. How can we integrate the past and present? And how can we predict the future from the present?

I will provide a precise description of the fundamental concepts at the heart of the International style, an architectural movement emerging in the 1920s and 1930s that wanted to make a clean sweep from the past. I will examine the many frequently strong criticisms against this movement by philosophers and architects of different schools of thought.

I will show that the vigorous and apparently rigid stances are not actually dogmatic. I can even say that the general framework of the debate on the International style is characterised by disunity and fragmentation. Le Corbusier, Gropius, Aalto, and Mies van der Rohe on one side and Lloyd Wright, Loos, Kahn, and Libeskind on the other strictly defend their positions and are supported by philosophers such as Heidegger, Ortega y Gasset, Adorno, and Benjamin. I will conclude the chapter with a description of the concept of no place proposed by the anthropologist Marc Augé: I will argue that the corruption of the International style has fostered the creation of places without life, that is to say, of places unfit for habitation as intended by Heidegger.

In Chapter Six—Continuity and discontinuity in psychoanalysis, I will continue to discuss the issues of the previous chapter and I will also consider the relationship between psychoanalysis and postmodernism. Some psychoanalysts who endorse postmodernism argue that we have participated in an out-and-out social mutation that requires new and innovative ways of thinking. In fact, according to these psychoanalysts, the old and traditional ways of thinking are obsolete and inadequate for describing new subjectivities and new psychopathologies. Other psychoanalysts contradict this theory and argue that the analytic ways of thought proposed by Freud are sufficient for understanding the new phenomena. I believe that there is a third position between the excessively pessimistic "everything has changed" and the excessively optimistic "nothing has really changed". Such a position is certainly harder and more difficult to take but, in my opinion, it cannot be avoided. In fact, I think that today we must continually deal with a subject characterised by a "radical nomadism" and subjectivity no more definable and containable in rigid symbolic structures. In this sense, I think it is necessary to avoid identifying the phantasmatic dimension with some of its historical forms and appearances.

Erik H. Erikson (1964, p. 125) has defined fidelity as "the ability to sustain loyalties freely pledged in spite of the inevitable contradictions of value systems". However, I think that it is not a sign of fidelity to rigidly adhere to a certain worldview that does not consider the sociocultural complexity it aims at understanding. Rather, such a rigid adhesion could be seen as a defence of the orthodox and traditional view.

In Chapter Seven—The haste in the world around us, I will discuss the issue of time for elaboration, defined by the psychoanalyst André Green as *le temp mort de l'analyse* (the dead time of analysis) and by the architect Francesco Venezia (2011, p. 29) as the conceptual basis of an architectural project slowly taking shape. "The slower the settling of thoughts for building up this sort of conceptual basis, the faster the conception and the realisation of the project."

In Chapter Eight—The uncanny in architecture, I will start with Freud's essay *The "Uncanny"* (1919b) to argue that contemporary architects should design and build places, both public and private, hospitals and houses, that represent the distinction and/or the non-distinction between self and non-self, chaos and order, separation and non-separation. They should conceptualise spaces able to contain many complex requirements, compositions, and decompositions of the subject, constructions, and deconstructions. I think that such spaces should be able to care for and be hospitable to those parts of the mind often assessed as hostile or uncontrollable. In other words, the parts of the mind that we want to eliminate, repress, ban, or militarise.

I will discuss the architectonic research of Frank Gehry and I will provide an analysis of one of his works, specifically the Gehry House in Santa Monica. In my view, this work clearly represents the possibility of constituting a space that is both able to contain and to overturn its order, a space that guarantees recognition and hospitability to those mental aspects difficult to normalise and to put into traditional architectonical contexts.

In Chapter Nine—Psychoanalysis and architecture: the need for an interdisciplinary debate, I will try to make a comparison between the language, aims, work methodologies, and continuous osmosis between the theory and practice of both psychoanalysis and architecture. I will attempt such a comparison while remaining respectful of the epistemological statutes of the two disciplines, but without a diminished passion for seeking interactions between them. I believe that the deeper meaning of psychoanalysis and architecture is, first, to live in the immediacy of the direct emotional experience; second, to presuppose a fine ability to listen; and third, to provide a more weighted analysis of what has happened in the here and now of a psychoanalytic session or of a technical assessment of the ways in which its construction has led to certain aesthetical qualities of a building.

In Chapter Ten—The house, I will make a comparison between architectural theories relating the structure of the human body with that of the house[3] and the various modalities in which homes are represented in dreams. These modalities assume the function of a clock, compass, and thermometer in the analytic relation. I will assume that the mathematical figure of the Möbius strip can represent passage from the traditional monolithic home, closed and characterised by rigid distinctions between inside and outside, to the disembodied home, dematerialised and telematic, without defined borders and without any possibility of rigid distinctions between inside and outside. The home, intended as a metaphor for the warm and comfortable uterus but also as a sort of prefiguration of the outside and of autonomy, is conceived as the background for some reflections on the psychoanalytic setting. Crucial in such a setting is the construction of the external space that, although it cannot directly refer to the psychological home, should increase the possibilities of listening to the internal world and of staying in emotional contact.

In Chapter Eleven—Therapy places, I will consider hospital architecture and, specifically, mental health departments. The old psychiatric hospitals were designed and built according to a logic of neat separation between sane and insane, normal and abnormal, and so on, with the clear aim of reclusion and exclusion. The closure of the old psychiatric hospitals has not led to a renewed conception of spaces suitable for mental pain. In this sense, these new hospitals cannot be conceived of as truly therapeutic. There is a lack of reflection on therapy and assistance models that can be at the basis of a specific architectural project. There is no model capable of proposing routes, trajectories, and functionally and formally specialised spaces connected to those interstitial places where informal communication can be encouraged. I will propose the architectural model of the monastery or convent as a reference for planning new collective psychiatric structures. Such a model consists of various parts: there are places absolutely private and intimate like cells and other areas where a minimal degree of ritualised social relations is possible through a silent presence like the courtyards. Further, there are places dedicated to proper ritualised social relations like the church, and others where communication must always be controlled, but it is certainly less ritualised than the refectory. Finally, there is a place for meetings and public debate like the chapter house. I will argue that this type of place can be considered the prelude to the world outside and to social life. I will conclude the chapter by describing the collaboration between psychiatrists and psychologists and the Genoa University Faculty of Architecture: this experiment concerns research on the chromatic requalification of an old mental health centre.

Chapter Twelve—The analyst's consulting room, which is fully illustrated with images, will consider the architectural achievement of the analytic space. I will underline how the construction of a specific therapeutic place has evolved from the room of its inventor, Sigmund Freud, into today's consulting rooms. I will stress that such an evolution has been influenced both by different psychoanalytic ideologies and by various cultural, architectural, geographical, and climatic aspects. I will describe how these influences have characterised the composition of the room and the furniture in it. Through the presentation of some clinical vignettes I will show how the organisation of the external space figures very deeply both in the making of the internal world of the analysand and in the transference relationship with their analyst. I will argue that this happens because patients often view the space of the analyst's consulting room as a sort of representational extension of the analysts themself.

In Chapter Thirteen—Some notes and suggestions on a possible partnership between architects and psychoanalysts, I will deal with the issue of ethics in architecture, and issues between certainty and responsibility and between creativity and attention to the context, to people's social and existential needs. I will argue in favour of architecture and town planning able to interpret the needs and even the desires of citizens: this can be done only by listening to them and making them participate in the designs and in their realisation. I believe the main aims of critical and wise town planning are to construct green areas, to facilitate communications between the different parts of the city, to reduce private traffic, to lower energy consumption, and to improve forms of ecologically sustainable systems in order to reduce pollution.

Sigmund Freud argued that every psychoanalyst must necessarily know of literature and wrote (1907a, p. 92): "We probably draw from the same source and work upon the same object, each of us by another method. And the agreement of our results seems to guarantee that we have both worked correctly."[4] *Mutatis mutandis*, I believe the same can be said for architecture: the dialogue between architectural and psychoanalytic knowledge in a fruitful relationship with the individual and social history can provide important insights into the complexity of the symbolic system that unifies people, houses, and cities.

In this sense psychoanalysis and architecture can come together in the service of conceptualising and designing homes, analysts' consulting rooms, and, more generally, new mental health services. Such a convergence can allow for the improvement and increased possibilities of psychic and spatial containment in a continuous coming and going between inside and outside.

CHAPTER ONE

The origins of a meeting

Ithaca has given you the wondrous journey:
Without her you'd never have set out.
She has nothing left to give you any more.

If you find her poor, Ithaca has not deceived you.
As wise as you've become, with such experience, by now
You will have come to know what Ithacas really mean.
(Konstantinos Kavafis, *Ithaca*, 1911, p. 37)

To belong to our home place and to set in new contexts

In Kavafis' poem the island of Ithaca is a metaphor. It is the destination at the end of an experiential journey during which the traveller becomes aware of the human condition and asserts the autonomy of his conscience and the freedom to define himself. The arrival is of no importance: the meaning of the journey is found in the adventures experienced in a dangerous world. The only monsters the traveller encounters are those existing in his archaic imagination. They annihilate, devour, and paralyse. Because man has to face the unknown outside of himself, he is forced to confront the unknown inside of himself. The only truth he can make reference to during the journey is his place of origin. This is a place that prompts the questions encouraging man to start his journey and this place of origin accompanies and transforms him throughout. In the end, one's place of origin is where answers and peace are found.[1]

It is likely that my birth in Taranto, a city in Apulia (a region in the south of Italy that was once the capital of Magna Graecia. Situated in the middle of a gulf, Apulia faces the part of the Mediterranean known as the Ionian Sea) has favoured the making of a professional life at the crossroads of different specialisations and interests. It is also likely that Genoa, where I have settled for reasons of work, has become my Ithaca due to a sort of recognition and recovery of my roots. Genoa, a city in Liguria (a narrow region in the north of Italy at the border with France) is a superb seaside town like Taranto: it has a large port and is located in the middle of a gulf in the Ligurian Sea.

The focus on the relationships between the home place and the new context must be wide and able to comprehend various points of view.

In *The Four Quartets* (1943, p. 17) the poet Thomas S. Eliot writes: "Home is where one starts from." However, from a different perspective, in his *Mediterranean: A Cultural Landscape* (1987, p. 7) the writer Predrag Matvejevic seems to reply to Eliot in this way: "Eventually the place of embarkation will be less important than the place of destination, and what we have seen and how." Both Eliot and Matvejevic's perspectives are able to consider the various and conflicting features of emigrating.

To emigrate is to be confronted with the new and the unknown: it means allowing yourself to be traversed by the unknown without allowing yourself to be assimilated by it, without being annihilated by dismay, and without feeling threatened. At the same time, emigration fuels the need to firmly preserve one's roots and allows them to grow in the face of otherness: this means to not ignore that your original identity is always inside of you, but rather to slow down that hard work of transformation that aims at reaching a separation from our origins. Emigration means having experienced the loss of the container object. Such a feeling is strictly connected to the removal of the indigenous reference points. The ethnologist and philosopher Ernesto De Martino (1952) has called it "territorial anxiety" and the psychoanalysts Leon and Rebeca Grinberg (1984) "protective deficiency".

The subject desires integration into a new culture and thus he has to face an opposing resistance to integration that places him in a state of affective ambivalence. "The person who emigrates faces a sort of double absence: the absence of the world that she has left behind and, at the beginning, the absence of the world in which she lives now." (Algini & Lugones, 1999, p. 13)

In her poem *Homesickness* Marina Tsvetaeva (1934, p. 102) sorely expresses a feeling of indifference from which we can see a glimmer of hope:

> Houses are alien, churches are empty
> everything is the same
> but if by the side of the path one
> particular bush rises
> the rowanberry …

Migration implies crossing not only a geographic border, but also a cultural and existential one. This is because the border represents the utmost place of transformation and transition. In other words, the fact of being in transit implies a complex process of psychic transformation and discussion at the relational and cultural level. The border defines a whole psychic dimension in which we can stay for a significant time. In fact, a true process of reformulation of identity requires time (De Micco, 2014b).

Let's think about Freud's long journey:

> Freud was born in a border town and went to live in Vienna, a city near the border of Western Europe. Later, he went to study in Trieste and then in Berlin, both border cities. Is this a coincidence? Perhaps we can say that, by gladly accepting the decisions of destiny, Freud developed a great passion for frontiers, ridges, crossroads … borders, forks, deviations, in few words, for that line that cannot be precisely placed and able to connect and separate different areas. (Ricci, 1995, pp. 18–19)

Leon and Rebeca Grinberg (1984) argue that the migration experience is an out-and-out rebirth experience. This is because, in such an experience, it is necessary to again travel through a complete developmental path in a foreign country. In a certain sense, the migrant experiences again the condition of the child who, at the beginning of life, does not know the meaning of language and must orient herself through the emotional undertones of communication. The more dreadful and distressing these tones, the less comprehensible they are. The more chaotic, emotion-laden, and persecutory they sound, the less acceptable and representable they will be.

This situation involves learning to tolerate and perhaps to endorse an ambivalence both insurmountable and fruitful. This is difficult to do without running the risk of losing focus, that is to say, running the risk of falling into an unstable equilibrium between security and insecurity, the known and the unknown, recognition and disorientation, identification with the origins and identification with the stranger.

In ancient Greece, the centre of the agora was where the moneychangers could be found. Anyone who wanted to start a journey had to pass through the peristyle, to stand up and be counted, to approach a moneychanger in order to finally improve her future purchasing power (Nunzio, 1976).

The psychiatrist Flavio Pavan argues that this ritual has a hidden symbolic meaning:

> Going out into the open space is a prelude to separation from the protection of the mother country. In a condition of relative absence of references in which the traveller has to face the fear of a painful experience of isolation and alienation, the ritual offers her a person with whom to identify. This can inspire her capacity to adapt to new realities and to acquire new horizons free of the most threatening aspects. The position of moneychangers in the centre of the agora is umbilical. In fact, it indicates the future separation and gives testimony to the choral interest of community for the experiences of others. Community members consider these experiences of exploration and the return of one any of them as possibilities of growth for all of them. (1984, p. 256)

The psychoanalyst Giovanna R. De Ceglie writes of symbol formation and notes that:

> The Greek word *symbolon* means a sign of recognition. The symbolon was an object that was broken in half by two people, each retaining one piece. After a long absence from one another, when reunited they would match the two pieces together as a sign of recognition of their relationship. The symbolon is a representation of our need to

> grow and separate without losing our sense of belonging to our origins … Without the symbolon we would not manage separation … Without separation we would not be called upon to exercise the function of creating symbols and with them to furnish our internal home. (2005, p. 103)

Recognition of our self occurs through a type of prior disorientation caused by otherness, that is to say, in the house of someone different from us, a foreigner. We are forced to expose ourselves out of our own houses (Pesare, 2007).

The philosopher and sociologist Jean Baudrillard (1990, p. 197) writes: "The other is what allows me not to repeat myself for ever."

The philosopher Gianni Vattimo (1989) points out that the achievement of a continuous oscillation between belonging, displacement, and reintegration is the only possibility for a contemporary human being to dialectically experience a new world. Such a world is certainly full of differences, but also offers a great wealth of wisdom and freedom.

According to the anthropologist Franco La Cecla:

> To lose yourself is … either the state of origins, the need and the land from which you start or restart to direct yourself. There is a cultural process between losing and directing yourself. Such a process is to make the external and fortuitous occasions favourable, that is to say, to make the unknown hospitable and comfortable. For example, to direct yourself could mean … all frustrations, failed attempts, acquaintances, long waits, senses of a new reality, life preservers made up of people and places. Day-to-day all these things start as an elementary network … that becomes more and more complex and permits both to recognise and include the remaining unknown sites and to part from and return to more familiar places. (2000, pp. 16–17)

The back and forth between losing ourselves and meeting ourselves again, between the house of the other and one's own house can also be a possibility for balancing the necessary separateness of the impersonal and the pre-individual dimension of the mind. That is to say:

> The separateness can be meaningful only if we can keep it in fluctuation with the impersonal and pre-individual dimension of the mind. Such a dimension ensures permeable borders and

> allows sharing and empathising. Then, the differentiated and the undifferentiated are the two focal points in the formation of the subject. (Ambrosiano & Gaburri, 2013, p. 19)
>
> Creativity … implies a capacity to regress and to not be differentiated or, more precisely, to become more complicated and complete. The human psychic development risks being (and generally is) the output of a progressive depletion. For realising some of our many starting potentialities, any one of us slowly forgets the most of them. Only one who can psychically return to the conditions in which these potentialities could be represented can see the external stimuli in a new way and thus think about new solutions from the inside. (Semi, 2014, pp. 178–179)

Between eradication and hyper-adaptation

To build up new points of reference, to get accustomed to new sights, to settle into new contexts, and to continuously provide necessary mediations and translations between them allows us to "learn to learn" (Bateson, 1972). This means reconsidering features taken for granted and becoming involved again. In other words, this means allowing fantasies of a new beginning in opposition to those feelings of having sacrificed, blocked, or censored some authentic aspects of the self in order to adapt to the environment. As stated by the philosopher and historian Tzvetan Todorov (2002), the individual can remove himself from his country, language, and childhood traumas because members of the human species can continuously modify themselves.

An obstacle to communication and to an exchange without suspicions is certainly the language and the accent. This is because the accent immediately identifies a foreign person or a stranger.

As the anthropologist and sociologist René Girard (1982, p. 153) points out, "the person with the accent, any accent, is always the person who is not from here. Language is the surest indicator of the being with."

However, linguistic difference includes not only "a vocabulary and a syntax to learn, but also facial expressions and gestures to recognise and symbols to appreciate … Joys and afflictions have not the same translation everywhere" (Pélicier, 1964, p. 2719). Thus, some inevitable errors of interpretation of the surrounding world and its messages are always possible (Frigessi Castelnuovo & Risso, 1982).

I believe there is the risk[2] of adopting a compensatory mechanism of hyper-adaptation to a new environment, I mean, a superficial and artificial assimilation into the new culture without an authentic working through. In this sense, a person runs the risk of creating a sort of robotic false self with conformist features, which rigidly submits to rules and is inhibited in its affects.

Beyond the rhetoric of enhancement provided by hybridisation and hybrid cultures, so-called multicultural societies offer an unsettling and unstable panorama. In fact, in such a panorama, the uneasiness of identity appears multiple and painful due to a total lack of tools for subjective appropriation of radical anthropological transformations caused by the migration itself. Immigrants often experience a dramatic collapse of their symbolising apparatus (De Micco, 2014a). The discomforts of such a collapse are often hidden behind masks of perfect integration that are built up by privileging certain attitudes that act as camouflage. Actually, nomadic identities are built along uncertain and unstable cultural boundaries and continuously struggle to find a psychic place in which to live and a symbolic space in which to lay roots (De Micco, 2012).

According to the psychoanalyst Silvia Amati Sas (2010), if our unconscious were penetrable by the mentality of others, it would be as if our mind were pervaded in a natural, not disturbing, and free-from-anxiety (that is to say, free from alienation and perplexity) manner. In this manner our mind would become part of the obvious and the implicit natural world living in us and that surrounds us.

However, the sociologist Georg Simmel (1908) argues that the foreigner learns to adapt in a more conscious and penetrating (though painful) way compared to those who live their belonging as a right without a conflicted relationship to their environment. An accent that identifies a person as a foreigner or a stranger can constitute an obstacle to communication and generate suspicion.

According to the sociologist Richard Sennett (2008), the changes required to modify relations between human beings and the physical world are so great that only a certain sense of self-displacement and estrangement can lead to concrete practices of change and to the reduction of our consuming desires.

In this hustle of psychoanalysis and sociology, the psychoanalyst Claudio Neri (1999) reminds us that although domestic objects can give us comfort, they cannot help us to recover the vital force, that is to say, the energy of life enhancement. This energy can only come with the meeting of a stranger.

On this point, the psychoanalyst Antonio Alberto Semi argues that:

> Only a careful consideration of the original effects and of the possibility of building up new representations up at every level of psychic life allows the individual to detach himself from the original internal objects and from every lost object. Such a detachment has certainly a human dimension because it permits the assessment of experiences with these lost objects as unique. Further, it permits the assessment of these objects as different in respect from those that are now represented as new and noticeable. It is only in this way that the nostalgia for the beloved and lost objects would not be held in grievance against possible new objects that cannot take the place of the old ones or give up to the narcissistic presumption of morbidly repeating a lost object and the relation with it. It is only in this way that the nostalgia will emerge as something clear, recognisable (because it was already recognised), and able to guarantee psychic continuity. This is because it represents such a continuity and even before the reality of desire. (2014, pp. 47–48)

Literary critic Jean Starobinski writes:

> Nowadays … nostalgia no longer indicates a lost homeland, but rather it goes back to those stages in which desire did not have to take into account the outside obstacle and was not condemned to defer its fulfilment … The problem appears in case of a conflict between the needs of integration into the adult world and the temptation to preserve the privileges of the infantile situation. (1966, pp. 116–117)

In short, nostalgia is conceived as a sufferance for one's lost childhood in the face of frustrations to which adult life exposes us. But perhaps we need to go beyond Starobinski's theory to hypothesise that migration exposes people to a condition of fragility because it reactivates areas of psychic life devoid of any form or structure. The ego perceives these areas in forms of widespread feelings of anxiety that completely escape cognitive capacity (Algini & Lugones, 1999).

These areas can lie dormant for a long time until a new existential condition (for example, an illness or, simply, old age and with it the need to reconstruct the pieces of one's life) allows them to find expression through nostalgic pain. One of the characters in W. G. Sebald's novel *The Emigrants,* whose recollections of his homeland had long been left by the wayside of his memory, begins to remember forgotten impressions. Sebald metaphorically links this condition to news published in a Swiss newspaper about the discovery of the remains of the Bernese alpine guide Johannes Naegeli in a glacier: "And so they are ever returning to us, the dead. At times they come back from the ice more than seven decades later and are found at the edge of the moraine." (1992, p. 23)

The psychoanalyst Nicole Berry (1982) argues that separation anxieties are related not only to separation from the mother, but also from the house. In fact, the house can be seen as the elective projection place of an archaic topography. Separation anxieties may flare up during the experience of relocating and moving into a new house, sometimes resulting in the formation of considerable psychopathological conditions (Fava & Gentile, 1984).

The psychiatrist and psychoanalyst Alberto Eiguer defines the different emotions and representations of psychological displacement as:

> the return of excitement, the end of the ability to represent, the confusion about space and time, and the nostalgia for internal objects or the fear of their revenge. But, above all, it is the unfamiliarity that appears as typical. This is because the eradication provokes an ego reorganisation through a rupture of the feeling of identity continuity or the strengthening of the splitting which appears as an attack to identity … The pain and the guilt for having wished this rupture reinforce the feeling of eradication more than they can appease it. (1999, p. 106)

For La Cecla (2000), to become lost and to settle down in a place are largely unconscious primary processes. These processes identify a map with a territory through analogy and correspondence. Such operations cannot be performed in a conscious way or through secondary processes based on distinction and topography.

The psychoanalysts Davide Lopez and Loretta Zorzi Meneguzzo (2005) take a position against the Kierkegaardian logic of either/or and endorse the Hegelian paradigm, both/and, in the context of human relationships. In the Hegelian paradigm, thesis and antithesis coexist in synthesis and this can be seen as a fundamental assumption of their approach to complexity theory. Such an approach focuses on the dynamic construction of the complementary and distinct and supplants the strict logic of identity and of constrictive binary patterns that force thoughts to polarise in an oppositional manner.

Leon and Rebeca Grinberg argue that the acquisition of a sense of identity is the result of a continuous process of interrelationships between spatial, temporal, and social integration. "The ability to continuously feel similarly to the same person during a series of changes is the foundation of the emotional identity experience. It involves the ability to remain stable through all the transformations and changes of life." (1975, p. 9)

The psychoanalysts Laura Ambrosiano and Eugenio Gaburri argue that:

> The game between the environment and a certain number of unknown but specific dispositions of the person leads immediately to a rich and complex interplay between object investment and identification, between the principle of pleasure and the principle of reality, between the primary and the secondary thought, and between oceanic resonance and differentiation … We are continually suspended between a kind of malleability, which blends all of us into pre-individual and undefined organisms, and a push to differentiated development. In fact, we continuously run the risk of merging into what Freud called the "primordial soup" at one extreme and of becoming rigid and closed on the basis of a fantastic subjectivity immune to the influence of the other at the other extreme. (2013, pp. XVI–XVII)

The psychoanalyst Michael Balint (1959) distinguishes between ocnophil and philobat. The former is characterised by a strong attachment to people and places of origin. The subject lives with the illusion of being safe as long as they remain in contact with an object that signifies security. In contrast, the latter tends to live independently and seeks pleasure in adventures, travels and, in general, new emotional experiences. The philobat illusorily believes that he does not need objects (in particular, special objects) at all and wants to be completely self-sufficient. According to the Grinbergs (1984), Balint's categories are not *per se* an index of mental health. Ideally, equilibrium is achieved between ocnophilism and philobatism so that one can act in one way or the other depending on the circumstance and situation.

Psychoanalysis and psychiatry

From the outset, psychoanalysis has contaminated my psychiatric training and, in turn, psychiatry has contaminated my analytic training. Even when explicitly and obstinately anti-institutional, my psychiatric work was supported by my personal analysis and my work in the consulting room. In turn, my activity as a psychoanalyst greatly benefited from my experience as a psychiatrist specialising in serious mental illness.

The feeling of being on the border increases one's sense of freedom (such a feeling depends on the possibilities available for being able to switch from one situation to another) on the one hand and challenges one's sense of identity on the other. This sense of identity is often confused with the need to belong to something and is linked to primitive evolutionary mechanisms that lead to forms of idealisation and/or splitting. A more evolved and developed use of one's own ideological, scientific, cultural, or personal beliefs can lead to unsaturated positions and to reparative tendencies. In these tendencies, concern and responsibility for the life and the destiny of the individual and the community predominate (Grinberg & Grinberg, 1975).

The psychoanalysts Laura Ambrosiano and Eugenio Gaburri argue that:

> When the ego ideal gives way to the conformity pressure, it ends up being completely guided by the group's ego ideal and he cannot have any personal position … In these circumstances, even the super-ego is degraded and thus the archaic and megalomaniac part of the mind (the one that offers the individual indisputable mafia-like rules, rigid ideologies, or a saturated worldview) dominates. (2013, p. 127)

An Argentinian psychoanalyst who immigrated to Italy many years ago, Gianfranco Nicolussi (1996), says that those who emigrate to another country become foreigners for life. Even if they were to return to their country of origin, the country would no longer be a part of them in the same way in which it was prior to their departure. To return is to emigrate again. The place of origin to which the immigrant returns is no longer the one left behind, and the person who left is no longer the person who returns.

The Iranian psychoanalyst Gohar Homayounpour writes:

> There was nobody more Iranian than me outside of Iran and nobody less Iranian than me in Iran; as it is, I have trouble recognising myself now. Where has all my steadfast love for my country gone? What am I to do with this new knowledge about myself: the mirage that has been taken away from me, while behind it I had to come face to face with myself as an absolutely non-patriotic citizen? … It seems we are destined to suffer guilt if we have become incapable of seeing our motherland as flawless, and have recognised that our paradise is nowhere to be found, especially not in our homeland, and that our paradise is forever lost. (2012, pp. 58–59)

When the writer Marcel Proust returned to Illiers, his childhood home, he had the impression that the landscape had got smaller. The Illiers landscape was no longer as big as it was when he had looked at it through the eyes of a child. Only the adoption of creative writing allowed him to recover the apparently reduced size of the landscape (Mancinelli, 2012).

In *Invisible Cities* the Italian writer Italo Calvino (1972) writes: "The city exists and it has a simple secret: it knows only departures, not returns."

In his poem *La Vuelta*, Jorge Luis Borges beautifully describes a similar concept:

> At the end of my years in exile
> I returned to my childhood home
> and its space continued to be foreign to me.
> …
> And how much brittle new moon
> will infuse the garden with its tenderness
> before I recognise my house
> and it becomes a habit once again. (1923, pp. 50–51)

My own eccentric identity made possible my involvement in the creation and management of *The Salt Road* (*La Via del Sale*), a Genoese journal of psychiatry. I can say that, for some years, such a journal inspired a fruitful and intense cultural debate. The road has always metaphorically represented the possibility of a transit and of traversing the unknown and thus the desire of knowledge. For example, Freud presented *The Interpretation of Dreams* in a letter to Fliess dated 6 August 1899 in these terms:

> The whole thing is planned on the model of an imaginary walk. First comes the dark wood of the authorities (who cannot see the trees), where there is no clear view and it is very easy to stray. Then there is a cavernous defile through which I lead my readers—my specimens with their peculiarities, their details, their indiscretions, and their bad jokes—and then, all at once, the high ground and the prospect, and the question: "Which way do you want to go?" (1899, p. 290)

One of the oldest salt roads in Europe began in the port of Genoa, crossed the Apennines and the Alps, and permitted merchants to move their goods through the continent. The name of the magazine emphasised practicality and openness. The editors were to be road workers who would restore and keep the road open and traversable. In the magazine's first editorial, mental health workers, psychiatrists, psychologists, social workers, and nurses were invited to reflect on and write about the relationship between psychiatry, psychology, psychoanalysis, medicine, and the humanities:

> In brief, we would like to gather emerging issues, areas of painful working-through, and collective thoughts *in statu nascendi*. We would like to be able to understand what's going on in the different areas, to propose a common reflection (of course, respecting different individualities) and to leave space open for original contributions. (Schinaia, 1997b, p. 12)

I was also a member of the editorial board of *Psiche*, the Italian Psychoanalytic Society's journal of psychoanalytic culture. The first *Psiche* editorial clearly expresses the aims of the journal:

> It would be interesting to try to bring the subject matter of the psychic apparatus into other fields of knowledge, that is to say, to introduce such a subject matter into areas where it has never been considered important or necessary. This means to

> stimulate a debate and a discussion; that is to say, to bring out this unspoken thing that stays within us and gives substance and form to all our knowledge. In this sense, *Psiche* should act as a two-way bridge. It would receive languages and experiences different from the psychoanalytic one and, at the same time, it would promote psychoanalytic discourse within other disciplines. (Preta, 2002, p. 9)

Because of my interest in cultural intersection and interdisciplinarity, I have been a long-time member of two boards of the European Psychoanalytic Federation: the Interface Party and the Outreach Platform. As a member of these boards I was involved in the study of the connections between psychoanalysis and other disciplines both scientific and humanistic. Further, I have taken part in various events of the Genoa Festival of Science, organising and participating in debates and symposia with philosophers, scientists, sociologists, historians, and architects. In 2003 the architect Enrico Pinna and I founded Architecture, Modernity and Sciences (AMS), a cultural association in Genoa focused on issues emerging from the interrelationship between architecture and mental health-related disciplines. By specifically looking at contributions from Europe and America, the AMS focuses mainly on the issue of "quality of life".

The members of AMS are architects, historians, psychoanalysts, psychologists, psychiatrists, philosophers, engineers, musicians, professionals, and entrepreneurs. In short, we are a large number of curious people. Therefore, the reciprocal influences between exterior and interior spaces are the main issues in the AMS's unconventional and lively exchanges. These dialogues sometimes become passionate public discussions, especially between analysts and architects. I owe the idea for this book to these countless meetings with different and various people, ideas, and theories: I can describe these meetings in many ways—creative, rigorous, open, eccentric, and always vital.

The ethnologist and anthropologist Marc Augé (1994, p. 67) points out that the French proverb *chacun son métier, les vaches seront bien gardées* (the literal translation is: *if everyone does their proper job, the cows will be well supervised*. In other words, if everyone does what they are actually supposed to do, everything will take a turn for the better) is reactionary. This is because "we must abandon the restrictive idea of cultures as autonomous and independent from one to another". In his autobiography (1985, p. 52) Bion writes: "Certainly, it is not the successful building of the Tower of Babel, but the failure that gives life, initiates, and nourishes the energy to live, to grow, to flourish."

The psychoanalyst Thomas Ogden says:

> Conversation, in which two people are talking with one another, involves a different sort of structuring of language and structuring of experience. The spoken conversation resonates with an unconscious conversation in which the two people are thinking together … It takes two people to think; that is, it requires the creation of a form of unconscious thinking comprised of the conjoint thinking and feeling of two people, which enables them to think in a way that neither individual alone could think/feel. It is that experience of thinking with another person with whom one is in conversation consciously and unconsciously that I believe has the potential to create conditions in which psychological change may occur in both the patient and the analyst. (2013, pp. 634–635)

In her novel *Cassandra* (1983), the writer Christa Wolf approaches the Greek heroine by considering herself as a stranger in a land in which she does not understand the language. This position of reciprocal linguistic unfamiliarity between the author and her character does not mean a complete lack of communication between them. Rather, it allows a deep relationship based on a long-distance dialogue between different eras and worlds that can communicate by using different languages. Wolf maintains that we can understand only what we can share with other: in this sense, conviviality and empathic participation (and not the correspondence between homeland and language or between language and ego) are the bases for comprehending the others.

In her poem *The Silence of Plants* (1993–1997, p. 269), Nobel Prize winner Wisława Szymborska writes:

> After all, we share a common journey.
> When traveling together, it's normal to talk …
> Both of us at least try to know something, each in our own way,
> and even in what we don't know there lies a resemblance.

The architect Anthony Vidler writes:

> So might we begin to interpret our present intradisciplinary experiments not as failed total utopias, nor as lost disciplinary practices, but rather as elaborate conversations between private subjects in a newly constituted public realm: an interior constructed as an exterior in order to capture and analyse ... a collective private void in public. (2007, p. XII)

The psychoanalyst Virginia De Micco (2014b) argues that neither an alleged repertoire of traditional meanings of the culture of the migrant's country of origin nor a translation of meanings and interpretations of their host country can be a response to the migrant's need to re-signify their own psychic experience. Rather, a possible response to this need can come from a process of open psychocultural working (such a process can be seen as a counterpart to the dream work). To borrow a beautiful expression of the anthropologist Gananath Obeyesekere (1990), this process aims at transforming the fantasy material into cultural substance.

More generally, I believe we can say that the conversation among different scientific and cultural idioms can lead to new forms of language and experience. It is worth noting that the output of such a transformation must not be conceived as the sum of the initial languages and experiences, but rather as something more that has an autonomous and original life.

CHAPTER TWO

Fruitful contaminations

> Then, what do you love, extraordinary stranger?
> I love the clouds ... the clouds that pass ... up there ...
> up there ... the wonderful clouds!
>
> (Charles Baudelaire, *The Stranger*, 1869, p. 1)

Contacts, proximities, and intersections

Through a continuous process of crossbreeding, the contributions from different disciplines (for example, philosophy, natural and social sciences, architecture, literature, arts, and psychoanalysis) can lead to fertile connections and fruitful contaminations. These intersections can force us to deal with cultural differences and thus to feel and understand emotions. This is possible because our mind is not something rigidly subdivided in distinct parts or modules. The openness to the novelty, to the outside, and to the unknown, is an achievement, not something ideologically postulated *a priori*. This openness deals with the promotion of desire and interest. It can modify worn-out or emotionless languages. I want to stress that these languages appear to be insufficient for describing and representing the value of a novelty and not includable in already established knowledge contexts. In other words, these languages lack the symbolic and representational importance necessary to pass from automaticity to authenticity and from habit to risk. Further, they do not allow a new way of storytelling through the recovery and construction of elements of shared thought.

In the book *Œdipe africain* (African Oedipus) (1984) the psychoanalyst Marie Cécilie Ortigues and the philosopher Edmond Ortigues argue that the possibility of sharing the various forms of "knowledge" can help us listen to the other narratives with respect rather than invade them with previously elaborated theories or stereotypes. In this sense, the hope is that the meeting between various disciplines can help bring forth a meaning able to respect the human subjectivity. According to this meaning, human beings tend to learn what society offers to them through proper and original modalities.

The philosopher and psychoanalyst Cornelius Castoriadis (1989) argues that free and non-functionalised imagination is the fundamental property of human beings.

The architect Aldo Rossi (1981, p. 35) writes: "Not in purism but in the unlimited contamination of things, of correspondences, does silence [of a project] return."

For many years, the psychoanalyst Lorena Preta has supported the need for fruitful contaminations between the different disciplines in the full respect of their scientific and epistemological statutes. She aspires to constitute a new way of thinking, one that would be unstable and incomplete, as well as germinal and transformative. Further, she praises the notion of "unobservable", a term designating everything we don't yet know. This lack of knowledge would be the source from which we could obtain fantasies and imaginary backgrounds. The lack of knowledge is generative because it permits an imaginative stimulation. In this sense, we should not speak of knowledge in general, but rather of passion for knowledge. This is because a process cannot be confined inside a single discipline and represented only within the limits defining it. Knowledge exists in different places (Preta, 1990, 1991, 1993).

The borderline character of every discipline produces areas of interest that could otherwise be excluded: it makes room for nomad ideas and unstable and inconclusive elaborations. Such ideas and elaborations are open and sometimes transgressive and eccentric. Because of their unsaturated nature, they are open to translations, changes, interactions, interferences, and original output and can be the bases for new praxes. Of course, the main risk of staying inside such a polysemy of expressions is confusion and fragmentation. However, I think it is worth the risk.

The philosopher Edgar Morin (2004) uses expressions such as interdisciplinary migrations, border violations, multidisciplinary objects and projects, and cognitive schemata, aiming at reorganising clandestine notions and illegal common-law marriages, to refer to a continuous and dynamic process where official and institutional ideas or positions are in dialectic tension with unrecognised or heretical ones (that is to say, with every idea or position in contrast with an established order).

The act of knowing is not a linear process: it is a swinging and dynamic process of projection and introjection upon which the relational dialectic between inside and outside is based.

The psychoanalyst Wilfred Bion underlines the importance of the "process ... of awareness of incoherent elements and the individual's ability to tolerate that awareness" (1985, p. 195). He points out that the no-thing is an indication of those mental processes through which we can tolerate the limitations of knowledge on the one hand, and avoid saturating them through pseudoscientific arrogance on the other. Further, we cannot transform them into nothing because of our inability to tolerate the lack of the no-thing (Bion, 1965). In this sense, Bion writes:

> If it is true that the human being, like nature, abhors a vacuum, cannot tolerate empty space, then he will try to fill it by finding something to go into that space, presented by his ignorance. The intolerance of frustration, the dislike of being ignorant, the dislike of having a space that is not filled, can stimulate a precocious and premature desire to fill the space. ... In other words, the practising analyst has to decide whether he is promulgating a theory, or a space-filler indistinguishable from a paramnesia. ... The question is if these paramnesias, the answers immediately comprehensible, those that can be used to fill the space of our ignorance, lead to an extreme danger; if the powers of the human mind are equal to their being destructive. (1987, pp. 301–303)

Every genuine progression challenges our capacity to tolerate the uncertainty of the "truths in transit" (Horovitz, 2007). Such an expression refers to small truths, probably slightly larger than a babble expressing a desire. However, we cannot exclude these truths because they support and promote psychic transformations. After all, the control of every theory consists of assessing whether it gives good answers to interesting questions or satisfying solutions to relevant problems. Such a control can also be done by recognising the temporal and contextual relativity of a certain problem and the fact that every answer has a temporary and approximate nature (Argentieri, 2013).

On 8 October 1936, Freud writes to Binswanger:

> I've always lived only in the parterre and basement of the building. You claim that with a change of viewpoint one is able to see an upper story that houses distinguished guests such as religion, art, etc. … If I had another lifetime of work before me, I have no doubt that I could find room for these noble guests in my little subterranean house. (1936a, p. 156)

On this point, the psychoanalyst Jacques Lacan (1966, p. 116) writes that Jung himself told him the following anecdote about Freud. In 1909 the first president of Clarke University in Worcester, MA, the psychologist Stanley Hall, invited the father of psychoanalysis to give five lectures. So, on 20 August 20 1909, along with Jung and Ferenczi, Freud boarded a transatlantic ship named George Washington in Bremen. Ten days later, when they were approaching the port of New York and could see the Statue of Liberty, he told Jung: "They don't realise we're bringing the plague."

In this sense, the notion of unconscious is a sort of cultural cataclysm that continues to shock and surprise even today. The psychoanalytic point of view permits us to shed new light on the various scientific and humanistic disciplines. It does not propose any cultural colonialism or reductionism, but it also does not aim at an easy conciliation between the different disciplines. This is because we cannot renounce the specific epistemological status of the single discipline considered. That would mean building up an incomplete knowledge that denies the relevance of its unconscious determinants.

"Psychoanalysis must propose an open and not a defensive way of thinking: I mean, a way to extend our field of experience rather than to limit it. It must be able both to deal with every issue outside its area of expertise and to not take for granted its ability to give an answer." (Preta, 2015, p. 13) It is worth noting that I don't want to re-introduce here the old concept of applied psychoanalysis, that is to say, the subjective explanation and understanding of an interpreter of the arts who aims at interpreting on the basis of the unconscious mind and its decryption. I believe this perspective is too reductive and can even be pathologising because it does not consider the multiplicity of meanings the arts can bring. In Book VII of his *Seminar*, which Lacan dedicated to *The Ethics of Psychoanalysis* (1959–1960), we can find a shift from the so-called psychoanalysis *applied to* art to a psychoanalysis *implied in* art. In fact, according to Lacan's definition of art (but also of architecture) as an organisation around a void or in support of a void,[1] the problem is not to examine an artwork by comparing it to a symptom. Rather, the problem is to try to understand what the arts can teach psychoanalysis about the nature of its object of inquiry.

I believe we must think of new geometries of mind (Preta, 1999) and pass from one-dimensional to pluralistic situations. This means developing a way to provide a theoretical connection among various disciplines. Such a way should foster the construction of a space of transversal thinking: a place where it is possible to connect the ever-present fantasies of mind with innovations coming from the external world.

> The Freudian plague has shown how there exists a direct and continuous contact between certain mental areas and certain apparently distant experiences. For example, before Freud, sexuality was considered a sort of obscure object of the adult world and after him it has become the main organiser of mental life from birth. Reality and fantasy, sleep and wakefulness, conscious and unconscious become experiences strictly connected among themselves and mutually influenced. The continuous steps and the non-stop migration from one state to another produce transformations of which only a minimal part is consciously apparent to us. The intrapsychic contaminations (those contaminations taking place only in our mind) and the continuous contaminant relation between our mind and the external world are the conditions of our dialogue and of the non-stop human conversation. Such a conversation is something stimulating and risky at the same time. (Preta, 2004, p. 10)

The Argentinian psychoanalysts Janine Puget and Leonardo Wender (1982) talk about *mundos superpuestos*, that is to say, *overlapping worlds* in the analytic relation. Of course, such worlds are respectively that of the analysand and that of the analyst. Both are crossed by social contradictions and ideologies, so that we cannot refer to an impersonal transference-countertransference dynamic. In other words, this dynamic cannot be free from the analysand and analyst's cultural references (which are often the same ones). In his introduction to the Italian first edition of my *Pedofilia Pedofilie*, the psychoanalyst Francesco Barale (2001) points out that it is necessary that a good psychoanalytic reflection not be self-referential and closed in itself. Rather, it must patiently proceed by decentralising and knowing other dialogical and scientific contexts and other points of view.[2]

In a sort of manifesto on the ethics of scientific debate (titled *Psychoanalysis and Philosophy*), the psychoanalyst Roger Money-Kyrle (1956) discusses the mutual criticisms of philosophers and psychoanalysts. He argues that members of both parties tend to overstate a piece of truth that both philosophers and psychoanalysts have gradually learned to recognise. In this sense he appraises the constructive self-criticism and criticises the method of drastically condemning the opposing positions.

So, psychoanalysts are condemned to a sort of "methodological walleye". In the making of their psychoanalytic identity they must not forget that the internal world is the central place of their observation-relation but, at the same time, they must keep in mind its relationships with the external world.

The consonance of architects

Architects, as well as psychoanalysts, have a great passion for intersections, exchanges, and connections. Thus, passion for knowing and trying to build up new languages is what appears to associate the aspirations (and sometimes also the words) of psychoanalysts and architects. Both are involved in a continuous work of weaving and re-weaving competences, interests, and worldviews. Both require a cognitive and emotional position not conditioned (or not too conditioned) by preconceived ideas and able to avoid homologation, conformity, or a slapdash attitude. Such an emotional position has to deal with the threating presence of different languages difficult to translate in known idioms and does not provide any obvious certainty or security. It forces us to pay attention somewhere else. It recognises intuition as a resource. It makes imagination free. But, at the same time, it respects the specific languages of every discipline and it does not degrade them. On the contrary, it appraises them through an honest and continuous work of separation/integration.

In the context of the global space, the main political role of the border is to provide translations between socio-cultural dimensions that need to communicate (Fornari, 2011). The border is phenomenologically ambivalent. It is a place of production of relations and conflicts, discipline and innovation. It is a real *fabrica mundi* (Mezzadra & Neilson, 2013).

The architect Carlo Truppi writes:

> The border areas are often more fruitful than other ones, perhaps more explored and defined, but probably more rigid and sectarian. In fact, the study of similarities among disciplines provides a common legacy coming from different linguistic and conceptual contexts that could be later transferred to defined theoretical areas ... It is the first connection and syzygial structure of our work. To develop an alliance among different contexts and to produce a relation not based upon polarised positions or dichotomies. In this sense the exchanges among people are based on experience and competence, on cooperation and sharing. The relation is not hierarchical, vertical, or based on the power. Rather, it aims at developing the individual potentialities and an involvement that leads to appraise the different contribution and to strength the meeting points. It is something based on listening, patience, and open-mindedness. It is also based on the exploration of changes and ideas, on the practical experimentation. Further, it is also based on connecting the various points of view and it permits to give the right credits to the different contributions, to take on a task compatible with the personal preferences, to foster learning, developments, autonomy, self-affirmation, and, finally, creativity. (2004, p. 109 et seq.)

According to the architect Renzo Piano (2000), architecture is a frontier profession. It can exist only in so far as it accepts the challenge of being contaminated. If it does not accept this challenge, it is an armchair and rhetorical discipline. Piano also points out that "to live in a frontier means to avoid the borders. I chose to work through muddling and confusing different disciplines. I have not got any interest in the differences between arts and sciences, but in their similarities." (2004, p. 123)

Martin Heidegger (1954) used to say to himself that it is the bridge that gives the meaning to the scene.

The philosopher Michel Serres (1977, p. 28) writes: "The bridge[3] is a way connecting two banks or gives continuity to a discontinuity or mends a tear."

The philosopher and sociologist Georg Simmel (1909, pp. 3–4) describes the bridge as a symbol of the expansion of our will over the space. He argues that only the human beings can connect and divide. The action of connecting is always the condition of the action of dividing and vice versa. "Immediately and symbolically, bodily and spiritually, in every moment we are who divide what is connected and connect what is divided."

The writer and 1961 Nobel Prize in Literature winner Ivo Andrić writes:

> Of all the things created and built by humankind as a part of life's effort, nothing in my mind is better or worthier than bridges. They are more important than houses, more sacred, and more universal than temples. They belong to all and treat all alike; they are useful, always built for a purpose, at a spot where most human needs entwine; they are more durable than other buildings and serve no secret or evil purpose ... They are all essentially one, they are equally worthy of our attention, because they show the place where humankind encountered an obstacle and did not stop before it, but overcame and bridged it the way humankind could, according to understanding, taste, and circumstances ... Thus, everywhere in the world, wherever my thoughts wander or stop, they encounter faithful and silent bridges like an eternal and ever insatiable human desire, to connect, to reconcile, and to join everything that challenges our spirit, eyes and feet, to stop division, contradiction, or parting ... Finally, everything that this life reveals itself by—thoughts, efforts, looks, smiles, words, sighs—they all sway toward the other shore, to which they are directed, as if toward a target, and once reaching it, they gain their true meaning. They all have to overcome and bridge something—disorder, death, or the lack of meaning. For everything is a transition, a bridge whose ends fade away into the infinity and toward which all earthly bridges are nothing but mere playthings, pale symbols. And all our hopes are on the other side. (1963, pp. 156–157)

In 2000, Jan Henriksson, a Swedish professor of architecture, was interviewed by the psychoanalyst Ulla-Britt Parment. He said that the training of architecture students must include not only the technical and instrumental part, but also the formation of a critical thinking for highlighting what is the truth, what resembles the truth but actually it is not. He stressed the relevance of conflicts, which should be considered crucial for producing something new and not disturbing what was rationally planned. He defined the turnover between order and chaos as a stimulus for creative thoughts and actions. Parment (2000b) agreed with him and stressed how psychoanalysts, as well as architects, must share a common perspective on training. Such a perspective must be based on creativity, personal capacities, and few inhibitions in the freedom of thought.

I think that to work on metaphorisation, on analogies, and on correspondences allows building up an open, free from boundaries, and curious kind of thought. From hermeneutics we pass to hypotheses and conjectures. In this sense the border areas become places of interconnection where we can go through the narrow passages of what seems to be divided (Truppi, 2004).

The architect Daniel Libeskind (2004) argues that, when Goethe was asked about his favourite colour, he said: "I like the rainbow." From this quotation, he points out that, if architecture is good, then it includes all the colour spectrum of life; if it is bad, all the colours fade and then vanish.

I believe it is also necessary to combine talent and rule, creativity and sense of measure, openness to visions and methodological rigour.

In polemics with the surrealists' "automatic writing" the writer Raymond Queneau (1938) argues that the idea of an equivalence between inspiration, exploration of the unconscious, and liberation (in other words, an equivalence between chance, automatism, and freedom) is radically false. According to him, the kind of inspiration that leads us to senselessly obey every impulse is another form of slavery. In this sense, the classic author who writes a tragedy by following a certain number of rules that he knows very well, is freer than the poet who writes everything that passes through her mind. In fact, this poet is slave to a certain number of rules of which she is not aware.

Aldo Rossi is suspicious of the supporters of irrationality. He thinks they are unprepared and argues that they are unable to understand irrationality itself. In this sense he writes:

> This freedom compels me to maintain my love of order, or of a disorder that is always moderate and reasoned … Although I love

> what is uncertain, I have always thought that only small-minded people with little imagination are opposed to discreet acts of organisation; for it is only such efforts of organisation that in the end permit contretemps, variations, joys, disappointments. (1981, pp. 54–55)

The architect Enrico Pinna (2002, p. 111) stresses how, from a space organised and measurable, the architect should be able to refer to an aesthetic and incommensurable dimension. The strict relation between creativity and measure has not been sufficiently studied and assessed. A work can be conceived as a device composed of parts rigorously measured whose aim is to produce an emotion. In an interview with the journalist George Plimpton (1959) on the art of writing and storytelling, Ernest Hemingway demystified the commonplace according to which creativity is only connected to talent and inspiration. He proposed the iceberg theory, according to which the mechanism of imagination is based on solid knowledge processes.

The philosopher Umberto Curi writes:

> In the ancient map, the inscription *hic sunt leones* (here be dragons) indicated the unknown or not sufficiently explored or mysterious regions of Africa and Asia. This inscription had lasted until the exploration of Africa was completed. It indicated not only that a region was unknown or unexplored, but also that it could be frightful and threatening. However, the focus on the possible resources and treasures of these regions led to not worry and to start travels for knowing the unknown. Thus, finally, *hic sunt leones* was cancelled from the maps. It was understood that the gifts obtained after the discovery of these mysterious regions (although they could not be considered completely safe yet) were precious and fundamental. (2010, p. 19)

The writer Italo Calvino (1988, p. 16) stresses this point: "Lightness for me goes with precision and determination, not with vagueness and the haphazard."

Bion (1965, p. 75) writes: "An explorer's knowledge of instruments must be such that he can use them in situations of stress. The analyst must use instruments that are altered by the circumstances they are devised to study."

Expeditions into the unknown are fundamental because of new discoveries and the gratifying rewards. However, they absolutely require adequate gear, logistic support, and a series of tools that progress the research. All these things help avoid dismay and unproductive confusion.

Metaphors, analogies, correspondences

In spite of her personal mentality, the individual must make an effort to change and become open to the new (Gaburri & Ambrosiano, 2003). Such an effort should permit us to hold together the need for general categories and interpretation criteria for giving an account of a set of events, but also for dealing with the unpredictability and the irreducible variety of the different aspects of reality. This is possible through a continuous work of interconnection (Donghi & Preta, 1995). For example, the first phases of the formation of a new theory imply aspects of repetitiveness and creativity often difficult to differentiate. Thus, we are forced to refer to tradition and to what we already know. In this case, redundancy can be avoided only if the observer makes good use of discretion; that is, only if she makes use not only of her knowledge, but also of her intuition and imagination.

If we do not want to transform our field of application into a sort of bazar of strange and confused solutions, we must consider that, before their formalisation, ideas live a life made of contrasts, juxtapositions, and changes both in the single mind and in the social context.

> Before being formulated in a hypothesis or in a theory, the ideas are a mass of many things; they are temporary hybrids showing all the tensions of research ... Incursions and suggestions, intersections and passages ... all these things can be seen as useful navigational instruments for the search of new routes ... In this way we make a nomadic or travelling use of concepts. (Preta, 1992, pp. X–XI)

The models are able to contain and give a meaning to emotions. Because they are at last imaginative conjectures, they cannot be definitive, unalterable, or immutable. Sometimes only certain parts of them last, sediment, and become attached to the theoretical construct.

We know that the construction of a new theory or model (or of some of their parts) can generally take place by using already known theoretical constructs and referencing the culture present at the moment. In the first phases of theory construction, the mechanisms of metaphorisation can be the most relevant. Through these mechanisms, images, languages, and theoretical constructs are freely used and, in a certain sense, recreated. At the metaphorisation processes we can later add those of analogy (according to which a quality of a certain system can be imported into another one) and of correspondence (according to which a structure can be imported into a different field). It is clear that the degree of similarity increases from metaphor to correspondence. The relation among theories can be based on the process of juxtaposition and not on the direct comparison, that is to say, on the possibility to take advantage of the co-presence of various hypotheses. This model of research reproduces the irregular and multi-layered structure of the mind that needs complex and different interpretations and experiences.

Once a new theory becomes more defined and coherent it is not necessary to stand on the shoulders of past thinkers or to refer to their theoretical vocabulary. Thus, an autonomous language for the new ideas emerges. In this sense, the metaphorical or analogical use of words, images, or concepts taken from other disciplines assumes an historical value. In other words, it loses the strong indicative value that it had in the original theory and assumes new proper characters. From the start of *Papers on Metapsychology* (1915, p. 117), Freud points out that if a certain number of defined concepts or constructs actually form a specific science, they are immediately accessible and definable. The researcher must start from a description of the phenomena, a gathering of data, and a system for putting them in relation. In this phase she cannot avoid referring to abstract ideas taken from different perspectives. Once reworked and redefined, these ideas will be the fundamental concepts or constructs of the new science. In the beginning of *Metapsychology,* Freud argues that these fundamental concepts:

> must at first necessarily possess some degree of indefiniteness; there can be no question of any clear delimitation of their content. So long as they remain in this condition, we come to an understanding about their meaning by making repeated references to the material of observation from which they appear to have been derived, but upon which, in fact, they have been imposed. Thus, strictly speaking, they are in the nature of conventions—although

> everything depends on their not being arbitrarily chosen but determined by their having significant relations to the empirical material, relations that we seem to sense before we can clearly recognise and demonstrate them. It is only after more through investigation of the field of observation that we are able to formulate its basic scientific concepts with increased precision, and progressively so to modify them that they become serviceable and consistent over a wide area. Then, indeed, the time may have come to confine them in definitions. The advance of knowledge, however, does not tolerate any rigidity even in definitions. Physics furnishes an excellent illustration of the way in which even "basic concepts" that have been established in the form of definitions are constantly being altered in their content. (1915, p. 117)

Eight years later, Freud (1923a, p. 254) stresses again: "There is no incongruity (any more than in the case of physics or chemistry) if its [psychoanalysis'] most general concepts lack clarity and if its postulates are provisional."

This process of theoretical definition has occurred in psychoanalysis but also in architecture. On the other hand, both psychoanalysis and architecture cannot illusorily close in a sort of *a priori* specialised purity: they must recognise the common cultural features of the different disciplines and the need of a communicative exchange between different perspective in order to reach a systemic point of view on knowledge. On the other hand, both must avoid rough methodological errors and apparent facilitations leading to confusion and lack of distinction. The architect Roberto Secchi (2005) makes some examples of these errors and facilitations. He argues that we cannot accept all the analogies between the realm of inanimate objects and the realm of living organisms and the metaphors from biology,[4] in spite of their appeal and grandeur.

Marc Augé (1994, p. 97) warns us against the defensive relativism and some common expressions as *de gustibus* or "everyone has his own truth". This is because they represent the contrary of tolerance and indicate "a refusal to recognise ourselves in the other and thus to damage our sense of security about our identity".

I think that the methodological recommendations of the psychoanalyst Maria Ponsi (2013) for comparing different psychoanalytic theories count also for comparing architecture and psychoanalysis. There is no doubt that the variety of ideas present in a pluralistic perspective is a sign of creativity and cultural wealth. However, there is also no doubt that such a variety implies a very strong effort for making a real comparison among the various approaches. This is true especially when a set of common criteria for assessing the evidence upon which these approaches are based must be chosen and defined. However, in spite of the need to recognise the stable and invariable aspects of the object of observation, it is important to risk a possible fragmentation of the unified thinking and to challenge the consequences of a confused eclecticism. This is necessary when we want to verify if the different points of view can be juxtaposed and integrated or if they must be considered as incommensurable (Bernardi, 2003).

CHAPTER THREE

The metaphorical architecture of mind

> Psychical objects are incomparably more complicated than the excavator's material ones and … we have insufficient knowledge of what we may expect to find, since their finer structure contains so much that is still mysterious.
>
> (Sigmund Freud, 1937d, p. 260)

The architect transforms emotion into form whereas the analyst transforms emotion into language. Most of the metaphorical encyclopaedia used in psychoanalysis draws analogies between the psychical and the physical—the city, the house, rooms, windows, furnishings, as well as landscapes and theatrical spaces:

> All this dreamy-fantastic imagery, that redoubles the outside into the inside world, is absolutely fundamental for a description of psychic life. It is based on a topography and an interior and exterior architecture at the service of the psychological representation of imagination. (Petrella, 1993b, p. 654)

The psychoanalysts Domenico Chianese and Andreina Fontana (2010, p. 33) point out that, according to Freud, there is a karstic river running under and beyond the established dominance of the *logos*, "a karstic river that appears not only in images of Gradiva, Moses, or Leonardo, but also in the antique collector's passion, in archaeological fantasies, in idealised images of Rome, in reflections about civilisation."

The art historian Aby Warburg writes:

> I consider man an animal, handling things whose activity consists in establishing connections and separations. Such an activity makes him lose his organic feeling of ego. In fact, he can grasp concrete objects devoid of the nervous system because they are inorganic and thus extend his ego in an inorganic form. This is a tragedy for man. He handles things and goes beyond his organic being.[1] (in Didi-Huberman, 2002, pp. 360–361)

A Jungian metaphor

Many analogies used in psychoanalysis aim at organising mental space in an up-and-down structure, according to surface and depth; or in terms of what is clearly visible versus what is inaccessible; interiority and exteriority, inside versus outside.

Jung makes the following analogy between a building and the psyche:

> We had to describe and explain a building whose upper storey was erected in the nineteenth century, the ground floor dates back to the sixteenth century, and careful examination of the masonry reveals that it was reconstructed from a tower built in the eleventh century. In the cellar we come upon Roman foundations, and under the cellar a choked-up cave with neolithic tools in the upper layer and remnants of fauna from the same period in the lower layers. That would be the picture of our psychic structure. We live on the upper storey and are only aware that the lower storey is slightly old-fashioned. As to what lies beneath the earth's surface, of that we remain totally unconscious. This is a lame analogy, like all analogies, for in the psyche there is nothing that is just a dead relic. Everything is alive, and our upper storey, consciousness, is continually influenced by its living and active foundations. Like the building, it is sustained and supported by them. And just as the

> building rises freely above the earth in space, so our consciousness stands as if above the earth in space, with a wide prospect before it. But the deeper we descend into the house the narrower the horizon becomes, and the more we find ourselves in the darkness, till finally we reach the naked bed-rock, and with it that prehistoric time when reindeer hunters fought for a bare and wretched existence against the elemental forces of wild nature. (1931, pp. 31–32)

Such an image comes from an enlightening oneiric experience and would represent the existence of the collective unconscious as an archetypal cumulation of all humanity. In such a fund, "in accordance with the phylogenetic law, we still recapitulate in childhood reminiscences of the prehistory of the race and of mankind in general" (Jung, 1931, p. 32).

Jung uses such a bold passage from the contemporary world to prehistory for placing in opposition childhood and adulthood, the difficult and dark life of nomadic hunters and enlightened modern times. In this sense, he certainly proposes a linear and Eurocentric view of human development.

The meaning of Freud's archaeological metaphor

The similarities between analytic work and archaeological activity are probably what best characterise today the peculiarity of psychoanalytic practice compared with other kinds of psychotherapy (Petrella, 1988). The positivistic yearning upon which Freud's archaeological metaphor is based and the narrative creativity of his constructions are connected and intertwined through a common thread.

> The methods of archaeological excavation and those of psychoanalytic investigation have had more or less the same evolution or trajectory—a progressive departure from a focus on a specific object to bring to light to a stratigraphic analysis of the ground. The aim of this trajectory is to slowly redefine the thread of the story. (de Mijolla-Mellor, 2013, p. 132)

The archaeological metaphor remains on a problematic continuum in which scientific-historical knowledge must deal with emotions, passions, and their metaphors. The psychoanalytic work is not simple excavation. It places the person before their passions and upsets the order of representation. In this sense, says Freud (1937b, p. 260), "for the archaeologist the reconstruction is the aim and the end of his endeavours while for analysis the construction is only a preliminary labour."[2]

At a 1936 conference on "Freud and the Future", the writer Thomas Mann says:

> The attempt of psychoanalysis is also to understand the infancy and childhood of humanity, the primitive, and the myth. Freud himself has recognised that all the natural science, the medicine, and the psychotherapy were for him nothing but a return (as long as his entire life) to the original young passion for the history of humanity, for the origins of religion and ethics. (1956, p. 112)

Such a deep mythological interest finds expression in adequate narrative models. This happens sometimes to support hypotheses that are bold or insufficiently corroborated by scientific data, as for example is the case with *Totem and Taboo*.[3] Certainly, such hypotheses were necessary for supporting Freud's theoretical constructs. The work of excavation, the scientific reconstruction of the past, and the analytic construction are the basis of the enormous building of Freudian theories. In this context I would like to consider the role of fantasy, creative imagination, and interpretative suggestion in the work of archaeologist Sir Arthur Evans. In his reconstruction of the Knossos Royal Palace and in the discovery of the existence of a Minoan-Mycenaean civilisation, Evans clearly omits important historical information and detail and deliberately uses reinforced concrete for the supporting walls. If we consider the methods used to restore Knossos we can clearly see that, although it is recognised as scientific and is based upon his deep knowledge and intuition, Evans's reconstruction is largely an ingenious and imaginative invention. Further, we can clearly see how such an invention inspires many people to approach the Knossos Royal Palace with curiosity and sensibility. By referring to the reconstruction techniques used in the rediscovery of Knossos, Freud argues that:

> In the face of the incompleteness of my analytic results, I had no choice to follow the example of those discoverers whose good fortune it is to bring to the light of day after their long burial the priceless though mutilated relics of antiquity. I have restored what is

> missing, taking the best models known to me from other analyses; but, like a conscientious archaeologist, have not omitted to mention in each case where the authentic parts end and my constructions begin.[4] (1905a, p. 13)

It is this way of dealing with archaeology that allows us to understand why Freud himself points out that his clinical cases can be read as short stories on the one hand, while on the other:

> The ruined walls are parts of the ramparts of a palace or a treasure house; the fragments of columns can be filled out into a temple; the numerous inscriptions, which, by good luck, may be bilingual, reveal an alphabet and a language, and, when they have been deciphered and translated, yield undreamed-of information about the events of the remote past, to commemorate which the monuments were built. *Saxa loquuntur!*[5] (1896c, p. 192)

For the close and deep links between science and storytelling described in his work and the narrative ways through which he expresses his scientific revolution, Freud is awarded not a scientific prize but the eminent Goethe Prize for literature.[6] In *Creative Writers and Day-Dreaming* (1908, p. 143) Freud writes: "If we could at least discover in ourselves or in people like ourselves an activity which was in some way akin to creative writing! … Creative writers themselves … so often assure us that every man is a poet at heart and that the last poet will not perish till the last man does." Freud also says (1907a, p. 8): "But creative writers are valuable allies and their evidence is to be prized highly, for they are apt to know a whole host of things between heaven and earth of which our philosophy has not yet let us dream." In *Delusions and Dreams in Jensen's Gradiva* Freud also argues:

> An author, we hear them say, should keep out of the way any contact with psychiatry and should leave the description of pathological mental states to the doctors. The truth is that no truly creative writer has ever obeyed this injunction. The description of the human mind is indeed the domain which is most of his own; he has from time immemorial been the precursor of science, and so too of scientific psychology … Thus the creative writer cannot evade the psychiatrist or the psychiatrist the creative writer, and the poetic

> treatment of a psychiatric theme can turn out to be correct without any sacrifice of its beauty. (1907, pp. 43–44)

In *Delusions and Dreams in Jensen's Gradiva* (1907) we find the zenith of Freud's archaeological metaphor. This essay is a sort of "Pompeian phantasy", in narrative and creative terms, about the adventures of a young archaeologist, Norbert Hanold, the eponymous hero of Jensen's novel. Hanold recovers his capacity to reawaken some parts of his self that were hidden and buried. He cannot do it through science because it does not permit an understanding of the soul's affairs, the emotions, and the heart. Therefore, under the midday sun, the young archaeologist is alone contemplating the ruins of Pompeii with a new capacity to live his senses, that is to say, using the eyes and the ears of an imagination permitting him to live again the dead and to recover Pompeii.

> Gradiva (which means the one who walks solemnly and is the name that the main character attributes to an archaeological find, a young girl portrayed in an ancient old relief) is a moment of euphoria at the realisation of an imaginary archaeology. That is to say, it is about the discovery of the buried and hidden city where everyone can live again ... At last the stones speak of a past that offers clues about the present and in the future. (Petrella, 1990, p. 963)

Rome

In a later work, *Civilization and Its Discontents* (1930), Freud uses the image of the city of Rome to argue "that in mental life nothing that has once been formed can perish, that everything is somehow preserved and that in suitable circumstances (when, for instance, regression goes back far enough) it can once more be brought to light" (p. 69). He points out that if we want to visualise the unconscious we can do it by visualising the eternal city throughout time. We see the *Roma quadrata* (Roman Square) of the Palatine, the Rome of the Septimonium, the Rome enclosed in the Servian Wall, and the many eternal cities of successive emperors. In Rome, nothing that has ever taken place has disappeared. We can see all previous phases of the city's development next to the more recent ones. "Where the Coliseum now stands we could at the same time admire Nero's vanished Golden House" (p. 70). It is worth noting that Freud gives up using the metaphor of the past of Rome for representing the psychic past. This is because "demolitions and replacement of buildings occur in the course of the most peaceful development of a city. A city is thus *a priori* unsuited for a comparison of this sort with a mental organism." (p. 71) According to Petrella (1990), Freud's reference to Roman archaeology seems to be a sign of faith not in the availability of the object to reveal itself, but in the capacity and in the patience of the human being to approach it. Such an approach can take place through the fragile power of his or her senses and in the critical elaboration of fantastical figuration. In agreement with Freud, Wilfred Bion argues that the patient hides an ancient and buried civilisation and he underlines the role played by the most archaic part of the unconscious. However, taking his cues from Freud's doubts about the relative inadequacy of the archaeological metaphor, Bion writes that:

> Analogy of an archaeological investigation with a psychoanalysis was helpful if it were considered that we were exposing evidence not so much of a primitive civilisation as of a primitive disaster. The value of the analogy is lessened because in the analysis we are confronted not so much with a static situation that permits leisurely study, but with a catastrophe that remains at one and the same moment actively vital and yet incapable of resolution into quiescence. This lack of progress in any direction must be attributed in part to the destruction of a capacity for curiosity and the consequent inability to learn. (1967, p. 94)

The psychoanalyst Christopher Bollas (2000) agrees with Bion's position and argues that if Freud wants to defend his metaphor perhaps his dialectics could lead to further elaboration. It is a matter of fact that destructions (not only the transference of events that allow recovery of the past) part of the unconscious and their prominence depends on how we desire to view the eternal city of our unconscious life. In this sense, we can see both what was preserved and what was destroyed. Certainly, for architects, cities, and clients, destruction and creation are very similar and even complementary activities (Emery, 2011). The relationship between past and future lies in the transition from destruction to construction. In the deep unconscious city many new buildings have substituted the previous ones after a demolition. A new structure is now erected where before there had been another. For the person who lives through these moments, there will be always two constructions in the mind: the destroyed and the existing one.

Anyway, I agree with Fausto Petrella when he argues that, beyond all criticisms, the result Freud obtains is:

> An effect of spatialisation and concretisation of psychic life, that is to say, the incorporation of the subjective experience into an objective-practical order … The mental phenomena can be conceived as stones and, in this sense, can deal with the metaphorical and semantic field of the stone. If they are transferred according to the orders of mineralogy or architecture, they can assume a dimension accessible at the level of meaning. (1988, p. 80)

In this way Freud shows and gives life to his interest in nineteenth-century archaeology.

Freud tempers his reservations about archaeology in order to make it constructive and functional with respect to psychic life.

The philosopher Paul Ricoeur (1965) defines the Freudian endeavour as an *archéologie du sujet* (archaeology of the subject), that is to say, a perspective where subjectivity is not simply and naively identified with consciousness and can turn regressively to the origins of consciousness. In this sense, subjectivity is characterised in terms of anteriority; of something that comes first in every kind of conscious rationality, more or less as a sort of primitive background (Oudai Celso, 2006). It is worth noting that, since his schooldays, Freud had been a friend of Emanuel Löwy, a professor of archaeology in Rome and adjunct professor in Vienna. Freud speaks of him in a letter to Fliess (1899, pp. 372–373) in which he underlines Löwy's great intellect and remembers their long conversations lasting into the night. Max Schur, Freud's personal doctor, writes about the passion of the father of psychoanalysis for archaeology:

> In a letter to Stephan Zweig of 7 February 1931, Freud has argued that he has actually read much more of archaeology than of psychology. He considered the new archaeological excavations in Crete extremely exciting and he was very disappointed that fate did not allow him to see their conclusions. He was also a collector of antiquities and he said that such an activity was a vice only a bit less intense than that for smoking. (1972, p. 221)

In a letter to Wilhelm Fliess dated 28 May 1899, Freud compares himself to the figure of Schliemann:

> I have bought myself Schliemann's *Ilios* and enjoyed the account of his childhood. The man found happiness in finding Priam's treasure, because happiness comes only from fulfilment of a childhood wish. This reminds me that I shall not be able to go to Italy this year. Better luck next time! (1899, p. 281)

In another letter to Wilhem Fliess, dated 21 December 1899, Freud gives an account of a patient's dream, and writes: "It is as if Schliemann has dug up another Troy that had hitherto been believed to be mythical." (1899, p. 305) Once, on a ship, Freud meets Wilhelm Dörpfeld, Heinrich Schliemann's assistant, and is so excited by such a direct connection to the discoverer of Troy that he cannot approach him out of panic and envy.

The self-comparison between Schliemann and himself is certainly evocative and can be appreciated because it allows the immediate understanding of the many important links between archaeology and psychoanalysis. However, we can assume that at the time Freud could not foresee that, compared to Schliemann's contributions to archaeology, his objective contribution to the understanding of the human mind would be even greater for psychology and philosophy (Oudai Celso, 2006, p. 52).

CHAPTER FOUR

The space

> A pair of wings, a different respiratory system, which enabled us to travel through space, would in no way help us, for if we visited Mars or Venus while keeping the same senses, they would clothe everything we could see in the same aspect as the things of Earth. The only true voyage, the only bath in the Fountain of Youth, would be not to visit strange lands but to possess other eyes, to see the universe through the eyes of another, of a hundred others, to see the hundred universes that each of them sees, that each of them is …
>
> (Marcel Proust, 1923, pp. 343–344)

The phenomenology of space

Through his anthropoanalytic approach (*Daseinanalyse*), the psychiatrist and neurologist Ludwig Binswanger (1946) distinguishes between the geometrical space (measurable by natural sciences and mathematics) and the anthropological space (immeasurable and unthinkable but "emotionally attuned"). The anthropological space conceives the human being as not in a space, but as disclosing a space that must be seen as "distance and proximity" to the world objects and as presence and projectuality in the world itself. Specifically, he describes a pragmatic space or an oriented space (action space) on the one hand and a soul space on the other. Through these concepts he describes the closed, restricted, static, and encircled character of the schizophrenic experience of space and the abolition of the borders between personal and external space. A further peculiarity of this character is the loss of somatic borders and liquefaction of self. Thus, this self is confused in a spatial indeterminacy. The person perceives his or her body as fragmented, vulnerable, and inhabited by other people.

The philosopher and phenomenologist Maurice Merleau-Ponty (1945) distinguishes between the spatiality of the position of the external objects (or of the "spatial sensations") and the spatiality of the situation typical of the corporeity. "I don't merely have my body, but I live in my body and, through it, I live the things." (Merleau-Ponty, 1995) The body is fundamental for orienting. All the places in the space come from it (Lanfredini, 2014). The spatiality of the body is the sum or the totality of co-implicated (not naively juxtaposed) parts. The body schema is a "dynamic form … a Gestalt … a global awareness of my posture in the inter-sensory world, a 'form' in Gestalt's psychology sense of the word" (Merleau-Ponty, 1945, p. 102). More precisely, it is a form in front of which "privileged figures against indifferent background" (p. 103) can appear. This can occur only because the body is "spatiality of situation" (and not merely of position) and thus attracted by its task and always open to the world around it.

> Bodily space can be distinguished from external space and it can envelop its parts rather than laying them out side by side because it is the darkness of the theatre required for the clarity of the performance, the foundation of sleep or the vague reserve of power against which the gesture and its goal stand out, and the zone of non-being in front of which precise beings, figures, and points can appear. (Merleau-Ponty, 1945, p. 103)

Starting from the reflections of Merleau-Ponty, Franco La Cecla (2008) argues that the environment intended as "surrounding space" is an interaction between the presence of an inhabitant and the presence of a place. These two presences are similar because the body is not in the space, but inhabits the space. At the origin of the space we can find the subject's conquest of his world.

The psychiatrist Eugène Minkowski points out that, at the phenomenological level, schizophrenia shows the dissolution of the difference between the inside and outside. This dissolution produces confusion between the self and the external world and, specifically, between the body and the things outside of it. According to Minkowski:

> For us the space is not reducible to geometrical relations, that is to say, relations we establish as if we (as simple curious spectators or scientists) were out from the space. We live and act in the space and both our personal life and the collective life of humanity occur. Life extends itself in space, but it does not have itself a proper geometrical extension. Extension and perspective are necessary for life. (1968, p. 407)

Minkowski distinguishes between a light space and a dark space. In the former everything is clear, obvious, defined, unproblematic. It is an immediately socialised space and it is defined through the notions of distance, extension, extent. In the latter everything is dark, mysterious. Its main feature is the depth. "This space will not be socialised anymore. It will be mine but not subjective or personal as it is generally intended. This is because I will attribute an objective character to everything happening in this place." (ibid., p. 438) These considerations are crucial if we put them in relation and oscillation with those features that objectively but not evenly determine the external space. "On the contrary, we risk producing an artefact, a bad description. That is to say, we risk not considering the moment of the need for a body alive and full of spaces and relations." (Petrella, 1993b, p. 652)

The philosopher Michel Serres writes:

> My body (and I can't do anything about it) is not identified in a unique and specific type. It works in a Euclidean space, but this is enough. It sees in a projective space. It touches, caresses, and handles in a topologic variety. It suffers in another variety, it feels and communicate in another one. And we could go ahead in similar descriptions until we want … Thus my body is not in a unique space, but it is in a complex intersection of many spaces, that is to say, in a set of connections and links that can take place in such a variety of spaces. It is not something already stated, that is to say, something that it is always there. This intersection and these links

> must be always built up. A person who is unable to build up such links and intersections is generally called insane. His body explodes because of the lack of connection among spaces. (1977, p. 30)

According to Gestalt theorists, the human experience cannot be subdivided in its elementary components. They propose that we consider the whole as a higher-level or emergent phenomenon irreducible to (or more than) the sum of its single parts. In the *hic et nunc* (here and now) of every kind of connection, every living being is in contact with the surrounding environment, which can be animated or inanimate. Such an environment provides the living being a kind of support. This is because the features of the relation do not correspond to those of the single individual implementing them. This implies that the relation is the common thread accompanying the whole life of a person. In this sense, the relation can be seen as an enduring navigation between inclusion and separation of our psychological space in the surrounding environment. In this view, a house can be conceived as a catalyst for psychical development as well as what allows learning to be in contact with the outside world (Pesare, 2007).

Some brief notes on space in psychoanalysis

Freudian psychoanalysis has provided a description of the psychic apparatus as constituted in various parts or places and defined each time as systems or areas with distinct borders. Such a description has endorsed the spatial dimension and the notion of topic[1] and has permitted to Freudian psychoanalysis the study of mental life with the methods of natural science and thus taking it away from philosophical and moral disciplines. "That is to say, internal space is not real in the sense in which we say external space is real. But it is not a hypothesis either, in the normal scientific sense of this term." (Gaddini, 1976, p. 92) It is a fictional and invented space, represented in a reflecting way through an imaginative metonymy or a metaphor. Finally, Freud never deals with the internal or inside space as a meaning. He simply installs the category of space in his first topical and then structural description of the psychic apparatus.

In the seventh chapter of *The Interpretation of Dreams* (1900, pp. 48–49) Freud himself writes: "We may, I think, dismiss the possibility of giving the phrase an anatomical interpretation and supposing it to refer physiological cerebral localisation or even to the histological layers of the cerebral cortex."

> This enabled him (Freud) to find and describe mental phenomena in scientific terms for the first time, to locate them spatially in the various systems of the structure, and to find and describe the dynamics and economics of those phenomena within the sphere of the relations between the different systems and within each system. (Gaddini, 1976, p. 94)

In the nineteenth lecture of the *Introductory Lectures on Psycho-Analysis*, Freud tries to describe the first topic by characterising the space as full of tensions and dramatisations:

> Let us therefore compare the system of the unconscious to a large entrance hall, in which the mental impulses jostle one another like separate individuals. Adjoining this entrance hall there is a second, narrower, room—a kind of drawing room—in which consciousness, too, resides. But on the threshold between these two rooms a watchman performs his function. He examines the different mental impulses, acts as a censor, and will not admit them into the drawing room if the displease him. You will see at once that id does not make much difference if the watchman turns away a particular impulse at the threshold itself or if he pushes it back across the threshold after it has entered the drawing room. This is merely a question of the degree of his watchfulness and of how early he carries out his act of recognition. If we keep to this picture, we shall be able to extend our nomenclature further. The impulses in the entrance hall of the unconscious are out of sight of the conscious, which is in the other room; to begin with they must remain unconscious. If they have already pushed their way forward to the threshold and have been turned back by the watchman, then they are inadmissible to consciousness; we speak of them as repressed. But even the impulses that the watchman has allowed to cross the threshold are not on that account necessarily conscious as well; they can only become so if they succeed in catching the eye of consciousness. We are therefore justified in calling this second room the system of the preconscious. In that case becoming conscious retains its purely descriptive sense. For any particular impulse, however, the vicissitude of repression

> consists in its not being allowed by the watchman to pass from the system of the unconscious into that of the preconscious. It is the same watchman whom we get to know as resistance when we try to lift the repression by means of the analytic treatment. (1916–1917, pp. 295–296)

Psychoanalysts still tend to propose the Freudian idea of spatial fiction or to propose new ones, for example the third space, the transitional space, the collapsed space, the negative space, the oneiric space (Leavitt, 2013). "The mind is not a material thing—you can't see it, measure it, or even locate it … But since … the mind is not a material thing, we use metaphors to think about mental functioning that are drawn from the physical world." (Ogden, 2013, p. 635)

It is worth noting how the psychoanalysts Willy and Madeleine Baranger (1990) have conceived the notion of relational space between analyst and analysand as a bi-personal field (such a notion is inspired by Merleau-Ponty's phenomenology, whose aim is to found a psychology of the "human being in situation", that is to say, a psychology that could understand the psychical phenomena in the context of the interpersonal relations). The Barangers define the analytical situation as a bi-personal field in which, through a reciprocal interaction, it is possible to know the bi-personal unconscious fantasy, that is to say, the fantasy shared by the two complementary parts. In spite of the differences between their theoretical models, first the psychoanalyst Francesco Corrao and then the psychoanalysts Antonino Ferro, Giuseppe Civitarese and Domenico Chianese use the image of a field full of tensions, forces, and sensations that sometimes appear to assume a physical and theatrical weight.

The concept of an analytic field borrows from physics in that it is comparing the interplay of invisible psychic forces with the interplay of forces in such fields as electromagnetic fields and gravitational force fields. The metaphor of an analytic field places emphasis on the ways in which force fields are generated by the interaction of differing "poles" and on the way in which forces of enormous strength can be generated by events that are invisible (Ogden, 2013, p. 635).

Two of the main lectures of the 15th Congress of the Italian Psychoanalytic Society (this congress was held in Taormina in 2010 and its main issue was the clinical perspectives coming from an exploration of the unconscious) describe crossings and passages from one space to another.

The lecture by Stefano Bolognini—"Secret passages to the unconscious: styles and exploration techniques"—opens with the country house frequented during his childhood. He describes a small bricked-up door that makes one think of mysterious spaces beyond it. From this description he passes to the analytic situation where we can individuate "many secret passages that we discover with our patients. Perhaps there is no need to ascertain who (between the analyst and the analysand), in the analytic field and during the process, has found them … The secret passages allow fluidity, speed, and unexpected savings." (Bolognini, 2010, p. 602 & p. 605)

The lecture by Antonino Ferro—"Shuttles to the unconscious: reveries, transformations in dream, dreams"—considers "all the media allowing the expansion of the degree of oneiricity in the session and thus a transformative improvement of the unconscious itself as communication medium for the unconscious" (Ferro, 2010, p. 620). He defines a series of operations brought together by the analyst and the analysand as *shuttles* from and to the unconscious.

The psychoanalytic inquiry on the mental process of space begins with Winnicott's research (1971) on the first mental organisation of the self. At the beginning the child lives in a subjectively erected reality, where everything is under his omnipotent control. From this point of view the child thinks he can *construe* his mother through his desires. He will have to gradually leave this omnipotence to build a vision of the shared objective space. In this space the mother is autonomous, that is to say, she lives independently of the child's will. However, there is a third reality between these two and it is called transitional space. This space is both subjectively built up and objectively perceived. Thus, the transitional experience has the features of both forms of reality and allows the child to move toward a shared objective reality without being subjected to trauma. Further, it allows the development of the capacity to live in the objective reality by maintaining at the same time a nucleus of subjective omnipotence. This nucleus permits the child to express authenticity and passion.

It is worth noting that the transitional space is not only a phase of human development: it is also the potential space between the individual and the environment. It is the space in which each mental creative process in all the subsequent ages of the human being, that is to say, before in the playing and after in the cultural life, takes place. "This intermediate area of experience, unchallenged in respect of its belonging to inner or external (shared) reality, constitutes the greater part of the infant's experience, and throughout life is retained in the intense experiencing that belongs to the arts and to religion and to imaginative living, and to creative scientific work" (Winnicott, 1971, p. 14). This space allows us to develop a reflective personal autonomy and represents "the substance of illusion" (ibid., p. 4).

In *Elements of Psychoanalysis* (1963), Bion defines the mental space as a space occupied (or even taken) by emotions that, through their disposition, quality and quantity, configure and order it.

Bion (1965, p. 121) writes: "I suppose that Euclidean geometry derives from the experience of 'the space'. My suggestion is that its *intra-psychic* origin is experience of 'the space' where a feeling, emotion, or other mental experience was." The first and fundamental element of psychoanalysis is the mental space. It is the dynamic relationship between a container and the contained. This relationship is permeated by emotions and tends to make the container receptive and to give meaning to the content. The second element is the D«-»PS oscillation and it is based upon the discovery of a chosen fact giving coherence to the many different objects of PS. It deals with the configuration and the narrative order of emotions themselves. The mental space is open to infinity and to the multidimensional.

Influenced by Winnicott and Bion, Eugenio Gaddini argues that the physical self gradually acquires an early sense of self that can be defined as a sort of primitive space:

> In other words, the nascent mental area of the self is a space without structure, without a boundary of its own, without form and without time ... This space of the baby-mother sphere, which is objectively a common space but subjectively its own, fed and filled in this sense by bodily experiences, could be defined as the "space of things" ... [In this] ... space *sui generis*, which is pre-dimensional ... there is no place ... for symbolic operations. Since they remain strongly rooted in somatic functioning, the experiences remain "things" ... The transition from the space of things to the space of the individual self ... is actually the result of a tumultuous series of successive changes in the spatial experience ... With the delineating of the individual self ... loss of self anxiety decreases and a first mental image of the self, a circle, a circumscribed enclosed space, begins to form. (1976, pp. 97–102)

We can say that if we are born with a certain disposition of evolution in our organism and in our mental life, we can imagine that we are also born with a certain disposition of phantasmatic development. This disposition can realise itself only if the environmental conditions allow its realisation (Racamier, 1999).

As we can see, the psychoanalyst deals with both the internal space and the external space. The outside space is more extended than the inside one and contains many influences and constraints that have relevant effects on the inside space.

> But that inner reality is also partly based upon early environmental realities—in terms of which much subsequent experience may be perceived and interpreted. ... Not all of the analytic experience is to be understood in terms of inner reality or as projections by the patient. The analyst, as much as a parent, has a real impact upon the patient. (Casement, 1990, pp. 130–131)

The complex interrelations between the inside and the outside, as well as the definition of the borders separating them and of the bridges connecting them, are at the basis of all the psychoanalytic models of mental functioning (Sabbadini, 2014).

Thus, we can say that a clear-cut distinction between the internal and the external spaces is very difficult, if not impossible. I believe such a distinction could lead us to renounce a full, rich, and anti-ideological perspective on the human being and her environment. We need to cross and be crossed by spaces of different quality and variety. Georges Perec writes (1974, p. 10): "To live is to pass from one space to another, while doing your best not to bump yourself."

The influence of the external space

The spatial experience is correlated to the features of the relational space, the social space, the cultural space, and, of course, the physical space at one's disposal. Further, "we can say that the quality of an architectonic fact is directly connected to the intensity that a work succeeds to set with the surrounding space. The more is the intensity the architecture creates in the space, the more is the quality of the artefact itself." (Botta, 2007, p. 19)

If all the factors at stake are not adequately considered, then we actually do construction but not architecture. The space can influence and direct human movement. In virtue of their spatial organisation, some spaces can invite us to active movement, other ones to an inactive attitude; some spaces can facilitate a meeting, other ones can impede it.

The British architect Geoffrey Scott (1914), pupil and librarian of the art historian Bernard Berenson in Florence, writes about architectonical space. He points out that, when we are at the bottom of an aisle and in front of a long perspective of pillars, we almost impulsively tend to walk forward. This is because the features of that space seem to force us to do so. On the contrary, a space symmetrical and proportional to our body does not invite us to move in one way or another. It gives us balance and control. A movement without motivations contradicts our physical impulses. It is not humanised in any way.

If the space suggests a movement whose goal cannot be reached, it contradicts its aim and thus is ambiguous for its beneficiary. The beneficiary will be puzzled and uncertain in front of "a space that both invites an action and does not allow this action" (Racamier, 1957, p. 47).

For example, a definitively closed door is a semantic ambiguity because it is a symbol of communication, openness, contact, and connection between inside and outside. The ambiguity can carry negative, destructive, and often unexpected meanings and give the idea of a perverse use of space (something close to the use made in psychiatric wards) (Petrella, 1993a).

> To inhabit is to exist. This is because to inhabit is very similar and near to the existence, the dreams, and the imaginary things that put it in motion. All these things are one and the same with the processes of territorialisation, here intended as an anthropological feature, that is to say, as the relationship between the human being and the places (and, through the places, the space in general). So, to inhabit is something plural that can lead to a plurality of routes, ways of being, stories, imaginary things, all things having inside them proper logics and reasons. (Fiorani, 2012, p. 7)

To inhabit means to build places to tell the stories of life and make a narrative of the places, that is to say, to house the staying and the acting, the desires and the memories. The philosopher and sociologist

Henri Lefebvre distinguishes between the representations of space and the spaces of representation. The former are conceptualisations of the space, permitting us to know and use its properties, whereas the latter are features related to lived experiences. "Representational space is alive: it speaks. It has an affective kernel or centre ... It embraces the loci of passion, of action, and of lived situations." (Lefebvre, 1974, p. 42)

The knowledge of this space has become increasingly subtle, uncertain, and complex. As a consequence, the same has occurred for the knowledge of the single places, of their knowledge and experiences, and of the interactions between place and community that have taken place in the course of time. From here a representation aiming at understanding the existential value, the emotional and perceptual side of territory has taken place. This side has allowed creating the emotional maps, the ethnocartographies, and the performative mappings. All these things represent the city in its relational and existential meanings, not as a simple expression of the logos (I mean, a rational structure) (Fiorani, 2012, p. 75).

Scott (1914) argues that architecture gives us three-dimensional spaces that can contain our people. Further, he adds that architecture always commends the space and the space is nothing without architecture.

The architect Juhani Pallasmaa writes:

> The lived world is beyond formal description, because it is a multiplicity of perception and dream, observation and desire, unconscious processes and conscious intentionalities, as well as aspects of past, present, and future. As the design process itself in today's computerised practice is distance from this "impurity", "the flesh of the world" to use Merleau-Ponty's significant and suggestive notion, the very existential life force of architecture tends to be weakened or entirely lost ... Artistic phenomena take place simultaneously in two worlds: the realm of matter and that of mental imagery ... Without the tension between its simultaneous material reality and its imaginary mental suggestion, an architectural work remains shallow and sentimental. (2012, pp. 260–261)

This is more or less what the architect Daniel Libeskind calls the invisible:

> I think that what is called physical space must not shock us too much. The physical space is good for physicists: It is not the

> architectonical space. In this sense, it is curious that most architects still speak as if architecture were based on physics … It is evident that a certain building is not made of glass and bricks. That is to say, although it is made of glass and bricks, a building is constituted by something else. What is such a "something else"? It is the invisible! For example, let's consider the room in which I'm going to enter. There is no doubt that it is a physical place surrounded by walls delimiting what it is outside and what it is inside … But the room in which I'm going to enter is made also and above all of each room in which I've entered before and of those I want to enter, of each room I've really visited and of each room I've only seen in the books (maybe these rooms do not exist anymore). Further, they are made also and above all of my adaptation to the environment, of the game of imagination allowing 'feeling' the factual situation of the room, differentiating, and modifying it … The physical rigor of the place, the construction technique, the materials, the type are only elements of my perception: I can even say that they are a part of that invisibility surrounding me when I enter in a room or I make a project of it. This invisibility certainly comes from the function and the aim of a place, but implies also something broader moving me as a fundamental perceptive experience. It is the character of the architecture of the room, that is to say, that sensation connecting the room with my internal activity, with those peculiar sensations that are more meaningful if I enter the room late in the evening or early in the morning, or when the oblique light of the walls suddenly seduces me as a magic lantern full of lights and colours. (in Terragni, 2013, p. 22)

It seems that Libeskind read *The Little Prince* by Antoine de Saint-Exupéry (1943, p. 89): "Be it a house, the stars or the desert, the source of their beauty cannot be seen!"

I think that the beautiful definition of *invisible* by the psychoanalyst Jean-Bertrand Pontalis (1988, p. 325) can be a sort of counterpoint to Libeskind's words: "The invisible is not the denial of the visible: it is in it, it inhabits in it, it is both its horizon and its starting point." According to this statement, Pontalis seems to refer to *The Little Prince* too: "What is essential is invisible to the eye" (p. 82).

CHAPTER FIVE

Architecture between past, present, and future

Architecture aims at Eternity.

(Sir Christopher Wren, 1750, p. 351)

The genius of origins

In his *On Airs, Waters, and Places,* Hippocrates suggests to physicians that they acquire some knowledge of town planning and architecture, and carefully examine the environment, specifically the quality of air and water, weather, meteorology, the features of soil, the geographical position, and even the political situation (Hippocrates believed democracy healthy and tyranny harmful). According to him, virtuous physicians should consider the seasons, the wind, and also the specific characteristics of every country and the peculiar features of its waters. For proof of Hippocrates' words, consider the sense of care felt at a place of wellness and rest such as the thermal baths of Saturnia or the magic purification permeating everyone who stops by the hot springs at Bagno Vignoni in Val d'Orcia in Tuscany.

On the other hand, first Plato and then Vitruvius coherently argue that the town planner and the architect should have some knowledge of medicine for building good and beautiful homes and cities (Emery, 2010).

The philosopher Gaston Bachelard starts *The Poetics of Space* (1957) by analysing four ancient elements, that is, air, water, fire, and earth, and describing the internal features of a place (spots, shelves, drawers, cupboards, basements, attics, hiding spots for things and children). He writes not only of small things, but also of the enormous intimacy and dialectics between inside and outside in the construction of a "happy space" (*éspace heureux*). Such construction deals with the meanings of a place, with the foundation of links with the earth, and with people living on earth with us.

Jacques Austerlitz, a professor of history of architecture, is the main character in Sebald's eponymous novel. At a certain point he says that:

> Someone … ought to draw up a catalogue of types of buildings, listed in order and size, and it would be immediately obvious that domestic buildings of less than normal size—the little cottage in the fields, the hermitage, the lock-keeper's lodge, the wing for viewing the landscape, the children's bothy in the garden—are those that offer us at least a semblance of peace, whereas no one in his right mind could truthfully say that he liked a vast edifice … At the most we gaze at it in wonder, a kind of wonder which in itself is a form of dawning horror, for somehow we know by instinct that outsize buildings cast the shadow of their own destruction before them, and are designed from the first with an eye to their later existence as ruins. (2001b, pp. 23–24)

In his book *L'Arte di Abitare la Terra* (The art of inhabiting the earth) (2011) the architect Ugo Tonietti guides us on a fascinating journey through certain areas of North Africa and the Near East. We find wonderful constructions built in innovative and original vernacular and structure, and showing an adaptive capacity for surviving in a primitive, fierce, and essential world. The residences Tonietti explores are carved into the stone and made of clay. In them we can have a direct perspective over worlds and environments in which the cultural superstructure is not too neat or strong and the interface of the technical and organisational elements is not cumbersome.

> In these residences, materials, techniques, and roles allow a very simple and quick modelisation of territory. Such a modelisation is sometimes founded on very clever systems of shared knowledge.

> As a consequence, all we see here is a (lost) image of attitudes and processes we can define as "original" (in the sense of coming from the origins of mankind). (Tonietti, 2011, pp. X–XI)

It seems that the most ancient constructions that have survived until now are contemporary to the appearance of the first rhythmic representations of the unison between human feelings and emotions and their constructive creativity. We find similar representations in the architecture that, through the sense of sight, transmits modularity, repetition, and symmetry (or, in a word, rhythm).

Recalling his conversations with Johann Wolfgang Goethe, the poet and author Johann Peter Eckermann (1936–1948) argues that the author of *Faust* always considered architecture as frozen music and music as liquid architecture.

When talking about the musical features of a work in *Eupalinos or the Architect* (1921), the writer and poet Paul Valéry stresses the power of a building to move the human being as well as the object that is loved does. The architect Eupalinos' distinction between three kinds of buildings (silent buildings, talking buildings, and singing buildings—singing buildings are very uncommon) is the main issue of the dialogue. It refers to the approval of the Muses and, above all, to the various abilities of their creator. Silent buildings are lifeless and lack grace. They are the most common and do not differ from stacks of stones. Talking buildings simply fulfil their function. Examples include prisons and courthouses. Singing buildings are difficult to describe because language itself is not sufficient to give an account of them. They shy away from every attempt at camouflage and they are the only ones respecting and raising to the highest degree *all* the principles at the basis of human creation. In general, human creations are useful when considered for our bodies and beautiful when considered for our souls. Both usefulness and beauty can contribute to solidity and temporal extension. According to Valéry, only architecture can balance all these features and push the creative power to the limit, as well as the mechanics of the effects arising from the construction itself (Scapolo, 2011). The same meaning is in this passage from *Invisible Cities* by Italo Calvino:

> I could tell you how many steps make up the streets rising like stairways, and the degree of the arcades' curves, and what kind of zinc scales cover the roofs; but I already know this would be the same as

> telling you nothing. The city does not consist of this, but of relationships between the measurements of its space and the events of its past ... As this wave of memories flows in, the city soaks it up like a sponge and expands ... The city, however, does not tell its past, but contains it like the lines of a hand, written in the corners of the streets, the gratings of the windows, the banisters of the steps, the antennae of the lightning rods, the poles of the flags, every segment marked in turn with scratches, indentations, scrolls. (1972, pp. 10–11)

The international style[1]

New ideas and projects allowing the transformation of cities need considerable time to be realised. Especially at the beginning, they are often harshly rebuffed. For example, consider how public opinion strongly refused the construction of the Tour Eiffel. Although widely considered a horrible and intolerable monster, it has become the symbol of Paris, of all France and probably of all modernity. In this sense, the psychoanalyst Salomon Resnik (2002, p. 33) writes: "Why shall we not conceive the Tour Eiffel as a big, bright metal tree, in a sort of alchemic fantasy of the new millennium? Why shall we not imagine the Tour Eiffel as a fundamental experience and a rite of passage from one century to another?"

The psychoanalyst Donald Winnicott (1971) argues that one of the main tasks of mothers is to propose a new object to their babies. This task is a real art. On the one hand, if a mother forces the issue and pushes the baby to approach to the new object too much, she will receive a rejection as a response. On the other hand, if she proposes a "period of hesitation" during which the baby will probably turn away and not show any interest, she will see that the baby shows a great interest in the new object.

Mutatis mutandis, in *Republic* Plato describes the city as a grazing land, that is to say, as a place where one might grow up, and in the *Timaeus* defines the space as the great wet nurse of society.

Antonio di Pietro Averlino (known as Filarete) (c. 1460–1464) compares the architect to a mother taking care of her child from conception to adulthood.

Through his works the architect creates or improves a certain taste. In this sense, he inherits the task of the mother guiding the self to a new place having new perspectives and objects. However, the architect does not inherit only the task of the mother but also that of the father as the architect Daniel Libeskind (2015, p. 37) points out: "Every design is like a son. It will have its life and development. You must love it, take care of it, and respect it. When you imagine something you must be ready to take the consequences. It does not matter what you see today but what you will see in the future."

An architectonical innovation must always be assessed first by eyes, second by nose, and third by mouth. This process is more or less the same of that of a sommelier who, for tasting and assessing a wine, must first taste and then ingest it. The development of a new aesthetic concept is a process requiring time and experience to be fully appreciated. However, such a process is possible only when the food (the architectonical innovation) is good and the ingredients fresh. To continue to use this metaphor, the food must be safe for the organism and original, that is to say, not a GMO. In other words, it must not be modified through the modern techniques of genetic engineering and, as a consequence, be a product of consumerist decadence.

With bitter irony, the writer Carlo Emilio Gadda (1959) focuses upon the many disadvantages the new (and inevitable) building techniques have brought to our houses along with the clear advantages: for example, the reinforced concrete and the structural clay tiles have caused phenomena like thermal disequilibrium and noise pollution. "The house of today—the reformed house, the transformed house—is unable to protect and defend its inhabitants and their nerves from this insulting stress." (p. 110)

New ideas, projects, and building techniques should always consider the basic needs of the inhabitant. They should respect the originality and authenticity of a place, its history, and its transformations. Of course, these features should be interpreted and not uncritically accepted. This should avoid conceiving lifeless and unexciting buildings or provocative and sensationalistic creations presented as buildings but actually only fascinating design objects (Venezia, 2011).

One of the fathers of modern architecture, Le Corbusier, argues that the first phase of a project is the critical assessment of the historical context and, as a consequence, of the mental operation of remembering or of placing the artefacts in a sort of mnestic map. However, in spite of his attention to these aspects, he theorises the need to break with the past and Modernism's utopia of *tabula rasa* through the construction of homes that are white, minimalist, and conceived as *machines-à-habiter* (machines for living in). Le Corbusier's "machinistic" poetics was based on the essence of geometry and on its role in the creative and cognitive processes (according to Juan Calatrava (2007), it is a harmonic geometry based much more on an instinctive and spiritual than an abstract and intellectual character). It is worth noting that this geometry is found on the right angle metaphor and was crucial in Le Corbusier's theories until his death. In fact, in 1965, a month before his death, he writes: "It is necessary to find the straight line again. This line comes across the axis of the fundamental laws: biology, nature, cosmos. The straight line is as inflexible as the sea horizon." (Le Corbusier, 1965, p. 172)

W. G. Sebald (1992, p. 145) seems to agree with Le Corbusier when he writes: "Memory … often strikes me as a kind of a dumbness. It makes one's head heavy and giddy, as if one were not looking back down the receding perspectives of time but rather down from a great height, from one of those towers whose tops are lost to view in the clouds." Thus, memory is seen as a hindrance or an obstacle towards something new that must deny its roots (or release from its genetic history) for reaching autonomy.

The architect Anthony Vidler (1992) points out that Le Corbusier intended *to forget* as synonymous with *to erase* the city both literally and figuratively. That is to say, he proposed a *tabula rasa* that allows a return of nature as a basis of a lost urbanism and creates monuments that are functional for modern life, that is, the bureaucratic skyscrapers.

The philosopher Michel Foucault (1984) is suspicious of everything that appears like a return (of something) and points out that history preserves us from historicism or, in other words, from a historicism that continually looks at the past to solve today's problems. For this reason he thinks that the modernists make the same error when they aim at erasing every reference to the past.

The architect Roberto Secchi argues that we cannot create good architecture by drawing on a clean sheet of white paper. This is because to make a project means to add our signs over the layering of signs already present on the topographic map or on the satellite imagery allowed by today's technology:

> This means to give up every redeeming wish and adopt a more responsible attitude. If we want to use a metaphor, this means to try to sow the seeds in a wild and abandoned place or garden, as long as it possesses a proper identity and follows a defined developmental trajectory. (2014, p. 425)

In this sense, the architect's subjectivity, creativity, and stylistic hallmark are not rejected at all, but can be exalted through the meeting with the specificity and the individuality of the place, which allows an authentic and original manufacture.

And in his 2015 encyclical letter, Pope Francis argues that it is not a matter of destroying and constructing new cities, supposedly more respectful of our environment but not necessarily more attractive to live in. Rather, it is matter of integrating the culture and the architecture of a certain place and thus preserving its original identity.

International style is a fundamental stage of architecture. Some of its supporters are important architects such as Le Corbusier, Walter Gropius (the father of Bauhaus), Alvar Aalto, and Ludwig Mies van der Rohe (the last director of Bauhaus architecture). The modern movement in architecture disapproves of the old and obsolete city and aims at substituting it with the new one. The new city is conceived as the cradle of the new human being (intended as an historical man). In the new city the building should appear neutral and deliberately planned, without any expression and applied decoration. Through it, the architect can impose his point of view on the world. Thus, the goal of modernists is the creation of an objective architecture that is free from subjectivity. In my opinion, this intention to destroy pre-existing things[2] cannot be realised. This is because each work is not a neutral space, but represents its creator's attitude and personality. In other words, it represents its creator's subjectivity a defined context and time. It is not intended as something abstract. I believe this is true also for the most shocking, controversial, and heterodox architecture, unconstrained by castrating academic rules.[3]

Jorge Luis Borges (1970, p. 46) writes: "both forgetfulness and memory are apt to be inventive". Creative work sits between forgetfulness and memory.

Gropius does the same as Le Corbusier did for the historical contextualisation of artefact: he refuses to recognise himself as a supporter of a rigorous rationalism. He points out that architecture (and thus his *modus operandi*) must answer also to psychological needs (or problems).

The architecture historian Ezio Bonfanti (2001) criticises Gropius's positions by accusing him not of rationalism but of functionalism. According to Bonfanti, Gropius conceives the psychological aspects in architectural planning as features that must be distinguished and separated from the rational ones. In this sense, these aspects are extra-rational and not integrated with rationality. Thus, Gropius's position is nothing but a mere formal, shallow, and insubstantial concession to the psychological.

The modernists' attempt to erase the clues and the signs of the past from architecture, to radically break with it, and to deny every form of subjectivity, is a sort of therapeutic programme aiming at eliminating nineteenth-century dreariness in all its forms. In a certain sense, the twentieth-century modernists salvage the "total-control paradigm" of the philosopher Jeremy Bentham (1786) and his panopticon.[4] Modernists' appeal to Bentham's positions is clear in their concept of "hygienic space" that stresses the transparency of construction material, the permeability of space, and the continuous streams of air, light, and circulation (Vidler, 1992).

According to the philosopher Walter Benjamin, "the cult of dwelling in the old sense, with the idea of security at its core, has now received its death knell. Giedion, Mendelsohn, and Le Corbusier are converting human habitations into the transitional spaces of every imaginable force and wave of light and air. The coming architecture is dominated by the idea of transparency ..." For this reason, Benjamin (1986, p. 264) sees in Le Corbusier's work the beginning of the end of the "house" as "mythological configuration".

> The idea of a "modern" architecture ... held two dominant themes in precarious balance. The one, stemming from the demand for cultural revolution and a sense of the exhaustion of traditional academic forms, stressed the need to remake the language of the art, to explode the conventions and out of the debris to construct a way of speaking adequate to the modern moment. The other, more tied to the tradition of utopian and materialist attempts to refashion the social world, called for a political and economic transformation that would precipitate society into a life of harmony in the new industrial epoch. (Vidler, 1992, p. 189)
>
> It was an absolute metaphysical aim of the internationalist path [of modernists]. This path attempted to simulate an abstract and linear way of construction, apparently uninfluenced by economic and politic conditions in order to fulfil the function to serve society. It was an attempt of being above everything for proposing an

> objective condition of habitat. The consequence was the design of depersonalised and absent places. (Celant, 2013a, p. 17)

Wilfred Bion (1959) argues that in life, especially at birth, we are exposed to a lot of psycho-sensorial experiences. On the one hand, if these experiences are not transformed in material to think and so in adequate mental functions, they become mentally indigestible experiences, that is to say, not metabolised psycho-sensorial elements. He calls them beta elements. On the other hand, if our mind can give an ontological meaning to psycho-sensorial experiences, they can be food for thought. He calls these metabolised experiences alpha elements.

When beta elements are not transformed into alpha elements and thus there is absence of food for thought, we have a poor quality product, an absence of thought, or junk food. This is a consequence of the architectonical and cultural degradation of International style. We can see how this degradation envelops hotels, stations, airports, malls, ships, districts, skyscrapers, streets, department stores, and so on. People go through these places but they do not actually inhabit them. That is to say, these places propose something like a false self to people, a fictional identity, a sort of cloning devoid of empathy for the minds of others, which are transposed and photocopied.

As we can see, it is a mere functional (sometimes pseudo-functional) or functionalistic operation, which does not allow for the creation of myths, memories, dreams, contemplations, or new visions.

I think that the following verses the poet Pablo Neruda dedicated to his beloved Valparaiso are beautiful:

> ... and window and window and window and
> window and window and another door another
> door another door another door.
> Until the hard modern infinity
> with its hell of squared fire,
> and the birthplace of geometry
> replaces the birthplace of human being.

La Cecla (2008, p. 79) argues: "Neruda's words ... show the difference between the city inhabited by people, where doors and windows are full of colours and confusions, and the city 'made by the fire squared by geometry' or the squared city of difficult modernity."

In his 2015 encyclical letter, Pope Francis seems to share the meaning of Neruda's poem and invites humanity to refuse to resign:

> If architecture reflects the spirit of an age, our mega-structures, and drab apartment blocks express the spirit of globalised technology, where a constant flood of new products coexist with a tedious monotony. Let us refuse to resign ourselves ... Otherwise, we would simply legitimise the present situation and need new forms of escapism to help us endure the emptiness. (pp. 61–62)

Criticisms of international style

The philosopher Martin Heidegger was invited to the Darmstadt Symposium on Man and Space in 1951. Architects, economists, and scientists were invited as well, as was the philosopher José Ortega y Gasset, who defended a position opposed to that of Heidegger.

In his essay *Building, Dwelling, Thinking* (1954), Heidegger points out that, in German, the three terms of the title have the same linguistic root (*bauen* = to build, *buan* = to dwell, *bin* = to be). Then, by making reference to the Saxon and Gothic roots, he notes that the meanings of these three terms are much broader than they can appear at first glance. In fact, they include concepts such as to stay, to hold, to be, to live in peace, and to feel protected by a familiar context. From these philological and etymological considerations Heidegger derives the possibility or the risk of losing the sense of living in a fluid time. He describes a way of approaching spaces that prevents their transformation in places, that is to say, in spaces in which human beings can live. We are because we dwell. To dwell means to stay on earth. To dwell means to embrace nature and accept its rhythms, to understand the divine silence without aiming at putting in its place, to recognise our death and be prepared for it without falling into dimming nihilism. The capacity of dwelling means taking care and thus having the possibility to construct and organise the space, that is to say, to start with the basic distinction between inside and outside. In this sense, Heidegger seems to see planting as a form of environtmental modelling and home construction a significant attitude of human identity, perhaps a structural necessity.[5]

According to José Ortega y Gasset (1952), humans possess this technique and are able to imagine the world. Thus, the act of constructing is the act of realising the human imagination. In this way humans move from nature and contrasts in order to construct a human world, that is to say, a world where humans can live. So, dwelling does not precede constructing, but it is something that humans themselves create. In this sense, as Ortega y Gasset says upon reflecting on the Darmstadt Symposium on Man and Space, humans are intruders and not part of this world. Their way of being in the world is not to dwell in it, but to seek wellbeing in it. As we can see, the different positions that Heidegger and Ortega y Gasset take represent well the conflicts of contemporary architectural thought.

The philosopher Theodor W. Adorno berates modernism and argues:

> The functional modern habitations designed from a *tabula rasa*, are living cases manufactured by experts for philistines, or factory sites that have strayed into the consumption sphere, devoid of all relation to the occupant ... The house is past ... These are now good only to be thrown away like old food cans ... The best mode of conduct, in the face of all this, still seems an uncommitted, suspended one: to lead a private life, as far as the social order and one's own needs will tolerate nothing else, but not to attach weight to it as to something still socially substantial and individually appropriate. (1951, pp. 38–39)

Many authors support the meaning and the importance of a return to the past. It is worth noting that many of them are not nostalgic in any way. Seneca (49 AD) describes the past as sacred and inviolable and stresses the importance of its eternal and unalterable possession. The poet and philosopher Novalis (1802) writes: "Whither are we going? Ever homewards." Or the poet Giacomo Leopardi in his *Zibaldone*: "Words like faraway or ancient are really poetical and enjoyable, because they give rise to undefined and extensive ideas" (25 September 1821).

Using the third person to talk about himself, in *Notre Dame de Paris* Victor Hugo notes:

> [The author] has already pleaded ... the cause of our ancient architecture, he has already loudly denounced many profanations,

> many demolitions, many impieties ... He will be as indefatigable in defending our historical edifices as our iconoclasts of the schools and academies are eager in attacking them; for it is a grievous thing to see into what hands the architecture of the Middle Ages has fallen, and in what manner the botchers of plaster of the present day treat the ruin of this grand art ... All the harm which false taste can inflict on good taste, they accomplish. (1932, p. 616)

The *Club des Hashischins* (the hashish-eaters club) was a Parisian group that aimed to explore drug-induced experiences, particularly with hashish. Members included Victor Hugo, Charles Baudelaire, and Theophile Gautier. Gautier (1846, p. 19) describes his entry to the club with these words: "I made my way to a remote *quartier*, a sort of oasis of solitude in the heart of Paris, which the river, in surrounding it with its two arms, seemed to protect from the encroachments of civilisation." Taking drugs allows access to a craved and almost impossible to reach internal city, thus going to a peaceful and idealised place. This place is conceived as uncontaminated by civilisation or by a confusing modernity.

We can find spiritualist and anti-progressive nostalgia in the work of Arthur Rimbaud, for example in his poem *Bad Blood* (1873, p. 267): "Science, the new nobility! Progress. The world marches on! Why shouldn't it turn back? It is the vision of numbers. We are moving towards the Spirit." Later, the writer Karl Kraus (1909) praises the narcissistic pleasure linked to nostalgia: "The origin is the goal" (p. 178) and "It is not the beloved who is distant but distance is the beloved." (p. 181) Walter Benjamin adopts Kraus's aphorism and uses it in the epigraph of his thesis XIV. However, Adorno criticises Benjamin because he finds that such an epigraph sounds like something conservative. Further, he stresses how the concept of origin should lose the character of static emptiness.

Franz Kafka (1946) writes that the future pushes the human mind back in the past, to the most ancient times. In *Requiem for a Nun* (1950), William Faulkner writes: "The past is never dead. It's not even past." (p. 152) In the same vein Christa Wolf (1976) argues that "what is past is not dead; it is not even past. We cut ourselves off from it; we pretend to be strangers." (p. 211)

In the segment *La ricotta* (curd cheese) in the film *RoGoPaG* (a 1963 film consisting of four segments, each written and directed by one of four film directors. The film's title is an abbreviation of the author's surnames: Rossellini, Godard, Pasolini, and Gregoretti) directed by Pier Paolo Pasolini, the actor and director Orson Welles plays the part of a Marxist director. At a certain point he says:

> I am a force of the Past.
> My love lies only in tradition.
> I come from the ruins, the churches,
> the altarpieces, the villages
> abandoned in the Apennines or foothills
> of the Alps where my brothers once lived.
> I wander like a madman down the Tuscolana,
> down the Appia like a dog without a master.
> Or I see the twilight, the mornings
> over Rome, the Ciociaria, the world,
> as the first acts of Post-history
> to which I bear witness, for the privilege
> of recording them from the outer edge
> of some buried age. Monstrous is the man
> born of a dead woman's womb.
> And I, a foetus now grown, roam about
> more modern than any modern man,
> in search of brothers no longer alive.

I believe these verses (they were later published in 1964) represent the most clear and desperate example of Pasolini's poetry, that is to say, his feeling of being a stranger in an increasingly conformed present and his fear of a future that seems a sort of cultural desert. In 1962, in the magazine *Vie Nuove* (New Ways), Pasolini replies to a reader's question, saying: "The idea that I am a modernist is a wrong idea and a journalist's mystification. Even in my most extreme experimentations I have never left the grand Italian and European tradition behind. We must take the 'monopoly of tradition' away from traditionalists."

In a different vein Martin Heidegger (1959) argues that the origin is both the source and the future. In this sense, he seems to adopt a relativistic perspective that can give a developmental meaning to the recovery of the past. The French historian Marc Bloch (1945) proposes a parable in which an oak is born from an acorn, but becomes and is an oak only under favourable environmental conditions. As we can see, he argues that the origin is not the history, which is represented by the process (in his parable, the passage from acorn to oak). This means that a certain phenomenon cannot be understood and explained only by referring to the past, but also by the context within which it has taken place and developed. It is worth noting that a series of consequential events is not always necessary for predicting and realising the next one. In this sense, sometimes tracing the origin and determining the cause cannot help. The Latin idiomatic expression *post hoc, ergo propter hoc* (after this, therefore because of this) is a logical fallacy and an unacceptable simplification. The *post hoc* (after this) does not imply the *propter hoc* (because of this); that is to say, something is not necessarily a cause because of its temporal antecedence.

Surrealists also fiercely criticise modernism. In fact, they are fascinated with a sort of return to an original, archaic, and uncontaminated society and they propose a worldview as much nostalgic as unrealistic.

André Breton, the father of surrealism (quoted in Vidler, 1992, p. 150), argues that modernist functionalism is "the most unhappy dream of the collective unconscious" or "a solidification of desire in its most and cruel automatism". The avant-garde poet Tristan Tzara (1933) strongly criticises Le Corbusier's and van der Rohe's modern rationalist architecture. He defines it as the absolute negation of the image of habitation and proposes the so-called "intrauterine architecture". This architecture is based upon the maternal and welcoming image of "uterine" construction that, from the cave to the grotto to the tent, comprises all the basic forms of human habitation.

Freud (1919b) argues that, in spite of their familiar origin, the mother's genitals or body can be experienced and interpreted as uncanny. He writes that, "in this case too, then, the unheimlich is what was once heimlich, familiar". (p. 225) With surrealists we easily find fantasies of coming back to the original maternal uterus. However, as Freud (1918) clearly points out in his descriptive analysis of the so-called Wolf-Man, the interiors of intrauterine existence are at the same time warm containers and the wellsprings of the uncanny, a refuge for unavoidably and incestuously unrealised desires and a possible place to bury human beings.

I believe that the apparently incompatible demands of total denial of the past on the one hand and of complete and idealised reinstatement of the past on the other should find a synthesis.

The architect Ugo Tonietti argues that:

> There are many and contradictory elements to consider. All of them are determinant factors. On the one hand, we aim at preserving all

> harmonies we link to the magnificent past urban settlements. On the other, we do not want to lose all stimuli offered by contemporaneity and to find a satisfying expression of it. (2011, p. IX)

I think that we must try to reach this impossible goal.

Like poets, architects use their emotions to work on the images of the past and on the visions of the future (Braghieri, 2013).

The nineteenth-century controversy between John Ruskin and Eugène Viollet-le-Duc is quite famous. Because of his idea of traditionalist conservatism, Ruskin thought that every sort of restoration work should be considered as immoral.[6] Thus, he argued that, first of all, it was necessary to preserve what still existed. For this reason, he allowed only routine maintenance or minor repair work[7] to extend as much as possible the life of ancient architecture. Ruskin argued that we must recognise the right for such architecture to die (at the right time, of course).

Eugène Emmanuel Viollet-le-Duc's creative romanticism was the extreme opposite of Ruskin's traditionalist conservatism. In fact, Viollet-le-Duc was a supporter of *ex novo* reconstruction in restoring building. According to Viollet-le-Duc, restoring a building does not mean maintaining, repairing, or reconstructing it: rather, it means completely restoring it to a state in which it had never existed prior to restoration. By applying these principles, he irreparably modified many buildings and monuments: it was quite paradoxical that after these modifications, the buildings could be saved.

A third way (the Italian way of restoration) between traditionalist conservatism and creative romanticism[8] appeared the most balanced. This is because it was able to solve the problems of restoration by finding a compromise between the extreme options.

The complexity and the overlap of various determinants can help us avoid two kinds of reductionism. The first comes from an excess of nostalgia or contemplation of past times aiming at reducing or avoiding a psychic trauma determined by a new external stimulus. In this sense, what is perceived is destroyed and reduced to something already known and experienced. The second kind of reductionism can be called that of the *horizontality without a past*: it implies the adoption of a point of view able to exclude the comparison with other alternative ones and to focus exclusively on the present. A possible elaboration of the meaning of the past is actually denied and the possibility of recovering a realistic diachrony of events is not allowed. It is not easy to synthetise different and conflicting demands as the reference to the past and the experience of the present. I believe that the main risk is an incoherent and unproductive eclecticism.[9] Unfortunately, I don't think that there are reliable valid alternatives available.

Something similar can be found in psychoanalysis. On the one hand, it is fundamental to assess whether the past occurs in the present, that is, to understand how past events and experiences actually influence present life both actively and unconsciously. On the other hand, a continuous revisiting of the past takes place via the psychoanalytic relationship. This allows the patient to reconstruct a version of her history not distorted by neurotic defences and false memories.

In an important manifesto for a new architecture the American architect Robert Venturi[10] writes:

> But architecture is necessarily complex and contradictory in its very inclusion of the traditional Vitruvian elements of commodity, firmness, and delight … I welcome the problems and exploit the uncertainties. By embracing contradiction as well as complexity, I aim for vitality as well as validity. Architects can no longer afford to be intimidated by the puritanically moral language of orthodox Modern architecture. I like elements which are hybrid rather than pure, compromising rather than clean, distorted rather than straightforward, perverse as well as impersonal, boring as well as interesting, conventional rather than designed, accommodating rather than excluding, redundant rather than simple, vestigial as well as innovating, inconsistent and equivocal rather than direct and clear … I am for richness of meaning rather than clarity of meaning; for the implicit function as well as the explicit function. I prefer both-and to either-or, black and white, and sometimes grey, to black and white. (1966, p. 16)

Ruins

In the 1950s, in opposition to a world used to the twisted images of an obsolete industrial machinery, Louis J. Kahn proposes to make reference to the beauty of the great ancient ruins and to the view of a simple world composed of few basic forms. In opposition to the vulgar rhetoric of Say's law, he indicates the civil dimension of construction. He reminds us that great monumental architecture can be built by using the simplest techniques and material (Braghieri, 2005).

Although Marc Augé (2003) affirms that future history will no longer produce ruins, but only rubble coming from the non-places of supermodernity, the question of memory and oblivion or of dissolution and permanence remains (Capuano, 2010). Augé himself seems to hope that, from the rubble of non-places, construction sites will arise and thus also the possibility to build something new and to find a sense of time (2003, p. 137).

In 1929 the French architect Auguste Perret admonishes his students with this famous aphorism (cited in Claude, 1944, p. 26): "Architecture is what makes beautiful ruins."

Talking with an imaginary student, Francesco Venezia interprets Perret's aphorism in this way:

> You must always remember, although it certainly depends on the contingent and temporary circumstances, needs, and conveniences, your project must have something that makes it eternal, once realised. In other words, the fate of your project realised must be that of being a ruin in the future and thus to talk to next generations. This means that it must be universal, at least to some extent. (2011, p. 15)

We are at the beginning of an era in which we fear constructions much more than ruins. Ruins are abandoned human constructions, places full of the promise of the unknown with all its epiphanies and dangers (Solnit, 2000).[11] We can see a nature able to suck the human being, I mean, a nature covering again with herbs, leaves, animals, and small bushes the ruins of the human products that constructed their destruction (Guarnieri, 2006). In ruins we can see the animals having their revenge over mankind and covering everything with leaves and shrubbery. Ruins represent an "un-nature" that creates its own destruction. "Ruins become the unconscious of a city, its memory, unknown, darkness, lost lands, and in this truly bring it to life. With ruins a city springs free of its plans into something as intricate as life, something that can be explored but perhaps not mapped." (Solnit, 2005, p. 89)

Giuliana Bruno, a professor of visual and environmental studies, describes modernist architecture as women unable to age well when they deny the physical evidence:

> Unlike the porous, permeable stone of ancient building, the material of modernism does not ruin. Concrete does not decay. It does not

> slowly erode and corrode, fade out or fade away ... Modernist architecture does not absorb the passing of time. Adverse to deterioration, it does not age easily, gracefully, or elegantly ... With concrete, there can no longer be lines emerging gently on the face of a building, line drawings on the map of time past. (2007, p. 79)

The quick and anonymous architectonic reconstruction of German cities destroyed in the Second War World and the consequent cover-up of the ruins (in this sense, ruins become *terra incognita*—unknown land) in which people lived during that war are clear examples of an unbearable feeling of loss and of a trace of something that cannot be fully accepted and that must be erased. In this sense, the collective memory is built upon the new origin myth of the reconstruction of Germany (Guarnieri, 2006). It is:

> Individual and collective amnesia, probably influenced by preconscious self-censorship—a means of obscuring a world that could no longer be presented in comprehensible terms ... The darkest aspect of the final act of destruction ... remained under a kind of taboo like a shameful family secret, a secret that perhaps could not even be privately acknowledged. (Sebald, 2001a, p. 10)

Sebald clarifies that Germany "developed an almost perfectly functioning mechanism of repression, one that allowed it to recognise the fact of its own rise from total degradation while disengaging entirely from its stock of emotions" (ibid., p. 12). Sebald finds dehumanising not only destruction *per se*, but also our capacity of living with and denying it.

An example of the great importance attributed to ruins and to their function of preserving the original project of the artist came in 1990 when the artistic and intellectual society of Barcelona opposed (unfortunately to no avail) the continuing construction of the *Sagrada Familia* (more specifically, they opposed the controversial work of sculptor Josep M. Subirachs).

On a July evening, about 500 people (many of them poets, writers, film-makers, architects, illustrators, and night owls) gathered in front of the cathedral and protested against what they considered to be an act of architectonic villainy, which did not consider that incomplete buildings always hold promise for the future (Puntì, 2012).

The architect Andrea Ugolini writes (2010, p. 13): "The attention to ruins and to something incomplete is first of all an ethical exercise of tolerant reception of a fragment and thus of a figurativity only apparently patchy and fragmentary."

Again, Francesco Venezia's words underscore the aesthetical importance of ruins, of their incompleteness, of their fragmentary nature:

> Ruins have an important place in human experience and psychic life. They have a poetical nature. Ruins allow us to travel with our minds, make lose in a deep temporal perspective without defined borders, feed our need of infinity. Of course, I here refer to a human infinity, which perhaps we can call unclear. For this and many other reasons we are ready to start long and sometimes trying travels. (2011, p. 91)

The French architect Laurent Beaudouin writes:

> Love for ruins comes from an impression of slow return to origins. In this slight return the building lose it artificial features and seems a real natural product. It thinks to escape from history and to become a fragment of geology. It returns to its origins and moves from a human time to a universal time, that is to say, a time without dates, references, or clear relationships. (2007, p. 89)

According to Marc Augé the meaning of ruins is neither historical nor aesthetical, but purely temporal. It is the duration intended as *hic et nunc* (here and now) of a fragment of the past:

> Contemplating ruins is not the same of making a journey in history, but of making an experience of time, more precisely, of pure time. About the past, history is too rich, too deep, and too various to be reduced to a directly observable symbol carved in stone … About the present, emotion is something aesthetic, but the beauty of nature is combined with that of ruins. (2003, p. 36)

Nature, origins, and ruins dynamically arrange themselves as scaffolding and a container for the present and as the promise of a future whose route is visible. However, I believe this can be done only if we are able to have respect for their mystery and to avoid saturated interpretations, analogical, symbolical, and allegorical explanations. In his novel *Mr Palomar*, Italo Calvino suggests something similar:

> A stone, a figure, a sign, a word reaching us isolated from its context is only that stone, figure, sign, or word: we can try to define them, to describe them as they are, and no more than that; whether, beside the face they show us, they also have a hidden face, is not for us to know. The refusal to comprehend more than what the stones show us is perhaps the only way to evince respect for their secret; trying to guess is a presumption, a betrayal of that true, lost meaning. (1983c, p. 97)

For the individuation of places

As reported by the architect Carlo Truppi, Frank Lloyd Wright argues that a human being is what he or she does. In this sense, he overturns the logic of a society in which the person exists in terms of what they do. On the contrary, Kahn argues, we do in order to exist. "The doing, or the way in which things are realised, implies a relation with what surrounds us and hosts our life. This is because the things define the places, they imprint them on our minds and thus they do not allow reducing them to cheap consumer goods." (Truppi, 2004, p. 118)

According to psychoanalyst Olivier Marc:

> Is it possible to call architecture something that is nothing but construction? Or, in other words, is it possible to call architecture something that does not talk to our soul and thus does not talk to our body any more? … Architecture seems to have lost its symbolic function and allowed development of many fields of application and new techniques. Thus, it seems to have come before simple building construction and after industrialisation of building construction. (1972, p. 142)

Georges Perec (1974, p. 89) defines "the uninhabitable" as "the architecture of contempt or display, the vainglorious mediocrity of tower blocks, thousands of rabbit hutches piled one above the other". I think we need to have a relational attitude permitting not the juxtaposition of architecture over place, but rather the realisation of a principle of continuity. However, if construction is mainly an act of decontextualising places and passing beyond their specificity (in this sense, construction means to subvert a place's rules), what remains of dwelling?

According Franco La Cecla (2015), the Italian expression *fare mente locale* (to think about something) indicates the capacity to inhabit the space that belongs to every culture and individual. It is the capacity to create mental maps for dwelling in a certain place. Unfortunately, the so-called "places specialists" (La Cecla critically uses this expression to define all architects, politicians, and administrators insensible to the active demands of everyone who wants to make use of places) have seized such a capacity to image, construct, transform, and use places. The Italian architect Carlo Ratti (2014) takes a position against an authoritative, commanding, and heroic architecture dictating its spatial system and denying the needs of its users and of the surrounding environment. He proposes open source architecture, that is to say, architecture open to participation in each of its phases. In this sense, he proposes collective, cooperative, and bottom-up architecture. It is architecture that uses the possibilities offered by computer science and the internet and thus allows the sharing of planning methods and techniques that can be adapted to specific demands.

In the 1927 paper *In the Cause of Architecture: The Architect and the Machine*, Frank Lloyd Wright introduces the expression organic architecture and says: "Let your home appear to grow easily from its site and shape it to sympathise with the surroundings if Nature is manifest there, and if not, try and be as quiet, substantial, and organic as she would have been if she had the chance." (p. 395) In the 1914 paper *In the Cause of Architecture: Second Paper*, he points out, "I still believe that the ideal of an organic architecture is the origin and the source, and basically the force and the meaning of everything we can call architecture." (p. 409) Further, in the 1957 paper *A Testament*, he writes (p. 402): "As natural building proceeds, the individual will see building as he is learning to see life. Idea to idea, idea to form, and form to function, buildings designed to liberate and expand, not contain and confine, the richer, deeper elements of nature."

The Austrian and Czech architect Adolf Loos[12] writes:

> May I take you to the shores of a mountain lake? The sky is blue, the water green and everywhere is profound tranquillity. The clouds and mountains are mirrored in the lake, the houses, farms, and

> chapels as well. They do not look as if they were fashioned by man; it is as if they came straight from God's workshop, like the mountains and trees, the clouds and the blue sky. And everything exudes an air of beauty and peace … But what is this? A discordant note in the tranquillity. Like an unnecessary screech. Among the locals' houses, which were not built by them, but by God, stands a villa. The creation of an architect. Whether a good or bad architect, I don't know. All I know is that the tranquillity, peace and beauty have vanished … An therefore I ask, why is it that any architect, good or bad, desecrates the lake … Like almost all city dwellers, the architect lacks culture. The city dweller is rootless. (1910, pp. 73–74)

In a 1949 paper, the psychoanalyst Raffaele Perrotti anticipates Augé's theory of non-places and notices that the design of the new Roma Termini railway station provided functionality and an appropriate architectonic aspect, but not an adequate psychological function:

> The station provides the first contact with the city. It is an anticipation of the city for those who arrive in it and the last image for those who leave it … The arrival is a boundary between past and future, something new, an achievement, perhaps an adventure or a hope for change. Similarly, the departure represents a separation (sometimes painful, sometimes softened by memories) scheduling a future appointment. In this sense, the departure resembles regret. Thus, the station has an unconscious and intensively affective symbolic meaning. It is a psychic medium between the traveller's past experience and the future experience of his destination. At an unconscious level, the moment he gets off the train, the traveller awaits a symbolic embrace from the city, that is to say, its welcome. This means that he makes a first contact with the city. This contact is made of many impressions. These impressions indicate the city's particular way of greeting, I mean, its unique welcome or goodbye (that sometimes implies an invitation to come back). Thus, to make this psychic deal, the station's architecture must refer to the spirit or soul of the city. That is to say, this architecture must represent all the features and hints of the city, all the things that identify it … I believe a psychologically neutral station is unconceivable … We can consider the disappointment of a traveller open to developing affectionate bonds with the Eternal City. Once he gets off the train,

> he finds himself in a modern and pleasant place, but one that is anonymous. He finds himself in a place where everything works very well, but where there is a sense of psychological disharmony (which does not arouse any interest or positive expectation). The question is this: if the traveller is absent-minded and thinks that he can find himself in some place (not necessarily in the Eternal City), will he come back to Rome again? (Perrotti, 1949, pp. 174–175)

The philosopher and anthropologist Pierre Sansot praises the social functions of railway stations:

> Once stations attracted people with time to spare in which they would notice small gestures and catch glimpses. The travellers or city inhabitants went to the restaurants near the station as if they could be places where something might happen and as if people could be more interesting than elsewhere. Near the station, monumental structures seem as though they could give more relevance to the most modest actions. Today, stations are no longer the temples of departures ... By removing the hall benches and hiding the waiting rooms, we made sure that men cannot take refuge in stations any more.[13] (1998, p. 173)

In spite of the criticisms of modernism, the architect Vittorio Gregotti argues that it is important due to its attention to social results (it is worth noting that Gregotti rejects postmodernism). In his book *Tre Forme di Architettura Mancata* (Three forms of failed architecture)[14] (2010), he points out that the apparent success of a certain way of creating architecture hides some dangers both for the artistic practice itself and for the consequences that it can have on the world in which we live. These dangers derive from three renunciations or three forms of failed architecture. The first is to give up the idea of modifying the present as a possibility of critically comparing it with the context. The second is to give up the idea of considering things in detail. The third is to give up the idea of an architectural work's lifetime as a metaphor for eternity. Gregotti's fear is that many contemporary architects, supporters of the contemporary and deconstructionist interpretations, have become simple illustrators. This means that they seem to propose that everything today can be sacrificed in the name of the triumph of a contingent event, and that the sublime can become perverted. In other words, they appear to be quite aware of the idea of proposing that (at least) a sketch of truth can be a foundation of an architecture of the possible and necessary (Gregotti, 2013).

In contrast to Gregotti, the author Tom Wolfe (1981) argues that the solutions proposed by postmodern architecture directly derive from architectonic rationalism and thus are not opposed to it, they simply reflect 1930s deformations and ghosts. He writes: "There are now new approaches, new isms: post-modernism, late modernism ... Which add up to what? To such things as building more glass boxes and covering them with mirrored plate glass so as to reflect the glass boxes next door and distort their straight lines into curves." (p. 4)

However, it is a matter of fact that, in postmodern architecture, the study of images is nothing but the search for exhibiting an architectonic object. This leads architects to focus on the issue of the form and to underestimate function and structure (the two other components of the Vitruvian triad). According to Rafael Moneo (2013), the analogy between buildings and objects completely denies the idea of architecture aiming at integrating within a contest, expanding and creating a defined identity.

The philosopher Nicola Emery (2007) proposes "difficult architecture"—architecture fully aware of the environment and opposed to formalism without any content. He argues that this formalism is a consequence of the contemporary spectacularisation, which leads to design, and constructs only in substantial and reified terms and which impoverishes the ecological, social, and relational meaning of architecture.

Non-places

Marc Augé introduces the concept of *non-place* in philosophical debate:

> If a place can be defined as relational, historical, and concerned with identity, then a space which cannot be defined as relational, or historical, or concerned with identity will be a non-place. The hypothesis advanced here is that supermodernity produces non-places, meaning spaces which are not themselves anthropological places and which, unlike Baudelerian modernity, do not integrate the earlier places: instead these are listed, classified, promoted to the status of "places of memory", and assigned to a circumscribed and specific position. (1992, p. 78)

Augé's concept of non-place is incisive because it refers to the issue of origins on the one hand and to the problem of psychological and anthropological solitude on the other:

> The ideal non-place is that in which all social relations can be interpreted only through observation. In a place like that there is no freedom at all. Every residence is assigned ... It is a place where solitude is the common condition. (2006, p. 81)
>
> There is non-place in every place, and in all non-places places can be recomposed. To put it another way, places and non-places, while they correspond to physical spaces, are also a reflection of attitudes, positions, the relations individuals have with the space they live in or move through. (Augé, 1994, p. 106)

Some years before Augé, the Italian philosopher Rosario Assunto (1984) strongly criticised the transition from the historical to the present city. According to his view, the former was first the space of representation and then of suitability, whereas the latter is characterised by the predominance of functional aspects over aesthetical ones. This predominance destroyed beauty and nature, serialised urban features, and transformed historical cities in "historical centres" often having the aspect of anonymous business centres.

According to the philosopher Fabio Merlini (2012), many constructions are no longer inhabitable in Heideggerian terms. Thus, we have a non-place when the space in front of us is not inhabitable. Merlini uses the term "schizotypy" to describe a place deprived of thresholds, that is to say, without any normativity of context but rather indifferent to any context.

There are a growing number of criticisms of International style, of the lifeless high-tech buildings, and of this pseudo-egalitarian and omnipresent functionalism from many different disciplines. Many stress the megalomaniac features that do not consider the *genius loci* and aim at eliminating every trace of past and memory. It is a sort of fantasy of parthenogenesis that denies every ancestry and every presence of mothers and fathers and thus the need of time and rhythms typical of the depressive position and necessary for a sufficiently good generational transmission.

The Swiss literary critic Jean Starobinski (1990) argues that the essence of modernity is the presence of the past in the present. The present both goes beyond and claims a right to the past. He coins the expression "low continuity" to describe those ancient places and rhythms that modernity cannot erase but only put in the background. Those places and rhythms are indicators of time going by and surviving. In modernity everything stays and past and present are intertwined. Steeples and chimneystacks are the rulers of the city and metaphoric visions of modernity (or, at least, of its appearance). Consider "supermodernity", which makes of the past and history nothing but a show, a display of exoticisms and particularities (Augé, 1992).

Lorena Preta (2006) writes about remains of the past and anticipations of the future.[15]

The philosopher Remo Bodei (2009) argues that, when nostalgia is manifest, things are no more subordinated to an unquenchable desire to return to a lost past. They are no more part of the dream of modifying time irreversibility, changing or maintaining the series of those events taking place only once in all eternity. Rather, things are vehicles in a voyage of discovery of a past containing a possible future.

Walter Benjamin writes:

> It's not that what is past casts its light on what is present, or what is present its light on the past; rather, image is that wherein what has been comes together in a flash with the now to form a constellation. In other words, image is dialectics at a standstill. For while the relation of the present to the past is a purely temporal, continuous one, the relation of what-has-been to the now is dialectical: is not progression but image, suddenly emergent. (1986, p. 462)

Enrico Pinna (2002, p. 114) finds in architects' sketches[16] "a primal force in which a past full of images and the attempt to transform and dynamically regulate the past".

The architect Oscar Niemeyer (1978) argues that function is not the only thing that matters. Beauty, fantasy, architectural hindrances constitute the essence of architecture. He reminds us that the concern to create beauty is one of the most relevant features of humankind. Such a concern can be found also in ancient times: for example, when our prehistoric ancestor painted the walls of his refuge before building it or in the construction of the pyramids. Niemeyer criticises functionalism because of its abuse of indoor mapping to outdoor, of right angles, of imposition of construction systems, of the unconvincing functional limitations.

He believes that functionalism cannot compare with inventive and lyrical past works.

What Niemeyer calls the perception of beauty (I refer here to beauty's endless game of existence, disappearance, and continuous change) deals with an intense, direct, and immediate emotional reaction.[17] Such a reaction does not come from social stimuli but rather from formal features and intellectual criteria. Meltzer (in Stokes, 1963, p. 44) argues, "in nature we can find reflected the beauty we already contain. But art helps us to regain what we have lost."

To remind us that even in the architectonic-urban intervention of Berlin's Potsdamer Platz (perhaps the most radical intervention of this sort planned in the last decades in Europe) we can find traces of previous constructions, Mario Botta says (2007, p. 11): "Nowadays, memory is a condition for filtering the contradictions and conflicts of globalisation, a way for going beyond the contrasts of the many past centuries. History is a necessary condition for dealing with the present challenges."

Renzo Piano writes:

> Berlin is strange, because it is a mix of nostalgia and amnesia. Everyone, myself included, asks: Will Berlin's good old times come back? Will life come back? Life will surely come back because Potsdamer Platz is in the heart of Berlin. I think the desert left by war was only a twist of fate. However, sometimes I say that I have got some doubts. What kind of life will there be? Surely the good old times will not come back. Thus, we have an unsatisfied wish. So, let's construe our present because nostalgia can be really dangerous. It does not make any sense to return to the past, to good old times. It is true that the past is fascinating. This is because of its romantic and ancient appearance. This is the reason for all the nostalgia and amnesia of Berliners. Berlin had wanted to forget all horrors, ghosts, and deserts. It made the remains of Potsdamer Platz disappear with the clear intention of forgetting. It has done the same thing with war and, more recently, with the Wall. There is no trace of the Berlin Wall. We are in a contradiction between nostalgia and amnesia. We will need a lot of time for dealing with this contradiction. However, there are all the fundamental features of an ancient urbanity. Life will continue, but something will be forgotten. Potsdamer Platz has to make itself forgive its presumption of newness. (2004, p. 136)

The Swiss architect Peter Zumthor (1999, pp. 24–25) writes: "Architecture is exposed to life. If its body is sensitive enough, it can assume a quality that bears witness to the reality of past life."

In a recent interview, Mario Botta (2013) affirms that architecture is always a mirror of the history and society in which it develops. It is hopeless to think we can have a beautiful city in a ghettoised and perverted society. In his book *Cities of the World* (1975), Elio Vittorini writes that beautiful cities produce beautiful people and ugly cities ugly people. I think it is clear that there exists a bidirectional relationship between man and architectonic context. In fact, if it is true that architecture reflects social identities, it is also true that it actively contributes to their formation. The ambition of a decontextualised architecture, which cuts off every link with the past and narcissistically represents only a sort of cold and objectifying creativity of the architect, has led to a consumeristically flattened and lifeless concept of dwelling. In this sense, Rafael Moneo (2013) points out how the shadow of "being everywhere" falls on our present world and how architecture, through the physical presence of a building, can release a place from this "being everywhere".

The coming together of architects and psychoanalysts aims at considering and designing places able to reunite mind and body, inside and outside, past and present, by avoiding dangerous and costly splitting.

CHAPTER SIX

Continuity and discontinuity in psychoanalysis

> The past no longer casts light upon the future; our minds advance in darkness.
>
> (Alexis de Tocqueville, 1835–1840, p. 819)

A social mutation or a wide and confused change in values?

As with architecture, psychoanalysis faces some problems of relation between continuity and discontinuity. Psychoanalysis is born as a great modern narrative and aims to universally define the internal world of contemporary man. It can propose itself as a modern narrative by inquiring about the individual stories and transcriptions of social reality. Postmodern culture introduces in psychoanalysis concepts and practices similar to those of the modern movement in architecture (as we have seen in the previous chapter, the modern movement aims to construe buildings representing the denial of the roots and the interruption of all links to the past). Claudio Magris fiercely criticises this culture (2005, p. 2): "Today the Modern, with all its faith in the progress and in the possibility of directing the course of history, seems like dusty junk. We are living and moving in a postmodern, global, and sophisticated

Middle Ages able to quickly transform the world through technology, but unable to give it a meaning."

For Sigmund Freud there is no contrast between individual psychology and social (or group) psychology. This is clear in the beginning of his essay *Group Psychology and the Analysis of the Ego*, which is a sort of manifesto:

> The contrast between individual psychology and social or group psychology, which at first glance may seem to be full of significance, loses a great deal of its sharpness when it is examined more closely. It is true that individual psychology is concerned with the individual man and explores the paths by which he seeks to find satisfaction for his instinctual impulses; but only rarely and under certain exceptional conditions is individual psychology in a position to disregard the relations of this individual to others. In the individual's mental life someone else is invariably involved, as a model, as an object, as a helper, as an opponent; and so from the very first individual psychology, in this extended but entirely justifiable sense of the words, is at the same time social psychology as well. (1921c, p. 69)

Differently from Freud, some contemporary psychoanalysts do refer to simple modifications of the social contexts and the implications for individual subjectivity. They emphatically describe an unprecedented social mutation and its anthropological implications.[1] They argue that this makes us unable to understand all the implications coming from the changes to which we attend. I think the positions we find among psychoanalysts on this issue are not well balanced and appear very controversial. I believe we can find two contrasting parties. On the one hand, we have the conservative psychoanalysts (for example, Glass, 1993; Leary, 1994; Melman, 2002) who hold strong or moderate positions. Supporters of the strong position argue that, if analytic theory and practice were open to newness, they would be corrupted and at risk of decline; supporters of the moderate position argue that the traditional psychoanalytic categories are sufficient to understand newness because there is nothing but new. On the other hand, we have the revolutionary psychoanalysts (for example, Stern, 1985; Chodorow, 1995; Hoffmann, 1998; Flax, 2000; Frosh, 2000) who argue that we must find radically new ways of thinking and that the traditional psychoanalytic perspectives are obsolete and unable to understand today's subjectivities. According to the revolutionary psychoanalysts, we must renounce universal theories and universal motivations and we no longer believe in the "great narratives" of the fathers of psychoanalysis. In my opinion, both parties are defensively extremist and unable to deal with the complex phenomena linked to socio-cultural changes.

The literary critic Remo Cesarani (1998, p. 21) writes: "There are neither earthquakes nor catastrophes in both history outside us and history inside us. We can find earthquakes or catastrophes only in our interpretative models." Even if it can be seen as an extraordinarily evident and strong transformation, postmodernity is actually characterised by delays, continuities, ideological and sentimental refusals, attachments, and nostalgias (Cesarani, 1998).

In the same vein, the philosopher and sociologist Jean-François Lyotard (1979) writes that postmodernity cannot be conceived as an era following modernity because of the strong connections between the modern and postmodern. The simultaneity of modern and postmodern forms of expression allows us to define postmodernity as modernity without illusions (Bauman, 1993), that is to say, a sort of suspension between what passed (and is no more) and what will be (and is not yet) (Bauman & Mauro, 2015). In this sense, we can avoid drastic historical interruptions.

The philosophers Agnes Heller and Ferenc Fehér write:

> Postmodernity may be understood as the private-collective time and space, within the wider time and space of modernity, delineated by those who have problems with and queries addressed to modernity, by those who want to take it to task, and by those who make inventory of modernity's achievements as well as its unresolved dilemmas. Those who have chosen to dwell in postmodernity nevertheless live among moderns as well as pre-moderns. For the very foundation of postmodernity consists of viewing the world as a plurality of heterogeneous spaces and temporalities. Postmodernity thus can only define itself within this plurality, against these heterogeneous others. (1988, p. 1)

Many emerging phenomena enter the hard core of mental experience and can remodel the unconscious transactions among human beings in new and often dramatic modalities. Examples of this phenomena are: economic globalisation, the internet and new media, time-space compression and change, growth of individualism and hedonism, the welfare crisis, the paradox of simultaneously increasing violence and conflict avoidance, confusion about role and sexual orientation, mass consumption, wastefulness, and passive impatience (Elliott & Spezzano, 2000). However, I don't think that all these phenomena, taken together or separately, can assume cataclysmic dimensions.[2] Further, I don't believe that the presence of all these phenomena indicates that we live in an era that has completely lost its original links with the past.

The sociologist Zygmunt Bauman (2000) argues that we should become erratic in our reflection. He rejects the concept of postmodernity and proposes that of "liquid modernity". The metaphor of liquidity and fluidity allows us to comprehend the character of this new phase of the history of mankind. It is the age of eradication without any possibility of taking roots again (Bauman & Tester, 2001). In this age our in-progress reflections require us to continuously question an uncertain and evasive reality and how every individual dwells and lives in it. "A merry-go-round comes to mind rather than marathon running; a life as a string of rounds, a sequence of new starts, often in unconnected places and unrelated surroundings." (ibid., p. 95)

The political theorist Anthony Elliott and the psychoanalyst Charles Spezzano (2000) argue that we must examine multiplicity, pluralism, and ambivalence so as to re-think psychoanalysis in the postmodern era. Elliott's postmodern perspective is not global at all; rather, it focuses on the fact that knowledge is singular, localised, and perspectival. Postmodernity challenges all undisputable truths by proposing careful doubts. It is a sort of anti-cynical and naive scepticism aiming at decomposing and interpreting the world. It is clear that such a perspective leads to a sense of insecurity (Bauman, 2000) and of uncertainty about things and the future. However, it is also evident that it can allow mankind to build its future and be responsible for it.

The psychoanalyst Robert R. Holt (2002) recognises that postmodernity has certainly made an important contribution to psychoanalysis in correcting its dogmatic and anti-scientific aspects. Nonetheless, he warns against authors such as Irwin Hoffmann and Donnel Stern, who, by starting from postmodern positions, arrive at radical constructivism of psychoanalytic theory and practice and thus at counter-productive exaggerations.[3]

A new subjectivity or the revival of an unchangeable past?

At this point, the question is: Are we to see the birth of a new subjectivity free from all debts with previous generations and of a new subject able to make a *tabula rasa* of its past?

Freud loved very much the following quotation from Goethe's *Faust*: "What thou hast inherited from thy fathers, acquire it to make it thine."[4] I believe this sentence should be put close to Freud's famous and often-cited statement "Where id was, there ego shall be" (1923b p. 74). Both Goethe and Freud focus on the importance of recognising the value of the past and the necessary and original generational transformations. Freud also writes, "it is a work of culture" (1923b, p. 74) in order to ethically stress the transformative meaning not only at the individual level but also at the social level of the analytic work.

At the beginning of the 1961 book *Between Past and Future* by philosopher Hanna Arendt, we find an aphorism of the poet René Char taken from his collection *Leaves of Ipnos* (1946): "Our inheritance was left to us by no testament." (p. 3) I think the aphorism draws attention to a typical modern paradox, that is to say, to the fact that every generation tends to forget the reasons and motivations of the previous ones. In Arendt's words, "the thread of tradition is broken" (p. 14).

The poet T. S. Eliot seems to share Arendt's considerations and to apply them to literature:

> In English writing we seldom speak of tradition ... Seldom, perhaps, does the word appear except in a phrase of censure. If otherwise, it is vaguely approbative, with the implication, as to the work approved, of some pleasing archaeological reconstruction ... Yet if the only form of tradition, of handing down, consisted in following the ways of the immediate generation before us in a blind or timid adherence to its successes, "tradition" should positively be discouraged ... Tradition is a matter of much wider significance. It cannot be inherited, and if you want it you must obtain it by great labour. It involves, in the first place, the historical sense ... and the historical sense involves a perception, not only of the pastness of the past, but of its presence ... This historical sense, which is a sense of the timeless as well as of the temporal and of the timeless and of the temporal together, is what makes a writer tradition. And it is at the same time what makes a writer most acutely conscious of his

> place in time, of his own contemporaneity. No poet, no artist of any art, has his complete meaning alone. (1932, pp. 3–4)

In his *Posthumous Diary* (1989) the sociologist and philosopher Georg Simmel writes: "I know that I shall die without intellectual heirs, and that is as it should be. My legacy will be, as it were, in cash, distributed to many heirs, each transforming his part into use conformed to his nature: a use which will reveal no longer its indebtedness to this heritage." (p. 47)

The deconstructionist philosopher Jacques Derrida (2001, p. 15) discusses the issue of heritage through a paradoxical hymn to the past: "First of all, we must know and reaffirm what has come before us (and thus we are ready to take it before we can choose it). However, we must be able to deal with what has come before us without being influenced by it." He cites Hegel:

> But this tradition is not only a stewardess who simply guards faithfully that which she has received, and thus delivers it unchanged to posterity … Such tradition is no motionless statue, but is alive, and swells like a mighty river, which increases in size the further it advances from its source … To receive this inheritance is also to enter upon its use … In this manner that which is received is changed, and the material worked upon is both enriched and preserved at the same time. (1833, pp. 2–3)

Inspired by Hegel's words, Derrida says:

> Receiving an inheritance is a contradiction (in fact, we simultaneously receive and choose something, that is to say, we take something coming from the past and we have to reinterpret it) because it is a proof of our finitude. Only a finite being can receive an inheritance. It is its finitude that puts him in this condition and allows him receiving what is bigger, older, stronger, and more longlasting than him. (2001, p. 17)

I want to bring to mind a famous quote by the philosopher Bernard of Chartres (the attribution to Bernard is by Archbishop John of Salisbury) (see his *Metalogicon*, III, 4): *Nos sumus sicut nanus positus super humeros gigantis.* "Bernard of Chartres used to compare us to [puny] dwarfs perched on the shoulders of giants. He pointed out that we see more and farther than our predecessors, not because we have keener vision or greater height, but because we are lifted up and borne aloft on their gigantic stature." (John of Salisbury, 1159) Contemporaneity can find meaning only through comprehending and recognising its historical roots.

The sociologist Norman Elias (1987) notes the dissolution of symbolic apparati and collective structures of subjectivity. These apparati and structures have certainly been restrictions, but also powerful organisers of pulsional life. The question is, will this dissolution or liquidity (Bauman, 2003) indicate the coming of new forms of organisation, perhaps ambivalent, changeable, metamorphic, transient, and thus negotiable in some difficult way? Or will it represent the clear impossibility of defining the subject, due to the absence of every sort of restriction or defined frame of reference? I think it is only apparently promising to appeal to the past for quieting feelings of disorientation, indefiniteness, and uncertainty about life. It would mean to act as *laudatores temporis acti* (people who praise past times), as Horatius called those old men unable to accept the newness of the present. In this sense, I think that trying to explain this disorientation only by appealing to a certain number of "holy books" or the force of tradition is hopeless.

Erik H. Erikson (1964, p. 125) writes: "Fidelity is the ability to sustain loyalties freely pledged in spite of the inevitable contradictions of value systems." However, continuously appealing to an obsolete world view (or, at least, refusing to update a world view to the socio-cultural complexity with which it should deal) is not fidelity at all, but only a sort of a totally uncritical acceptance of orthodoxy leading us to "howl with the wolves" (Freud, 1921).

Eugenio Gaburri and Laura Ambrosiano (2009) assert that analysts must continually challenge themselves and thus accept a personal and emotional involvement. They postulate that mourning and grief are fundamental for separating from original and primary objects. This separation allows us to deal with the fear of transience. The best space in which this separation can be adequately elaborated is the group. However, the subject must become at the same time independent of the group and open to the socio-cultural context. Gaburri and Ambrosiano interpret the reverie function as a discontinuous open-mindedness to contamination by others. A lack of this function leads to two kinds of conformism: social conformism or full identification with the group, and analytic conformism or uncritical acceptance of the positions of masters or of psychoanalytic institutions. The authors write also of "refuge-ideology" to refer to cases in which even the richest approaches (such as environmentalism, pacifism, or feminism) are taken as places to hide from the fear of thinking and feeling.

The philosopher Giorgio Agamben writes:

> Those who are truly contemporary who truly belong to their time, are those who neither perfectly coincide with it nor adjust themselves to its demands. They are thus in this sense irrelevant [inattuale]. But precisely because of this condition, precisely through this disconnection and this anachronism, they are more capable than others of perceiving and grasping their own time. (2008, p. 40)

In commenting on Agamben's words, the psychoanalyst Maurizio Balsamo argues:

> We can truly recognise an experience only by listening to what lasts in it beyond the time in which it takes place, by accepting what lays its foundations, and by constructing something new, never seen, and unexpected. The unexpected is similar to the present moment; it is not written in it but can come only from it. (2014, p. 4)
>
> Tradition is a chaotic universe of knowledge and feelings. It is able to concretely link architecture and man's ability to build and work. It is common sense based upon the repetition of personal experiences shared by persons and accepted by civil society because of their clear and proven rationality … For architects, learning from handicraft is crucial for respecting rules and shared habits. Following the precepts of tradition means dealing with reality slowly, to refuse the quickness imposed by trends and affairs, to start a work in terms of one's own ambitions. It means also assuming that one's own role is an expression of a collective knowledge. This knowledge is based upon both strict moral laws and undefined formal rules. (Braghieri, 2013, pp. 231–232)

Daniel Libeskind (2004) argues that buildings should not express feelings or nostalgia, but be able to speak the language of our time.

Mario Botta (2007, p. 47) argues that, "it is idle to make a contrast between the 'temporary and passing' proposals making reference to the International style and the proposals making reference to the forms of the past". Anthony Vidler writes:

> Nostalgia for a fixed abode inevitably falls into the paradox of all nostalgia, that consciousness that, despite a yearning for a concrete place and time, the object of desire is neither here nor there, present or absent, now or then. It is, as the philosopher Vladimir Jankélévitch (1974) put it, caught in the irreversibility of time, and thus fundamentally unsettled. (1992, p. 66)

We must avoid having analysts and architects do the same as certain characters in science fiction, having their clients live laterally and in parallel. These spaces are invisible and inaccessible and only resemble the space of history and life. We must take care not to contrast a globalised time and space with a slow-paced and nostalgic past. I think we cannot start an improbable, and today impossible, search for lost time. We can find a similar sterile juxtaposition in discussions about football. On the one hand there are supporters of a slow sport mostly based on individual technique and fantasy, and on the other supporters of a muscular, fast sport that lacks fantasy.

> The organisation of mental apparatus is such that the traces of experiences survive and create a sort of temporal gap. That is to say, there is a combination of different times: past, present, and future are juxtaposed and decentred. The oldest experiences come after the most recent ones. An affect in a new and recent relationship is directly linked to an affect in a childhood relationship. There is a continuous work of translation and copy. (Preta, 2006, p. 19)

It has been underscored many times that postmodern thinking is characterised by a great attention to subject and subjectivity (Flax, 1996). The psychoanalyst Stephen A. Mitchell (1988) argues that we have witnessed two crucial changes in psychoanalysis: first, the passage from a man dominated by his instincts or drives to a man as creator of meanings; second, the passage from the focus on child sexuality to the focus on recovering and revitalising the true self (which aims at creating its personal meanings). The attention to subject and subjectivity challenged many assumptions of the psychoanalytic theories, for example the issue of the existence of developmental models, the problem of sexuality, the question of identity, and even the psychoanalytic practice with all concepts like neutrality, abstinence, etc. In this sense, because of the complexity and historicity of subjectivity, metapsychological research has been put into question. In particular, it is a matter of debating the universalistic character of metapsychology and its attempt to organise all theories and to include all subjectivities (Capozzi, 2003).

If we take a look at recent psychoanalytic theories and at their variety of terms, concepts, and models, a question arises: should we talk of a single psychoanalysis or of many psychoanalyses (Wallerstein, 1988)? The psychoanalyst Robert S. Wallerstein (1990) is aware of the variety among the recent psychoanalytic theories, but nonetheless he is convinced that we can find a common ground or a least common denominator between them. Freud himself avoids *a posteriori* re-organising the differences and the contradictions emerging in the development of his positions and thus reaches a scientific completeness and coherence.

In *An Autobiographical Study* (1925), Freud points out that his theoretical model described in the *Metapsychology* could have been substituted or modified without impairing psychoanalysis in some way. Further, in the posthumous *An Outline of Psycho-Analysis* (1940) he does not re-conceptualise and re-contextualise systematically his original positions in light of the subsequent conceptual revisions (Wallerstein, 1997).

According to Ricci (1995, p. 189): "The city of psychoanalysis never offers citizenship. It is an open frontier, a bridge allowing passages and exchanges, a dock inviting new adventures, a courage able to deal with the incommensurable."

This is probably an example of what psychoanalyst Joyce McDougall calls a new "psychic economic", always based on the search for pleasure and its exhibition. In the recent past this psychic economic could be found in important social phenomena but was also marginal or limited to some fringes.[5] But today it can be found in many common and widespread social phenomena and it is often accompanied by a change in collective mentality.

Some Lacanian psychoanalysts (Melman, 2002) have recently indicated a transition from a culture based on representation and evocation of the desired object to a culture of presentation, in which we aim to reach the object itself automatically and instantly. In other words, we have moved from a culture based on desire repression (and thus on neurosis) to a culture promoting the free expression and satisfaction of desire (and thus on perversion). Psychic health seems to depend neither on an object of satisfaction, nor on a balance with the ego ideal.

I think that the writer and psychoanalyst Michel Schneider (2002) refers to the notion of repressive de-sublimation coined by the philosopher Herbert Marcuse in *The Obsolescence of Psychoanalysis* (1967) and by the analyst and sociologist Reimut Reiche in *Sexuality and Class Struggle* (1968) to describe a sexuality that is reified and thus deprived of sensuality. In this kind of sexuality, subjects become objects of their reciprocal performance demands. In this sense, they act in an extreme permissive way that, paradoxically, takes the place of the old sexophobic approach to morality in a late capitalistic society. This society does not increase personal freedom in any way, but rather its control over the individual. By following this line of reasoning, Schneider (2002) argues that the contract (Schneider here refers to a private agreement subscribed outside publicly shared and recognised norms) "is an essential part of pervert functioning. Everything potentially de-institutionalising, I mean, deregulating symbolic practices for make them part of a contract, can reinforce the pervert social mechanisms." (Schneider, 2002, p. 213) He underlines the social utility of legally regulating certain relevant parts of private sphere, in particular those subject to possible contractualisation.

I think that all these considerations must be viewed with caution. Certainly they contain a grain of truth but, if generalised and absolutised, they can lead to reactionary and conservative positions. Such positions can be seen in the middle of idealisation and denigration and clearly hark back to a past characterised by defined limits and boundaries and thus by precise organisational possibilities. This past clashes with the present world characterised by any possibility of delimitation and is so incoherent and disillusioned that psychoanalysis has some difficulties in dealing with it (Lebrun, 1997).

I believe the clearest form of contractualisation in our society is the subtraction of certain elements of the private sphere in favour of a certain number of norms permeated by impersonal forms of control. These forms of control come from a rigid and invasive interpretation of bureaucracy and normativity. They become ahistorical and unable to dynamically and adequately interpret private needs and their expression. Of course, I do not think that everything can be decided by the free market because of undesired effects of economical-political and ethical deregulation (Schinaia, 2000, 2010). In this sense, the worst-case scenario is the survival of the fittest. For this reason, I think it is important to maintain a balance between law and contract. This would allow us to make dynamic and protecting the social links. "Membership and identity are not carved in stone and are not lifelong commitments. They are largely negotiable and revocable." (Bauman, 2003, pp. 6 & 9)

"Postmodernity is better characterised … as a culture of imagination without illusions, a cultural space which admits the provisional and contingent form of imaginary structures." (Elliott, 2000, p. 142)

Between theory and lack of theory: the do-it-yourself analyst

To put it in another way, my questions are more or less the same as those of Remo Cesarani (1998) and Francesco Barale (2003):

> Can psychoanalysts continue to use their interpretative tools to try to reach their goals and thus to interpret, reconstruct, and reintegrate the relational life of a subject living nowadays? To put it in another way: can psychoanalysts continue to apply the analytic tools created, developed, and improved in a specific socio-historical context in a radically different one? (Cesarani, 1998, p. 23)

Is the subject of psychoanalysis changing? Are we attending to the passage from a self-questioning subject (Oedipus) to a radically nomadic subject? The self-questioning subject seems to be able to recognise his heterogeneity and diversity (perhaps we can talk of oddity), his incompleteness and openness, his net full of (conscious or unconscious, big or small) drives, relationships, differences, desires, and legacies. All these things constitute him via an endless dialectical movement. In spite of this situation, he can engage the challenges of his research because he is well supported by strong psychosocial organisers. Rather, the radically nomadic subject lives in a context in which subjectivities appear to dissolve themselves in the many uncertain flows crossing them and there is a lack of strong symbolic structures (Barale, 2003, pp. 20–21).

Domenico Chianese (2005) questions whether neurosis could still be a model or an "operator" (he borrows this term from a 1993 book of the psychoanalyst Paul-Laurent Assoun, in which the causal explanation applied to the Freudian notion of unconscious motivations is criticised) able to represent the collective contemporary form of distress or whether other operators (for example, perversion, borderline or melancholic states) could work better. Further, he questions whether the psychoanalyst has an ethical, therapeutic, and cultural duty to note and understand how the "gravitational field" in which the relationships between patient, client, and world is changed.

The psychoanalyst René Kaes (2005, p. 59) defines "meta-psychological authorities [as] all those formations and processes upon which the person's mind is based and structured. These authorities basically consist of the fundamental interdictions and the inter-subjective contracts. They are the organising principles of mentality and its framework and background." When the well-founded meta-psychological and meta-social authorities (I here refer to the main structure of organisation and regulation of social formations and processes: myths, ideologies, beliefs, religion, authorities, and hierarchies) fail or are uncertain, subjectivity becomes unstable.

I think we need questions and not clear statements. Questions allow understanding of the complexity of a certain situation, perhaps by dialectically being on the horns of a dilemma, whereas statements permit us to deal with reality in an unidirectional way and to avoid a possible meeting (or clash) in the case where something does not fit with the chosen interpretative framework. For example, we can consider a change in sexual habits as an example. This change is in fact often described as a revolution and this exaggeration can lead us to observe the objects of our inquiry fallaciously. I believe that this fallacy can lead us to trivialise and thus not examine in depth an extremely complex and multi-layered phenomenon.

Freud thought that our relationship with the outside world and ourselves did not depend on an object, but on the lack of an object. Of course, this is not an ordinary object but an essential and beloved object like the mother in the Oedipus complex. Thus, it is the loss of this object that allows humankind to enter stable ways of representation.

However, is it really true that, in this age of media, we are going towards a society not only without a father but also without mourning (this means the crisis of authority and the possible constitution of a creeping and voluntary substitutive fascism) (Barale, 2003)?

In this sense, we should consider progress as the acceptance that the sky is not only without God but also without ideologies, promises, points of reference, and precepts. Thus, we should accept that every one of us (individually or collectively) tends to self-determination. I think that, if we consider progress according to this meaning, it can increase our exercise of freedom and thus allow moving without any impediment, without any root or restriction and without any possibility of rethinking a certain choice. However, it can lead also to us trying to manically satisfy our desires and to pay attention only to present contingencies (Bodei, 2001), to avoid any delayed gratification and to demand the continuous presence of a satisfying object. In this picture, a lack of satisfaction is a scandal, a deficit, or a problem. Legislation modifies when new needs requiring an immediate satisfaction emerge. Thus, we have a legal right to completely satisfy these needs. Unfortunately, this means to legitimate a control of them via their pathologising.

The progress has always consisted in continuously defining the limits of science and, more or less synchronically, ethical prescriptions. However, today this processes of synchronization seems to be in crisis because the limits appear to be inconsistent and undefined. I think this is the same for identities and subjectivities. Excess is now a trend and sometimes appears more a prescription than a transgression. In other words, we have a prescription of the excess *per se*. Every exception becomes a habit and a variance something normal. "But to take place, rebellion needs there to be connections to cut, norms to infringe, solid identities to demolish, whereas it is not possible to rebel against the undifferentiated." (Vegetti Finzi, 2001, p. 67)

Further, this social mutation seems to take place via an indecent exposure of the object, whose continued and consumeristic presence does not allow it to form an adequate dimension for its loss. Thanks to publicity and mass media, perversion seems to have become a social standard and thus a principle of social relationships. In this sense, we can observe an increase of *disposable* phenomena, for example when you think your bodies or your partners are not up to your expectations. Quantity of relationships has been substituted for quality, which is often perceived as poor and consumable in a rush. Postmodern culture praises this supposed mutation and views it as an imposition of the inorganic and of an impersonal emotional universe characterised by anonymous and reified experiences.

In talking about removing and representing boys in today's culture, the philosopher Mario Perniola says:

> Phenomena like rock music and deconstructive architecture, science fiction and virtual reality, drugs and appearance, cyber-punk and splatter-punk, installation art and meta-literature, sport and

> theatre performances, must be attributed not to a living and trembling body but to a reified body. This is opposed to the spiritualistic vitalism, to mythological celebrations, to creation, to spontaneity, to true subjectivity. (2003, p. 134)

The question is whether it is really a sociological mutation or a wide social change that has lasted so long because it is amplified by mass media and publicity (that need to continuously propose new consumer goods) but cannot be considered stable and definitive.

The psychoanalyst Amalia Giuffrida (2006) asks if cultural and social change can involve a transformation of the phantasmatic unconscious configurations postulated by psychoanalysts. She continues by asking if the typical organisers of psycho-sexuality could have lost or changed their function of creating those sources of imagination that have characterised our society until now. Finally, she asks if changes in lifestyle could have been made to a new mythopoesis derived from the many different transformations of the original myths applied to the present social context.

The psychoanalyst Giuseppe Di Chiara (1998, p. 4) makes a clear distinction between "discontents of civilisation" proposed by Freud (1930) and psychosocial syndromes. The former are related to the fact that an individual must always face insurmountable conflicts in social life. The latter are related to those highly pathological social events in which certain defensive phenomena prevail and appear in the behaviour of big groups causing sufferings and problems often masked in useful and necessary acts. Because of this masked character, psychosocial syndromes are very similar to perversions.

I believe that it is right to pay attention to these intense and confused social changes and to those change vectors that quickly modify their trajectories. However, in doing so, we must be able to attach the right importance to those social changes that deny both belonging and absence in a omnipotent manner. This means not to draw catastrophic conclusions such as "everything has changed" or, on the contrary, comforting conclusions such as "nothing has really changed". I think we should stay in the middle between continuity and discontinuity by following Bion's famous dictum "without memory or desire". Thus, we should not look for redemption or rest in a dream of belonging or for not yet explored and experienced identities. These identities seem to propose benefits on the one hand exciting because they are unusual and on the other promising because they are still fresh and new (Bauman, 2003).

Psychoanalysts must accept the challenges of a society apparently deprived of its traditional references and in search of new ones able to substitute those experienced as obsolete and worn out. Francesco Barale (2003) rightly argues that psychoanalysts should avoid reacting to this turbulence by adopting fundamentalism or implicitly normative positions or by confusing the phantasmatic dimension with certain historical forms of it.

The psychoanalysts and psychiatrists Fausto Petrella and Vanna Berlincioni (2002) defend the argument that an analytic psychotherapy must revive the Oedipus complex. They do not recognise relational and pulsional realities alternative to its revival: "The great Oedipal narrative and its emancipating power makes way for other new formations, for local micro-narratives, for partial fragmented objects and their iconography." (Petrella & Berlincioni, 2004, p. 372)

André Green takes a position against what he calls "pragmatics of narrative knowledge (savoir) [because] free association breaks the narrative" (2005, p. 285).[6]

However, the psychoanalysts Glenn Gabbard and Drew Westen (2003, p. 825) note "an increasing flexibility in psychoanalytic practice and a recognition of the inevitability—and value—of the negotiation process that takes place in each analytic dyad".

The psychoanalyst Jay R. Greenberg (1995) argues that the psychoanalytic model and its rules can vary according to the particular features of the analyst's and the subject's subjectivities. Gabbard and Westen (2003) point out that adopting a flexible attitude does not mean that anything goes during an analytic session.

The complexity and heterogeneity of a subject are the bedrocks of postmodern thought. However, I believe that they should not imply uncertainty and relativism. The analyst should accept a certain degree of indeterminacy and the consequent suffering and consider himself a "do-it-yourself" therapist. This means, by starting from well-known perspectives, that he must be able to open the ways to new relational and cognitive routes via a careful selection of the different theories at his disposal and new ways of making experiences. A do-it-yourself analyst must refer to a polyphonic concept of identity, conceive it as something nomadic (or, at least, as something more nomadic than in the past), and inscribe it in circular patterns representing weak, changeable, and various expressive forms. They are temporary identities, perhaps preparatory to more stable ones, but certainly authentic and sustained by mutual relationships. They are conceived as identities that must be construed all along the analytic relationship and not as original entities to discover. The psychoanalyst Ruth Stein writes about being a do-it-yourself (a bricoleur) analyst and promotes the combination of different psychoanalytic theories in clinical practice. She argues that for an analyst it is important to have a tool kit for assembling various parts of different theories in an adequate meta-theoretic context. She writes:

> A tool kit serves a bricoleur (Lévi-Strauss's metaphor of the potter as the craftsman for our modern way of arranging knowledge), and theories are tools, as Wittgenstein (1953) says. There is constructive listening (Spence, 1982), and every analyst carries a tool kit, whether he displays it or not. And the more tools in the analyst's kit, the more sense his patient will make to him, the more vocabularies and images to grasp him with, and the more diversified affects to experience him with—through complex processes of intuitive combinations, permutations, additions, and subtractions of what these tools offer him. (1995b, p. 302)

Knowledge is built up, not discovered. It is contextual, not foundational (Elliott, 2000).

Fred Pine (1988, 1989, 1990, 2001) has proposed a reflection of how to unify different theoretical model in psychoanalysis and, at the same time, avoid the "great and all-embracing theories". He points out the need to refer to pulsional theory, self-psychology, object relations theory, and ego psychology, and to move from one model to another depending on the different movements and clinical situations. Commenting on Pine's work, the psychoanalyst Paolo Migone (2004) is in favour of the coexistence of various models and theories, but criticises Pine's proposal because it is too influenced by hermeneutics and radical constructivism.

Contemporary psychoanalysts deal with "a weak and elusive subject, not particularly thorough and sophisticated. Such a subject appears to be flattened in himself, more or less like new Narcissus contemplating his image in a thin mirror. He lives in a net of fast, manifold, weak, and elusive experiences." (Cesarani, 2001, p. 178)

By commenting on a clinical case of transexualism described by Ruth Stein (1995a), the psychoanalyst and sociologist Nancy Chodorow points out that the appeal to the conventional categories of psychoanalysis is a defensive epistemological trap with our new perspective on the complexity and multiplicity of gender. She argues that it is much easier to have a limited number of theories to bring to bear on what we hear, rather than to stay with uncertainty. According to the psychoanalysts Del Loewenthal and Robert Snell (2003), staying with uncertainty can be a plea for humility (and thus something that can promote therapeutic change) and a challenge to omnipotence of both patient and therapist.

Ruth Stein (1995b) polemically replies to Chodorow (1995) by arguing that we must assume a double position containing and embracing a dialectic relation between cultural (meta-) theory and immediate analytic experience. She argues that, in spite of the many difficulties and contradictions, we must bring together "micro (or particular) clinical" and "macro (or general) cultural" theories. The need to give meaning, to build coherent narratives, to construct plausible emotional explanations, stands in a tension with certain deconstructive processes of contemporary thinking.

Ruth Stein writes:

> The patient … needs coherence, not only plurality; he needs unity … not only dissemination; he needs self-construction and self-definition as an entity, something my patient so sorely lacked … A person who experiences and greatly suffers from a borderline personality, or from a fragmented or non-cohesive self, or from being in the paranoid-schizoid position, needs "centring," "constructing," "self-generalising" (through analysis, of course). Later, and if he wishes so, analysis can help him reach more sophisticated levels of being by making him aware of the potential endlessness of his self-choice and the creative differences within himself. One cannot treat an analysand as one treats the "subject" in certain contemporary theories—as an illusion, as a fiction, as a wholly artificial product of culture or language. (1995b, p. 304)

Remo Cesarani argues that:

> The interpretative tools of psychoanalysis are certainly a very strong and flexible heuristic model. This can be found both in Freud's experiences and in the continuous rethinking, corrections and changes of his model and in the controversial and often chaotic history of psychoanalytic schools that have discussed for many decades on the issue of the orthodoxy of Freud's model or on the acceptance of possible changes in it. (1998, p. 23)

Giuseppe Di Chiara argues that, in the crisis of modernity, psychoanalysis maintains a rationalistic position well informed of the irrational and its relevance. The change in the ways of being contemporary (Di Chiara here refers to the changes in the psychical agencies, in particular the super-ego, and the recurring loss of limits in the subjective organisations) and the Zeitgeist make us face a clinical reality not completely familiar to us and elusive in respect to our training as psychoanalysts (Bolognini, 2003). This means that this training must require continuous updates.

> In psychoanalysis, the rules, whatever they are, must be called into question and put thorough a theoretical and situational re-elaboration work. This work allows preventing us to worship the rules and losing their living meaning. (Israël, 1994, p. 33)

In this sense, we can neither propose a bold defence of the original rules and worship them or follow them in a bureaucratic and obsessive way, nor dissolve our identities thanks to the absence of any peremptory value.

If we put aside those theoretical positions that do not give any value to postmodernist theories and to their possible relation with psychoanalysis, we can see that there are many positions open to cooperation and emphasising the need for a comparison and a co-existence between the different psychoanalytic theories. In this sense, the ambiguity of postmodernity can be conceived not only as a danger but also as an opportunity (Elliott, 2000).

I believe that we must refer to different positions and to the plurality and complexity of our current perspectives. We must continuously and fruitfully develop these perspectives in order to place them in an adequate meta-theoretical context and test them with clinical experience. I think that this experience is what allows us to continuously decompose and compose our theories. Rethinking and reviewing our therapeutic technique permits us to save it from the micro-illusions of heuristic omnipotence and to ask questions about the point of view we want to take.

The psychoanalysts Luigi Rinaldi and Maria Stanzione write that:

> [Both flexibility and caution are useful] because they allow fully expression of the analyst's transference towards the patient in a

> clinical perspective in which the dynamic of transference/counter-transference is the main tool. Such a dynamic is what permits dealing with that part of our unconscious not submitted to repression and thus in principle inaccessible to verbal translation. (2012, p. 6)

Of course, the point here is not to defend a rough clinical-theoretical eclecticism, or to easily concede something to hermeneutics and radical constructivism, or to assume a sort of omnipotent intuitiveness, or to avoid reflecting on the compatibility or incompatibility between different theoretical models. Rather, the point is to propose a way of theorising both rigorous and free floating; a way that is deep and temporary, made not only of continuities and juxtapositions, but also of breaks and contrasts between different models.

Stefano Bolognini argues that:

> As well as many other Italian colleagues, during these years I have travelled a lot. We have visited the markets, the villages, the "sanctuaries", the houses [and sometimes the fortifications] of other psychoanalytic schools ... I have realised that, in general, Italian psychoanalysts are liked because they are open to dialogue and are not rigidly academic or don't have the super-ego attitude of their analytic culture. This culture is the product of a tradition of listening and studying, which is always interested in the different expression of our discipline around the world. (2010, p. 610)

The range and the ways of confronting different models (that always depend on sociocultural changes) can vary a lot and will be the subject of debate and discussion among those analysts who aim at dealing with the new expressive ways of psychical suffering.

Roger Money-Kyrle (1931, pp. 150–151) writes: "If we want to live forever, we must continue to adapt ourselves to environment and our environment must adapt to ourselves. Further, we must be able to predict and anticipate those adaptations that will be necessary in the future."

I believe Money-Kyrle's statement is a praise of both flexibility and rigour and can be valid for both psychoanalysis and psychoanalysts (perhaps also for architecture and architects) in the age of postmodernity.

CHAPTER SEVEN

The haste in the world around us

> When first one catches sight of the sea, crosses the ocean, and experiences as realities cities and lands which for so long had been distant, unattainable things of desire—one feels oneself like a hero who has performed a deed of improbable greatness.
>
> (Sigmund Freud, 1936, p. 247)

On travelling

Claudio Magris writes:

> We cannot travel without crossing frontiers. They can be political, linguistic, social, cultural, or psychological. Sometimes they are invisible, like those separating the different areas of a city, those between people, those inside us and our internal underworld that sometimes block us. We must cross the frontiers and also love them because they define a peculiar reality or individuality, give it shape and thus save it from vagueness. But we must not worship them or make them idols demanding blood sacrifices. We must keep in mind that they are flexible, temporary, and contingent. They are

> also mortal, I mean, they are subject to death, as well as travellers, but they are not causes of death as they have been and are many times. Here the adjective mortal means subject to death, a condition typical of the travellers, not possibility or cause of death, as the frontiers had been in the past and are sometimes in the present. (2005, p. XII)

Salomon Resnik (2006, p. 18) uses the metaphor of a journey through an unstable territory in need of reconstruction for talking of psychoanalysis: "I think psychoanalysis is an adventure or a journey through the dark areas of human being. Once you discover them, they suddenly become bright, sometimes so bright that they almost blind."

And when Kublai Khan asked Marco Polo if he was travelling in order to relive his past, he answered: "Elsewhere is a negative mirror. The traveller recognises the little that is his, discovering the much he has not had and will never have." (Calvino, 1972, p. 29)

I think that the lack of a real crossing and of an idea of exploring and touching an unknown place in the dromoscopic era[1] is a sign of the perversion of travelling today and of the resulting disorientation. Because there are many similar and almost identical environments, no place can be truly recognised. In a no-place we cannot recognise ourselves as members of a community and we feel like strangers. Magris writes (2005, p. 130): "Who is travelling? The ego of the traveller is little more than a glimpse, a hollow shape in which to imprint 'the mould of reality', a container to fill with things that give it a shape (full of his dislikes, his nostalgias, and his fears), as well as a container that gives a shape to the water it contains." In today's travelling we see a decreasing interest in the journey and an increasing interest in the arrival and for the destination. Every traveller is so quick in moving from one place to another that moving is only an obstacle between departure and arrival to be reduced as much as possible. This excludes everything in the middle space between departure and arrival and all the memories related to it.

Italo Calvino (1972, p. 128) writes: "You can resume your flight whenever you like … but you will arrive at another Trude, absolutely the same, detail by detail. The world is covered by the sole Trude, which does not begin, nor end. Only the name of the airport changes."

In *Austerlitz* (2001b, p. 14) Sebald has his main character say: "And indeed … to this day there is something illusionistic and illusory about the relationship of time and space as we experience it in travelling, which is why whenever we come home from elsewhere we never feel quite sure if we have really been abroad."

Franco La Cecla writes:

> Socrates told of a person who remained unchanged for an entire journey: "I think I know why: he had brought himself with him." "Bringing himself with him" means to invade the journey with our presence. In this sense, knowing new places means to deny every difference ... There is no possibility of understanding the forces of a place. We cannot get lost in a place because it is included in the order we bring with us. In other words, we don't allow it to interact with us. (2000, p. 28)

In the current economic model goods tend to perish more hastily than in the past[2] and thus are substituted by new ones. The aim is to support boundless market growth and thus, via a triumph of disposable items, to increase a consumeristic way of existence. Contemporary man's time for productivity tends to shrink more and more, and adolescence before and old age after appear to be longer and longer.

The Italian journalist and writer Luigi Pintor (2013) argues that, although progress seems to broaden our time and expand our life, it actually shrinks our time and shortens our life.

> The mythology of speed[3] relies on nothing but the elimination of the present in favour of a present that moves with desire and pressure ... In spite of the stability of this mythology, most speed leads to stalls, unproductive traffic systems, obstructions, inefficiencies. (La Cecla, 1993, p. 120)

Paul Virilio writes:

> With the speed of the continuum it is the goal (*objectif*) of the voyage that destroys the road, it is the target of the projectile-projector (of the automobile) that seems to trigger the ruin of the interval, it is the fleeting desire to go right to the end as fast as possible that produces in the opening out (*écartement*) of the travelling the tearing apart (*écartèlement*) of the landscape. (1984, p. 105)

Marc Augé writes (1997, p. 12): "The world still exists in its multiplicity. But this multiplicity has little to do with the illusory kaleidoscope of tourism. Perhaps one of our most urgent tasks is to learn again to travel, possibly in our close proximities, to learn again to see."

The term *emotion* comes from the Latin *emovere*. Thus, the meaning of emotion is historically linked to the movement, to the act of moving, to the migration from a place to another, from an interior to an exterior and vice versa. "Realise the moment in which that tension determining those set of relations that link the interiority to the exteriority occurs." (Delaunay, 1978, p. 349)

The reduction of the working age and the increase in unemployment go hand in hand with an increase in the time spent working[4] (in spite of the many disputes about its reduction) and its personalisation. In this sense, we can say that we tend to work less[5] than in the past but harder in terms of intensity and longer in terms of daily duration. We do not see a sustainable de-growth but rather a reduction in time for ourselves and thus for taking care of ourselves. In spite of the many ways we could use our free time (for example, sports, travelling), the fact that they are presented to us as packaged and ready-made strongly reduces our freedom of choice and imagination.

We must also stress the relevance of mass media and of its populist messages that place appearance above authenticity, speed of consumption of experiences above time necessary for their elaboration, and televised exhibitionism of bodies and emotions above discretion and protection of intimacy. Further, I think it is important to stress the relevance of the easy enrichment and the immediate and narcissistic achievement of goals and the increase of speed caused by economic globalisation and the internet (Schinaia, 2005a).[6]

In his 2015 encyclical letter titled *Laudato Si'*, Pope Francis writes:

> The continued acceleration of changes affecting humanity and the planet is coupled today with a more intensified pace of life and work, which might be called "rapidification". Although change is part of the working of complex systems, the speed with which human activity has developed contrasts with the naturally slow pace of biological evolution. Moreover, the goals of this rapid and constant change are not necessarily geared to the common good or to integral and sustainable human development. (2015, p. 17)

James Hillman (2001) writes: "Today the key word in every message is 'asap'—as soon as possible. Fast food, fast track, fast forward!" We can see the mortification of senses and of interests and a reduction of time for "the rite of the meal". This is clearly exemplified in the transition from fast food[7] to walking food.[8]

In the 1960s, members of the Archigram group proposed architecture as quick as an aerogramme or telegram. "Archi(tecture tele)gram" (Wolfler Calvo, 2007, p. 25).

In his book *Slowness* (1995) the writer Milan Kundera argues that speed is a form of ecstasy that the technical revolution has given to humankind.

> Modern age does not seem to recognise present, but only a mere flow of time, a becoming experience not as a possibility of learning or as a journey towards a goal that can give flesh and bones at every step of the journey. In modern age there is only dispersion, a continuous not being, a lack of values to refer to. (Magris, 1992, p. 30)
>
> Today ... the most important thing seems to be always on the run from ourselves, to cut relationships off instead of renewing them, to have something new everyday and at all costs. This leads us to exclude the work of founding theoretically and conceptually a project. Every project must appear as something never seen before. Here we have a sinister and recurring adjective: innovative! (Venezia, 2011, p. 32)

Pierre Sansot (1998) is against city planning that aims to eliminate those obstacles that slow down free trade and proposes slow city planning. Slow city planning would slow down the space of urban life, not only by eliminating those obstacles that slow down free trade. The French architect Laurent Beaudouin (2007) develops an idea of slow architecture moving from a micro-geography of continuous transitions to a genuine spatial choreography.

According to Giuliana Bruno, a set of principles and beliefs focused on time should give space to time:

> Make room. Look out the window. Look onto the street. Space out. Watch a building be. Take the time to eat your lunch. Take time. Get a haircut. Take your time. Massage your soul. Sleep. Dream something up. Revel in this mood. Get lost in the empire of atmosphere. As in the unconscious, something always happens when nothing does. (2007, p. 213)

"Poetry first of all admits man's dwelling into its very nature, its presencing being. Poetry is the original admission of dwelling … Do we dwell poetically? Presumably we dwell altogether unpoetically." (Heidegger, 1951, p. 398) This is Martin Heidegger's comment on a Hölderlin poem, more precisely that in which the following couplet can be found: "Full of merit, yet poetically, man/Dwells on this earth." (p. 392) The philosopher Fulvio Papi argues that the 1951 article of Heidegger is the most-read philosophical paper by architects. Vittorio Gregotti (2010) agrees with Papi when he writes about an architecture "able to deal with a long-term slowness … to return to a poetic way of building".[9]

In his book *Built Upon Love: Architectural Longing after Ethics and Aesthetics* (2008, p. 108) the Mexican architectural historian Pérez-Gómez writes "architecture fundamentally communicates not a particular meaning but rather the possibility of recognising ourselves as complete in order to dwell poetically on earth and thus be wholly human."

The architect Pallasmaa (2011, p. 119) distinguishes between poetic images and "seductively aestheticised images". The latter are like the effect of using cosmetics in order to make an impression, whereas the former are multisensory and speak to us like living metaphors.

We can find an antidote to haste inside monasteries:

> Monks do not watch the clock hand or the digital hour on the mobile phone's display. In spite of this, they do everything they have to do on time, with no haste or stress … In their lives, monks have been able to make the passing of time and its measurement through a clock overlap. This means that they have not divided the time into pieces, for example in the successions of the four seasons or of years, months, days, hours and seconds. They have been able to bring back time to the only measure that matters: the whole life. (Boatti, 2012, p. 58)

Francesco Venezia writes:

> Our buildings are based upon a conceptual basis, as well as upon a natural or artificial soil. We have slowly construed such a conceptual basis and we conceive it as a support base of the building itself … The architect's work achieves a good result when it is able to make a synthesis of two speeds, that of slowness[10] and that of quickness. The slower the time taken for conceiving the

> conceptual basis, the quicker the conception and construction of the project.[11] (2011, p. 29)

To describe the great impact of traumatic events in the first phases of human development, the psychoanalyst Anna Freud (1967) uses an architectural metaphor. In fact, she argues that the mind can be more damaged in the first phases of development than in later ones, just as the retaining walls of a house can be more damaged during their construction than after their completion.

The Italian expression *andare a zonzo* (to stroll) means, "to waste time wandering aimlessly". The origins of this idiomatic expression are unknown; however, it seems to fit perfectly well with the city described by Walter Benjamin, in which *flâneurs* had their walks, and in the *dérive,* the technique of psychogeographical exploration of a urban landscape proposed by the situationist theorist Guy Debord.[12] Today this city (that we can call Zonzo) is radically changed. It is no longer a space to live, it is not a place in which to experience new behaviours or alternative ways of life, in which strolling is a pleasure, an adventure, a free choice.

Inside the wrinkles of Zonzo, spaces in transit have grown up, territories in continuous transformation, in time and space, seas crossed by multitudes of "outsiders" who hide in the city. Here new forms of behaviour appear, new ways of dwelling, new spaces of freedom. The nomadic city lives in osmosis with the settled city. (Careri, 2002, p. 112)

The dead time of analysis

A crucial issue in psychoanalysis is the need for having a long time for introspection, that is to say, for an apparently "dead" time of waiting and transformation.[13]

In a poetic way Bion expressed the same concept in a 1964 letter to his daughter (1985, p. 199): "Be careful not to mistake plants having their winter rest for weeds or dead. They will look very much alive when the sap begins to flow and they wake from their winter sleep." This incubation period is necessary for that insight that always accompanies a creative and emotional transformation and a synthesis (Arieti, 1976).

Italo Calvino makes an excellent example of the need for a processing time by telling the following Chinese story:

> Among Chuang-tzu's many skills, he was an expert draftsman. The king asked him to draw a crab. Chuang-tzu replied that he needed

> five years, a country house, and twelve servants. Five years later the drawing was still not begun. "I need another five years," said Chuang-tzu. The king granted them. At the end of these ten years, Chuang-tzu took up his brush and, in an instant, with a single stroke, he drew a crab, the most perfect crab ever seen. (1988, p. 54)

The inevitably slow[14] phases of growth, processing, and insight, and of the construction of a real affective relationship, explain the reason for the choice of the "long way" (*voie longue*) (Chasseguet Smirgel, 1975). The long road is a road that people must take if they want to start a complete and rigorous analysis. In general such people have a spontaneous and intuitive knowledge of the psychoanalytic method and a genuine desire to know themselves and discover the real causes of their problems. In contrast, there are patients who always try to solve their conflicts by taking the "short way" (*voie courte*). This is because they lack an insight that allows them to deal with their conflicts or, more generally, they have particular narcissistic traits like anxiety and urgency.

There are two opposite tendencies, both of which can be harmful: on the one hand, the time reduction; on the other, the long duration of experiences. Psychoanalysts run the risk of the indefinite duration, that is to say, of a sort of never-ending present or of a sort of compensation for the limits imposed by a single session. In this sense, certain implicit values of the analytic couple (like regularity and continuity) precede other important ones (like transformation and change of each member of the couple) (Fachinelli, 1983).

In this sense, the analysis can increasingly become "a direct institutional relationship, with a defined duration, stability, and intensity. Thus, it can become more or less one of the many interpersonal relationships of our era." (Fachinelli, 1983, p. 52)

Of course, the change in historical conditions and, as a consequence, in the economic and cultural value attributed to the temporal dimension of experience, interferes with certain subjective features like memory and the experience and perception of time. These features come into play in the early phases of constitution of the analytic setting. For example, this happens through the categories of continuum and non-continuum, which cannot be qualitatively and quantitatively defined once and for all. I think that the point here is to consider these aspects adequately. It is one thing to consider them in a relatively flexible way, another to passively conform to them.

The renovation of the analytic setting

In the course of an analysis, a renovation of the setting can be necessary. This renovation does not mean "deregulation", that is to say, it does not mean to apply the technical rules of the analytic relationship in a self-sufficient and thoughtless way. Rather, it means to apply these rules in a flexible or firm way. Such an application concerns the way in which the analytic third or the law can be represented in the relationship.

In this vein, Thomas Ogden argues that, during an analytic treatment, the particular quality of interpersonal experience cannot depend upon the frequency of sessions.

Glen O. Gabbard and Drew Westen (2003, pp. 825–826) seem to agree with Ogden when they argue, "in general, the current psychoanalytic scene is witnessing a movement toward greater humility. This humility is reflected in tolerance for uncertainty—in our professional literature as well as in treatment hours." In a note of this paper (p. 826, note 1), the authors point out that "in a paradoxical way, this attitude toward uncertainty in the consulting room is likely to be associated with a more, rather than less, scientific attitude within psychoanalysis. Science is first and foremost about framing and testing hypotheses, not about establishing certainty—or its dangerous proxy, the subjective sense of certainty."

The psychoanalyst William W. Meissner (2004) finds disturbing the position expressed by Gabbard and Westen (2003). This position maintains that the psychoanalytic model and its rules must change according to the peculiar nature of the patient's and the analyst's subjectivities. Thus, Meissner argues that it is necessary to find a certain number of common criteria validated by experience. Further, he points out that flexibility must always be an exception and, if analysts must adopt it, it must guarantee those fundamental conditions necessary for the analytic process. "I think that every attempt to put an exceptional condition at the same level of a standard one can bring confusion." (Meissner, 2004, p. 247)

However, in spite of the many different positions at their disposal:

> Clinicians cannot ignore the fact that many things have changed in every context and situation: for example, in the form and quality of everyday life or in the effects on individuals of the new ways of life … In this sense, people change their sensibility and acquire a

> renewed perception of space-time and of relationships with others. The new emerging needs are not basic at all. (Petrella & Berlincioni, 2002, p. 172)

Today, the classical analytic setting cannot be defined as something *a priori*. In some cases, it can be defined as a situation that must be carefully prepared and continuously renewed. In other cases, it can be defined as a situation with some conditions that are not necessarily the best ones. I believe we need new analytic agreements able to account for new needs. This is simply because psychoanalysis cannot avoid the general norms that regulate social relationships among people.

The psychoanalyst David Liberman (1970–1972) proposes the term "meta-setting" to define the social, cultural, and economic environment around us.

> I believe that recognising the existence of external factors in our institutions and in our private practice should not necessarily imply that we adaptively and passively conform to these factors. However, this recognition could start a slow and painful reconsideration of certain past positions characterised by narcissism and by a certain degree of retirement from the social world. I believe these positions have characterised some historical phases of psychoanalysis. (Kluzer, 2001, p. 114)

Robert Wallerstein (1969, p. 126) asks the following question: "Is the patient fitted to the treatment, or the treatment fitted to the patient?"

According to the psychoanalyst Anteo Saraval (1988), both Liberman's and Saraval's positions can be endorsed.

The psychoanalyst Daniel Widlöcher (1999, p. 76) asks the following question: "How can we rigorously maintain the setting (in those cases in which psychoanalytic experience is necessary) and, at the same time, be able to be flexible (in those cases in which flexibility is necessary)?"

In conclusion, these are the two horns of the dilemma: on the one hand, we should avoid rigidity, and that can be called "a sort of mechanical organization of those factors external to the setting"[15] (Fachinelli, 1983); on the other, we should avoid building up an internal setting made of the vague, indefinite, and inexpressible (and so difficult to use at a psychoanalytic level) (Correale, 2003).

CHAPTER EIGHT

The uncanny

> The repressed is foreign territory to the ego—internal foreign territory—just as reality (if you will forgive the unusual expression) is external foreign territory.
>
> (Sigmund Freud, 1933a, p. 57)

At the beginning of 1919[1] Freud writes a brief but fundamental essay (*The "Uncanny"*, 1919b) based on a 1906 Jentsch article and on a 1914 book (*The Double: A Psychoanalytic Study*) by his pupil Otto Rank. Freud starts his essay by referring to the many difficulties in translating the title, more precisely the term *das Unheimliche*,[2] into other modern languages. The problem is that other languages do not seem to have an exact equivalent of this word. Freud himself writes (1919b, p. 221): "The Italian and Portuguese languages seem to content themselves with words which we should describe as circumlocutions."

> Its [of the term *Unheimlich*] peculiar linguistic status, its irreducibility to any closure axiom, its lasting dissimilarity in respect to those expressions that seem to fully understand its meaning, are all things profoundly "uncanny". Recognising that this term has something that resists definition and that holds language in check causes fear

> and discomfort. It means to take note of an insurmountable limit in using an apparently omnipotent tool like language. (Curi, 2010, pp. 29–30)

Freud accepts the definition proposed by Schelling who thought that the unfamiliar and frightening were nothing but what "ought to have remained … secret and hidden but have come to light". Freud (1919b, p. 225), similarly to Georges Bataille (1936, p. 11), says about poetry: "If poetry introduces the strange, it does so by way of the familiar. The poetic is the familiar dissolving into the strange and dissolving ourselves with it."

Heimlich and *Unheimlich* are ambivalent terms. They are in opposition but also in convergence and thus sometimes what is known, intimate, or familiar becomes its opposite, that is to say, what alienates, disorientates, or disturbs. Or, sometimes, it can be what fascinates. Freud argues that these fascinating features do not concern its content, but its mode of presentation. This is more or less the same for dreams. A nightmare is such not for what shows or presents, but for what happens between a certain presentation and our resistance in accepting it.

Actually, the uncanny element is nothing new or strange, but rather it is something that psychic life has been used to for a long time. In fact, it is an affect or an emotion transformed into anxiety by repression. "Among instances of frightening things must be one class in which the frightening element can be shown to be something repressed which recurs." (Freud, 1919b, p. 241)

The first cause of the uncanny comes from the return of something we believed definitively repressed, for example, animistic, magic, or totemic ideas. That is to say, all those ideas in which we don't believe, but that resurface and can cast a shadow over the status of material reality. Cases of this kind of uncanny can be the return to the childhood belief in the omnipotence of thought (for example, it can make us fear that we have killed someone just because we have not given a great importance to his death) or the apparent return of magical properties in things without any magical meaning. An example of this last case is the anecdote that Freud found in the English *Strand Magazine*: a furnished apartment in which there is a table with carving of crocodiles becomes the scenario of a frightening night. Very specific smells and strange figures begin to pervade the rooms as ghostly crocodiles haunt them (Freud, 1919b).

The second cause of the uncanny comes from the return of repressed childhood complexes such as those related to fantasies of castration or of the maternal womb. When they return, these complexes do not call into question the status of reality (in fact, these complexes have never been considered real) but rather the status of psychical reality. Freud makes an example of this kind of cause: "Dismembered limbs, a severed head, a hand cut off at the wrist ... feet that dance by themselves." (Freud, 1919b, p. 244) All these things are uncanny because of their "proximity to the castration complex" (Freud, 1919b, p. 244). Freud argues that the German word *unheimlich* appears at first glance as the opposite of *heimlich* (from *Heim*, house) and *heimish* (native/domestic), and thus the contrary of something known and familiar such as a house. However, if we pay attention, the two terms are not in strong opposition. Freud points out that "among its different shades of meaning the word *heimlich* exhibits one that is identical with its opposite, *unheimlich*. What is *heimlich* thus comes to be *unheimlich*." (ibid., p. 224)

Curi (2010, pp. 51–52) writes: "The word *unheimlich* makes us feel a series of emotions that we generally feel when we cannot interpret our experience clearly and unequivocally. It is as when we realise that a certain thing simultaneously comforts and discomforts us."

The philosopher and psychoanalyst Julia Kristeva writes:

> In the fascinated rejection that the foreigner arouses in us, there is a share of uncanny strangeness in the sense of the depersonalisation that Freud discovered in it, and which takes up again our infantile desires and fears of the other—the other of death, the other of woman, the other of uncontrollable drive. The foreigner is within us. And when we flee from our struggle against the foreigner, we are fighting our unconscious—that "improper" facet of our impossible "proper". Delicately, analytically, Freud does not speak of foreigners: he teaches us how to detect foreignness in ourselves. That is perhaps the only way not to hound it outside of us. (1991, p. 191)

However, we are no less disturbed when we realise that a certain process is both equal and opposite (thus symmetrical) in respect to that described:

> This happens when we understand that the non-house is inside our house, that is to say, that what we have always thought to be distant and different from us actually lives and dwells with us.

> The dissolution of "simple" imagination and of a comfortable dichotomous view strongly disturbs us. This is because we cannot put and subdivide in defined categories good and evil, familiar and strange, and also house and non-house. (Curi, 2010, p. 53)

The house not only provides protection, it also hides those things lying in the most secret of its parts. In its darkest areas it contains those things that cannot come to light because they represent its most sinister secrets.

Thus, the uncanny is both a gift and a menace. It is both inside and outside us. It is something different from us but also pertaining to our identity.

But the *Unheimliche* is also:

> What reveals the secret of the house and thus what the *Heimliche* is, what is peculiar to us. It is a sort of awakening or insight that allows us understanding of inexpressible meanings, that reveals the outside of the inside, the unfamiliarity of ourselves to us, the excesses of dwelling and familiarity. The *Unheimliche* must not be conceived as a mystery but as a return that allows the unveiling of secrets. (Borutti, 2006, pp. 153–154)

Anthony Vidler argues that:

> As a frame of reference that confronts the desire for a home and the struggle for domestic security with its apparent opposite, intellectual and actual homelessness, at the same time as revealing the fundamental complicity between the two, the *Unheimleiche* captures the difficult conditions of the theoretical practice of architecture in modern times. (1992, p. 12)

And he writes that he aims to deal with "a yet unfinished history that pits the homely, the domestic, the nostalgic, against their ever-threatening, always invading, and often subversive 'opposites'" (ibid., p. 13).[3]

Elvio Fachinelli (1974, p. 9) argues that psychoanalysis itself is "an uncanny knowledge and a knowledge of what is uncanny … ; it is a knowledge … that discovers and shows us what is uncanny in what is familiar and usual on the surface."

The historian Michel de Certeau strongly stresses the crucial role of the repressed towards all the symbolic orders:

> Any autonomous order is founded upon what it eliminates; it produces a "residue" condemned to be forgotten. But what was excluded re-infiltrates the place of its origin—now the present's "clean" (proper) place. It resurfaces, it troubles, it turns the present's feeling of being "at home" into an illusion, it lurks—this "wild", this "obscene", this "filth", this "resistance" of "superstition"—within the walls of the residence, and, behind the back of the owner (the ego), or over its objections. (1987, p. 4)

For a long time psychoanalysts have been tempted to refer to a mythical internal world of a man who is distant from those landscapes that he has contributed to shape, from the historical events, from the changes in the frontiers. After a phase in which psychoanalysts conceived the inside world as separated from the outside (this was probably a reaction to positivistic culture and its denial of the emotional-affective dimension in the observation of facts), they became aware that knowledge of the internal world required knowledge of the external world without censorship or omission. Internal territories are also external and external territories penetrate and transform the composition, the partitioning, and the borders of external territories through continuous and never-ending osmosis.

> Some experiences really are new. If we are not able to experience them as new, we have a defensive attitude before the possible turmoil and anxiety caused by something new. In this sense, we deny it by conceiving it as something usual. In this case, we reduce something unknown and strange to something familiar or part of our daily routine. Unfortunately, such denial and reduction exclude any possibility of thinking about the consequences that every change implies. Furthermore, experiencing something new can trigger persecutory or megalomaniac or omnipotent states of mind, which also exclude any possibility of thinking about our experience. (Preta, 1999, p. 7)

In his 1937 book *Surprise and the Psycho-Analyst: On the Conjecture and Comprehension of Unconscious Process*, the psychoanalyst Theodor Reik argues that, when an analyst is surprised by something unexpected that the patient said in a session, this means that something crucial is occurring. At first blush, the analyst experiences it as something without any meaning, because it comes from the uncanny and thus cannot be easily included in a known framework.

The uncanny in architecture

Anthony Vidler writes:

> Architecture reveals the deep structure of the uncanny in a more than analogical way, demonstrating a disquieting slippage between what seems homely and what is definitively unhomely. As articulated theoretically by Freud, the uncanny or *unheimlich* is rooted by etymology and usage in the environment of the domestic, or the *heimlich*, thereby opening up problems of identity around the self, the other, the body, and its absence: thence its force in interpreting the relations between the psyche and the dwelling, the body and the house, the individual and the metropolis. (1992, pp. IX–X)

Today, architecture should deal with places of care and containment that consider the distinction or indistinction between self and non-self, between order and chaos, between differentiated and undifferentiated. In other words, it should be able to deal with spaces able to contain multiple complex demands and the person's compositions and decompositions. It should also be able to host those areas of our mind that we have always considered inhospitable and thus to eject, repress, censor, or control.

We dwell in a space surrounded by thinner and thinner walls.

> Disorientation is a consequence of the permeability between different contexts. In this situation each context can lose its peculiarity and its temporary exclusive normativity. Thus, behaviours and expectations must be redefined according to new rules that change the meaning of the places ... These rules are defined by a trans-contextual normativity ... We must insist in confronting ourselves with an extended, transversal, and juxtaposed contextuality. (Merlini, 2012, p. 10)

Giordano Tironi (2007, p. 43) invites us to discuss the meaning and the limitations of dualisms such as natural/artificial, hybrid/pure, invention/clonation, original/copy, uniqueness/series, and so on. "These are increasingly complex, defined, intertwined and, I fear, next to confusion."

Most of our identity is outside us; for example, it is in the objects surrounding us, in the furniture and knick-knacks in our rooms, in our clothes, in what we do. Our skin is a sort of semi-permeable membrane allowing osmosis and dividing the internal from the external. When we move home and bring with us the objects contained in the old house, we lose parts of ourselves or areas of protection of our imagination.

"Our belief in ghosts will always be at least unconsciously authorised by the fact that we shall always linger on in our former houses, just as we assume that upon moving into a new dwelling, its former inhabitants will also still be there." (Bollas, 2000, p. 29)

Lorena Preta writes:

> Our human nature shows up as a construction. I mean, it is something that, although it is given as a specific basic feature, needs the meeting with an environment in order to develop and specify itself. This meeting helps our nature to distinguish itself from the natural world and even from the artificial world, which will be always part of it, more or less actively … Thus, the notion of human nature (more precisely, the experience of belonging to the humankind) implies an extended space in which the subject can expand herself or himself through a sort of movement allowing assuming the otherness. It does not necessarily imply an absorption leading to a lack of distinction able to cancel every difference. Rather, it implies a continuous work of modulation in order to reach an expansion and an increase. (2015, pp. 25–26)

An ineffective exchange regulation can lead us to project painful parts of our internal world on external objects and space. This space can be experienced as fragmented, crumbled, or odd and unrecognisable. In this sense, objects that appeared familiar and were daily life companions can become strange and threatening.

The psychoanalyst Harold F. Searles (1960) argues that the nonhuman environment and the daily life habitat (thus, animal and vegetable kingdoms, architectural structures of domestic and extra-domestic environments, furnishings, and furniture) play the same crucial role as the emotional and affective environment and the social context in determining and structuring our mind, in particular during childhood. Searles uses the term "relatedness" to refer to a sense of affective intimacy with both the processes of human life and those of the environment in which this life occurs. This relatedness helps mitigate man's existential solitude in the universe.

The sense of relatedness "mitigates the fear of death and helps the man in finding peace, stability, continuity, and security. Further, it can be an antidote against the feeling of voidness and futility." (Searles, 1960, p. 105) This sense of relatedness and this harmonic relationship with the environment are lost in schizophrenia. It seems that an identificative regression with the non-human takes place. This seems to allow patients to quit and defend from emotionally unsuitable and painful situations.

The psychoanalyst Jacques Hochmann (1982, p. 5) argues that a psychotic patient is really sure that most of his identity stays concretely outside him. "This identity is projected in his neighbours, in the objects surrounding him, in the furniture of his room, in his clothes, in other really concrete and physical objects that seem to be able to contain parts of his personality."

The philosopher and cultural theorist Mark Kingwell (2002) argues that the furniture of a certain room can provoke only the kind of thought that is possible in that room. The pieces of furniture are thinking objects themselves or features of humanity whose presence can be thought.

The psychoanalyst Julie Leavitt writes:

> In general, the material framework of the psychoanalytic space is a continuous expression of human projections we can meet at the level of material dimension. This is the same of Freud's description of ego as mainly and deeply bodily and material, that is to say … not merely a surface entity, but is itself the projection of a surface. (2013, p. 557)

If the situationist philosopher Guy Debord (1955) uses the term "psychogeography" to indicate those geographic-environmental influences on emotions and human behaviour, Leavitt (2013, pp. 559 & 563) points out that "the opposite influence. That is to say, a 'geopsychography' aiming at including the ways through which memories, emotions and behaviour influence the shape and the aspect of the material setting ... In this setting we can find traces of the present time through which memories can be lived in the present somatic experience."

Deconstructivist architects have put on the agenda for discussion the fundamental truths of architecture. Thus they draw upon deconstructivist and neoconstructivist forms explicitly aiming at challenging the conventional notion of *Heimlichkeit*. This occurs by removing the body classically conceived from its privileged position in architectural theory and practice. They categorically refuse both the idea of an accommodating architecture and the idea of being domestic.

> Let's consider the Falkestrasse rooftop remodelling located in Vienna [by Coop Himmelb(l)au], the Gehry Residence in Santa Monica, the Daniel Libeskind's collages that will give foundation to the Jewish Museum Berlin, the Koolhaas's urbanistic hypotheses, the Eisenmann's transcripts, the Hadid's fragmented geometries and the Tschumi's red enamelled steel follies. They are all projects starting from opposed biographies and perspectives to complex and irregular geometries and to an expressive use of structures. Their strength is in stressing the uncertainty, in conceiving the complexity as a dogma, in juxtaposing the signs to something indecipherable. (Neri, 2013, p. 23)

Frank Gehry's research

The architect Frank Gehry has studied how to create spatial containers able to overturn the ordered space as we know it. His work is a revolution from most of the architectural production that has been transmitted to us. It does not represent either a megalomaniac destruction of what is known, past, and codified, nor a sort of teenage wish for revolution or transgression that is without a cause and based on diversity, disorder, and hybridation. Rather, his work represents a change of meaning and of using our senses, a transformation of the *Unheimlich* into *Heimlich* without any intellectualisation, an immediate connection between space and body language or between unconscious and external habitat. Further, it represents a growth and an enhancement of those containing functions that, until today, living spaces have never had because they are unable to deal with those mental areas difficult to control, especially through untenable repressions.

Figure 1. Frank Gehry's house, Santa Monica, California.

Gehry's house in Santa Monica, California (Figures 1 and 2) does not appear as a solid block, but as a sum of various and apparently autonomous entities establishing an intense dialogue and a formal relationship between them and the external environment. The relation between inside and outside, that is to say, between opaque walls and transparent ceilings, allows for surprising visual effects. In this sense it gives the idea of an architectural route and not of something monolithic. "The power of Gehry's residence seems to reveal itself when the potential energy that emanates comes out." (Bruzzone, 2007, p. 27)

> The formal relationship between the dweller's existential reasons and his context ... passes through breaking up and decomposing an old idea of dwelling, according to which all was forced centralised and united. This breaking up and decomposition allow expressing

Figure 2. Frank Gehry's house, Santa Monica, California.

> its parts as architectural subjects in an unarranged order so that a free way of living can occur. This way of thinking ... rebuts every arranged communication and allows entities and structure being free and uncontrollable. (Celant, 2013a, p. 18)

The Junkerhaus (Figure 3) in Lemgo, Germany, is considered the clearest example of so-called schizophrenic architecture. In this sense, it is not only eccentric or fantastic; it is the only masterpiece by a schizophrenic architect, Karl Junker (1850–1912), who was never interned in a psychiatric hospital. The shapes and interiors of the Junkerhaus are actually in tune with the modernist construction of the time. Only in some rooms can we see the external projection of a schizophrenic world, for example in the spatial disposition of objects, furniture, and sculptures.

However, in the buildings planned by Gehry, the space is much more deconstructed than in other buildings such as the Junkerhaus. In fact, although the internal routes and the internal-external relationships appear to be apparently confused and incoherent, they actually are able to contain the split-off parts of a person suffering from a mental disease.

Figure 3. The Junkerhaus, Lemgo, Germany.

"Gehry's architecture looks like unfinished, incomplete buildings, still under construction." (Bruzzone, 2007, p. 22)[4]

The psychoanalyst F. Robert Rodman (2005) stresses Gehry's knowledge of psychoanalysis when he describes his billowing metallic buildings as breasts. It is clear that this description is related to the notion of a protective mother as an appealing model and can be seen as a response to modern man's need for comfort. In this sense, we can say that Gehry's work has two features: on the one hand, the external structure of his buildings tends to the notion of the masculine (that is to say, the protective shell within which emotions and affects may be expressed); on the other, thanks to Gehry's capacity for introducing sensual and elastic curvature to the volume of an object (they are all features that recall the wind and the tide), his work may be thought of as an atypical feminist architecture.

> It is the passage from Mies van der Rohe's suspended and packaged void (that is to say, a void that an individual can possess and manage) to emotional and expanding, bodily and sensual spaces interacting and breathing with the dweller. This allows the irrational to live

> with the rational, the superficial with the volumetric, the non-architectural with the architectural. (Celant, 2013a, pp. 17 & 25)

Of course, we must avoid easy and ideological transpositions and juxtapositions according to which spaces suggesting disorder, instability, or uncertainty (this is opposed to the repressive and detrimental spatial order typical of psychiatric hospitals and of many community mental health services) can provide a full containment of psychical pain. Even when architectural spaces are planned and organised for certain specific aims, they cannot radically modify by themselves human relationships and behaviours strictly entrenched in cultures, habits, and social conventions. However, these spaces are certainly containers of human emotion and action and thus can have a role in a subject's transformative processes, experiences, and behaviours. They can pass from the status of neutral, passive, and strictly functional object to the status of active, engaging, stimulating, and variable subject. In other words, they can become places able to adapt to the dweller's personal demands, to provide security, and to comprehend and accept diversity. I want to focus on mental health services. I believe that we need to conceive architectural spaces as complex environmental units (in this sense, they must comprehend resting spaces and interstitial sites able to favour intense exchanges and relationships between people) able to stimulate a completely new and genuine harmony between patients' and therapists' demands.

CHAPTER NINE

Psychoanalysis and architecture: the need for an interdisciplinary debate

> The appearance of things changes according to the emotions; and thus we see magic and beauty in them, while the magic and beauty are really in ourselves.
>
> (Kahlil Gibran, 1920, p. 51)

Christopher Bollas (2000) argues that the world of architecture (broadly defined here as the intentional consideration of the human built environment) and the world of psychoanalysis (broadly defined here as the study of unconscious mental life) intersect because the way in which we plan and dwell in the environment we construe reflects the unconscious forms of thinking that architecture aims to realise. Cities become holding environments that offer inhabitants differing forms of psychic engagement with the object world.

Even if a building springs from the typical idiom of a great architect, it certainly comes from the human imagination, in a dialectic that is largely influenced by many factors, such as its stated function, its relation to neighbourhood, its functional possibilities, its artistic or design statement, its client's desires, the anticipated public responses, and many other factors that constitute the architect's mental structure and thus his architectural design.

In this sense, psychoanalysis can be seen as a metaphor for architecture, especially regarding the topography of our mental and emotional life and, vice versa, architecture can be seen as a metaphor for psychoanalysis, a sort of "semantic pantograph" able to project the human mind outside and on buildings (Pesare, 2007).

In a certain sense, architects have a simplifying role: they are tools that allow their or their customers' unconscious wishes to find their place. Something similar can be said of psychoanalysis because, differently from other animals, man needs to tell and give a meaning to his fantasies and representations (Ferrari, 2011).

Aldo Rossi (1981, p. 65) writes: "architecture can be beautiful before it is used; there is beauty in the wait, in the room prepared for the wedding, in the flowers and the silver before High Mass".

The psychoanalyst Stephen Sonnenberg (2005) points out how Freud's experience at the Acropolis[1] can indicate the possibility of using the surrounding environment for proposing an analytic reflection. He describes his self-analytic experience at Berlin's *Neue Synagoge* and compares it to that of Freud at the Acropolis. From this description he starts developing hypotheses about what an analyst might do to promote patient introspection in the consulting room.

Esther Sperber argues that:

> Buildings always act as both symbols of their functions and the embodiment (some with greater success than others) of the function they represent. The analyst, like the building, also occupies both positions, symbolising in the transference all that the patient needs while also acting in the here-and-now as a new and better object and subject for the patient. The real building, insite, creates space for new modes of personal and social experiences in much the same way that the analytic insights foster new ways of being. (2014a, p. 123)

Adolf Loos (1910) writes that architects must make us feel emotions and feelings and clarify them. He offers an evocative example (p. 84): "A bank must say: here your money is safe in the hands of honest people."

According to the architect Jacobus Johannes Pieter Oud (1947, p. 18), "the genuine architecture, old and new, can and must evoke an emotional reaction. In other words, it must be able to transmit the aesthetic perspective of the architect to the person watching his building." In this sense, architecture promotes a continuous dialogue with the changes of our thoughts and with our most lasting ideas. There is a comparison between two territories: sometimes the external territory becomes small in comparison to the internal one, and vice versa. Both can be disturbing and calming (Pinna, 2013).

The psychoanalyst Mauro Mancia argues that the internal mother, the internal father, and the parental couple having a creative or sadistic relationship can be at the basis not only of man's oneiric representations but also of man's fantastic, pictorial, sculptural, musical, and architectural constructions. "I think that architectural constructions will give a meaning to the space occupied by the internal world's representations more or less as an enduring theatre that will tell the story of the internal objects and their relationships and how these objects will determine certain beliefs and values." (Mancia, 1995, p. 218) Mancia quotes a sentence that can be considered the spiritual testament of Antonio Gaudì: "*Originalidad es volver al origen*" (being original means returning to origins). He comments:

> The return to origins is the return to the most archaic relationship, that with our mother, by using our fantasy. This return sets forth the deep influence of Gaudì's unconscious in choosing certain shapes and not other ones in his work. Further, it allows Gaudì to make a unique imaginary journey in which he can describe adventures in a childhood place without physically moving (Gaudì has never moved away from Barcelona). (1995, p. 224)

Crossed definitions of architecture and psychoanalysis

A good definition of architecture is that of a knowledge that is partially the history of a profession, partially the evolution of a construction science, and partially a revision of certain aesthetical theories (Rabinow, 1982). Michel Foucault defines it as a τέχνη (*techne*) and not as an exact or inexact science. In Aristotle, *techne* refers to both creative and technical arts: it is "the name for a skilful activity (poiesis) that accomplishes its purpose in the production of a particular work" (Vassalli, 2001, p. 19).

On the other hand, by underlining the particular effect of the geographic environment over individuals' emotions and behaviour,

Guy E. Debord (1955) defines architecture as "psychogeography", in other words as the study and the manipulation of places for creating new physical environments and mental possibilities. In the same vein Esther Sperber (2014a) argues that architecture can be seen as the exercise of creating spaces able to expand the range of human activity and experience. "Architecture is always a sublimatory product, combining a rational, functional reality of building with a phenomenological experience of inhabiting space and dwelling." (Sperber, 2014b, p. 507)

The psychoanalyst Simona Argentieri seems to be near to architects when she defines psychoanalysis in this way:

> Sigmund Freud's conceptual construct is based on the intuition of the existences of an unconscious as a predominant area of human mind. Freud's concept is at the same time a metapsychological theory, a method of inquiry on how the mind works in normal conditions and, above all, a therapeutic practice. The peculiarity of an atypical discipline like psychoanalysis is that these three features are connected by an intrinsic circularity: every abstract concept comes from clinical experience. From this experience theory can be construed and from theory the method can be derived. (2013, p. 5)

Giovanni Vassalli argues that Freudian psychoanalysis is a τέχνη based on the Aristotelian model: "Analytic treatment according to these rules of the art is completed in a temporal projection to theory. In a second step the putting together, guessing, speculating and pondering is assigned to what is still a technical investigation. The subsequent theories should not be made in advance." (2001, p. 22)

In both architecture and psychoanalysis there is a continuous exchange and a reciprocal influence between theory and practice. Such an interaction allows architecture and psychoanalysis to modify and develop.

When architecture is an expression of a poetic attitude towards a certain state of things, it confronts itself with the unconscious universe of knowledge and images:

> On the contrary, when a spontaneous expression, a personal gesture, or a collective action is able to build a codified language, its approach becomes intrinsically conservative. That is to say, a natural expression enters into a formal law. A law means preserving

> and defending something acquired. The history of architecture is an endless cycle of revolutions and restorations typical of the history of mankind. In this sense, I believe mankind seems to aim at repeatedly constructing, destroying, and reconstructing rules of formal coherence. (Braghieri, 2013, p. 19)

The process of architectural design requires a synthesis of inward drives and outward pressures, one that is like the struggle to resolve the power of creation and the power of resistance. This architectural process is similar to the synthesis that takes place between analysand and analyst. In the design of a building, and in the creation of an analysis, a larger reality that cannot be grasped prior to its arrival is present; this new reality (for analyst, analysand, or architect) is itself a creative act (Danze, 2005, p. 123).

The psychoanalyst Peter Loewenberg writes that:

> The factors of reliability and security indulge the analysand's and client's most primitives fantasies of a completely satisfying and omnipotent union, which reproduces the primary narcissistic relationship with the infantile mother. In this sense, the building and the analysis are settings that facilitate the externalisation of internal relationships. In both architecture and psychoanalysis, the setting is also structured to enable the introjection of external spaces and relationships, qualities and forms, such as aesthetic grace, peace, and harmony. (2012, p. 41)

To paraphrase what Daniel Libeskind (2004) says about the relationship between music and architecture,[2] architecture and psychoanalysis are based first on direct experience and then on consequent analysis. There is nothing to prevent anyone from examining a song after having listened to it, deconstructed it, and explored its harmonies and tunes. However, before doing these operations, we need simply to be carried away by its sound. Often, buildings make their magic and genius felt in the same way as songs. In the same vein, an analytic session must be experienced without memory or desire, in the here and now (*hic et nunc*), in order to permit genuine and authentic communication.

I remember finding the same concepts in an interview with the rock musician Frank Zappa, who said that writing about music is like dancing about architecture.

What are the possible connections between architecture and psychoanalysis?

In the introduction to the monographic volume on the relationships between psychoanalysis, arts, and architecture of the International Forum of Psychoanalysis, Ulla Britt-Parment (2000a) points out that the aim of various authors is neither to give a definition of psychoanalysis, arts, and architecture nor to assess the similarities and differences between them. Rather, the aim is to evaluate the mutual influences of the different fields compared to each other and their capacity to learn from each other.

In 2005 the psychoanalysts Jerome A. Winer, James W. Anderson, and the architect Elizabeth A. Danze organised a congress on the relationships between psychoanalysis and architecture. The proceedings of this congress were published in a volume of *The Annual of Psychoanalysis* that was then edited as a book in 2006. In the introduction, they write:

> Is there any connection between psychoanalysis and architecture? Does psychoanalysis have anything to offer to the study of architecture? We soon realised that there is, in fact, a profound connection. Architecture refers to the built environment, the environment within which everyone lives, the residences, civic buildings, places of business, and houses of worship that people inhabit. An essential element of architecture is the experience of it. And psychoanalysis is the study of inner experience, of the interactions individuals have with the world around them, of their most intimate, emotional, and personal reception and apperception of whatever impinges on them. Architects, moreover, like all artists, design buildings on the basis of their own personal experiences, lives, preoccupations, and conflicts, and psychoanalysis offers a way of exploring the process of artistic creation. (2006, p. 4)

One of the most evident instances of splitting that can be observed in architecture is that between aesthetics and function, which has caused a sort of aesthetical distortion that has led to some architectural aberrations. Sometimes we find a lifeless and purposeless monumentality, an apparent haughtiness often lacking substance. Bollas (2000) argues that, because of their mass, monuments are like sepulchres, that is to say, signs of death within life. They are not authentic or genuine images but rather images substituting for something absent. They are a narcissistic and magnificent deal that does not consider the simplest needs, but they recall a false self, hiding the most basic demands and impeding reaching and enjoying a work.

> The Bible story of the Tower of Babel is not only about the origin of languages, but also of the megalomania of all attempts to concretely realise the grandness of fantasies, especially in architecture. Such a story has taught us that the megalomania oppresses the builder and the architect (and I think this is the same for the psychoanalyst!). The megalomania of the Tower of Babel deals not only with the archetypal image of the tower, but also with the fact that all its builders were speaking the same language (a unique language). Thus, it is about megalomania and unity, unification, uniqueness. The punishment was the global dispersion of people and the spread of different languages ... places, territories, idioms. The universalism of International style makes the same error or sin of Babel. Probably the God of the Holy Bible does not like the International style." (Hillman, 2004, pp. 59–60)

Between aesthetics and function

A dubious functionalism can be opposed to an arrogant monumentalism. According to functionalism, if conceived in a strong sense, function is everything (if conceived in a weak sense, function precedes the form). Functionality often becomes a critical and lifeless functionalism, lacking expression and aesthetic pleasure. In this sense, functionalism can be the prelude to building skyscrapers—boxes full of hermetically sealed offices and anonymous and grim dormitory suburbs that make our cities ugly.

Aldo Rossi pointed out that his projects and buildings should not be conceived in order to perform a specific function as functionalists thought. Rather, they have been conceived in order to perform many functions, since they can change in time. He writes (1981, p. 75): "I have seen old palaces now inhabited by many families, convents transformed into schools, amphitheatres transformed into football fields; and such transformations have always come about most effectively where neither an architect nor some shrewd administrator has intervened."

To this end, I would like to report two amusing anecdotes from Truppi (2004) about two famous architects.

The image of the roof of Notre Dame du Haut in Ronchamp (Figure 4) is one of the most beautiful and representative in the world of architecture. It is an enormous ark lying on the void and aiming at symbolising salvation. When Le Corbusier presented his project, the engineer Pierluigi Nervi was present, among others. He tried to make things difficult for Le Corbusier and he provocatively asked him how he thought to realise such a strange shape. Le Corbusier said in a huff: "We will realise it with cow shit!" In this sense, he wanted to reject an excess of concreteness that could prevent the constitution of a time for elaboration and imagination.

Frank Lloyd Wright conceived the Guggenheim Museum in New York (Figure 5) as a street, a road of arts, a museum-promenade, a part of the other streets of the city. He planned the museum with an empty central nucleus above a glass dome to allow visitors to see everything from every point of view. However, he had to deal with the worries of James Sweeney, at the time director of the museum, who doubted it was possible to hang the paintings on the curved walls. Lloyd Wright responded provocatively to Sweeney's worries by saying that the paintings could be thrown in Central Park's lake. The relationship

Figure 4. Notre Dame du Haut, Ronchamp, France.

between Lloyd Wright and Sweeney was highly troubled. Lloyd Wright conceived the Guggenheim Museum as an enormous masterpiece, a sort of big mother whose womb could contain many sons (paintings). Sweeney could not stand this view, probably because he considered it a threat to the record of contemporary art (Venezia, 2012). In fact, Lloyd Wright was correct as is evident by the great number of people who come to visit the Guggenheim and in the many exhibitions that are organised without any problems with hanging paintings.

These two anecdotes about architects' activity can refer to a general problem in the relationship between aesthetic (this term comes from the ancient Greek αἴσθησις (*aesthesis*), which can be translated as "perceiving with senses or intellect" and referring to αἴσθου (*aeistou*), meaning "I breathe in" or "I gasp") and function, the space of concreteness and the space of imagination, feelings, memories, and intelligence. James Hillman (2006, p. 27) warns us about the limit in the opposition between the natural and the artefact, as well as in the revival of the classical dichotomy between the raw and the cooked, the instinct and the culture, the given and the done. "The happy combination of the 'given' and the 'done' depends on the perspective they attend upon, that is to say, it is the development of the given world through the world done and built. Both these worlds are expressions of the peculiarity of *genius loci.*"

Figure 5. Solomon R. Guggenheim Museum, New York, USA.

In an interview with the psychoanalyst Valerie Tate Angel (2000), the architect Richard Meier answers the question of whether plan and form come before function by simply saying that we must think of space in terms of how people relate to it, mean it, think how to use it. Throughout the interview, Angel argues that this process is similar to the psychoanalytic one. In fact, during an analysis, the analysand does not know *a priori* what he will discover. The analysand starts from her symptoms and then, through analysis, discovers the roots of her problems rather than finding relief from her symptoms. Meier agrees that what occurs in an analytic relationship is similar to the work of an architect in imagining and conceiving a space. Most people do not know anything about space, about relating to or imagining it.

Let's consider how in psychoanalysis an excessively saturating use of interpretation can crush and sometimes even neutralise people's imagination, relation, and memory capacities. I believe that an interpretation must be given in a open way, at the right time, and thus in respect of the internal rhythms of the patient and of the patient-analyst couple at work, in order to promote and not neutralise the patient's vital, associative, and communicative capacities. I think that more or less the same can be said for architecture: "The complexity of a function must attend upon the optical-emotional use, the inquiry on the adequacy of the materials, the relationship between signs and practices and the links between techniques and contexts." (Truppi, 2004, p. 120)

As well as in psychoanalysis, in architecture "the time of the magnificence at all costs, of the events, of the creation of icons, of the constructions aiming more at exhibiting than representing seems to be near to an end" (Capuano, 2006).

> I believe it would be interesting to also conceive the architect's work as a daydream activity in which already existing experiences are transformed in architectural thoughts and in new forms. These thoughts and forms are products of the architect's capacity to dream the basic reality in terms of assessing the materials at disposal and reworking previous architectural theories and formulation. (Preta, 2006, p. 22)

By referring to a famous quote of Le Corbusier ("The purpose of construction is to make things hold together; of architecture to move us.") (Le Corbusier, 1923, p. 19), Libeskind (2014) argues that planning is not only constructing, but also having the fantasy, desire, imagination, individuation, and representation of human feelings.

Libeskind planned the Jewish Museum in Berlin.[3] It was probably one of the first public buildings aiming to provoke confusing feelings and unpleasant reactions. It does not aim to provide a rational comprehension of the Holocaust, but rather to give a sense of the unthinkable, of the void, of the unfamiliar, and of a dead end. In this sense, Libeskind's work seems to be able to reconnect its visitors' minds to affects that have been avoided, split off, or dissociated.

The American psychoanalyst Leanna Domash (2014) discusses the possible meaning of both the symbolic and physical voids of the Jewish Museum and argues that they are able to reactivate traumatic experiences. In this sense, they are probably linked to our inability to comprehend and mentalise the Holocaust. In spite of this, Domash feels that the building has a protective and mediating function. In this sense, she thinks that Libeskind has been able to represent both the horror and the sense of a holding environment within the same structure.

When man realises and organises the creative process of construction, he uses the language of architecture to express different contents from those required by survival needs. In fact, the construction act is limited only to realise a refuge in which man can repair himself and contain his objects. In other words, these different contents are not necessary: they are needs coming from a personal and collective aim to communicate. It is about the communication of a message via the forms of construction. This message is able to characterise a building and make explicit the ideas at the basis of the planning.

"The formal expression lays the physical basis for the surface of things and it is the way in which the most deep thoughts and desires are spread." (Braghieri, 2013, pp. 8–9)

However, I believe that it would be illusory and wrong to define a borderline between a form ordered by necessity and a form ordered by human aesthetical choices. In most buildings in which man has lived and worked from his beginnings, many different functional reasons and aesthetical qualities coexist and intersect.

The architect's daydream (reverie)

Gaston Bachelard in *The Poetics of Space* (1958, p. 6) writes that: "our memories of former dwelling-places are relived as daydreams that these dwelling-places of the past remain in us for all time."

Christopher Bollas argues that:

> When we traverse a city ... each gaze that falls upon an object of interest may yield a moment's reverie ... when we think of something else, inspired by the point of emotional contact ... and during our day we will have scores of such reveries, which Freud termed psychic intensities, and which he believed were the stimuli for the dream that night. But as a type of dreaming in their own right, the reveries wrought by evocative objects constitute an important feature of our psychic life. (2000, p. 35)

I believe that these reveries are important for those architects who are aware of the evocative potential of their buildings. These buildings can have a meaning only if they find a balance between the architects' oneiric visions and the dreams of inhabitants that enjoy the architects' works.

In this sense, according to Gaston Bachelard:

> The house shelters daydreaming, the house protects the dreamer, the house allows one to dream in peace ... The values that belong to daydreaming mark humanity in its depths. Daydreaming even has a privilege of auto-valorisation. It derives direct pleasure from its own being. Therefore, the places in which we have experienced daydreaming reconstitute themselves in a new daydream." (1958, p. 6)

About the painter Giorgio De Chirico's metaphysical city, Calvino writes:

> This city is made for embracing, containing, and holding our thoughts without any constraints. Here our thought can find their place and time: it is a suspended time, an invitation, a wait. Here our thoughts can stay on the mind's horizon: in it, they can continue the state of starting uncertainty and thus postpone the moment in which they will obliged to be defined and become thoughts of something ... In fact, the city of thoughts does not suggest only a single kind of thoughts, does not force anyone to think about meetings and appearances occurring in it or to investigate its mysteries. Light, shadow, facades, monuments, human and animal beings, and

> objects are so arranged that the mind can divert its attention from emotions, passions, and external influences.[4] (1983a, pp. 46–47)

The architect's reverie in planning and realising the analytic space should favour the reverie capacity of the analyst that, in turn, defines those holding conditions that should favour the reverie capacities of the analysand.

> The points of contact between psychoanalysis and architecture are strange and very interesting. Let's consider the dreams and their weird scenes showing surprising and original spaces. Dreams have taught us to see the body and its orifices as a house with doors, windows and terraces, whereas the landscapes and their features are expressions of the places of the soul. In these places the psychic apparatus takes the form of the most peculiar architectural and landscaping configurations. As well as for dreams, psychoanalysis has always viewed the mind as a material entity. In this sense, we can represent mental reality in usable and passable forms only if we conceive it as a material entity that takes place in a space. In psychoanalysis the Cartesian *res cogitans* and *res extensa* have the same qualities or, at least, the form can be represented to us only through the latter. (Petrella, 2014)

The professor of human geography Steve Pile (2005) stresses the relevance of dreams for architecture. By examining how dreams take form, he shows that something similar occurs in the creation of space. Further, he writes that dreams reveal our great yearning of a life in tune with our wishes (he conceives wishes as social products, not as something abstract, ahistorical, immortal, or unchangeable). After having used the hydraulic model, Freud focused on the archaeological metaphor for describing the unconscious mind whose traces allow understanding of the forms of a forgotten childhood life and the feelings related to it. By using such a metaphor, he refers to the palaeontology and prehistory of the subject and mankind and to the subject's historical era.

The professor of architectural history John Hendrix (2012) argues that the formation of dream images as first described by Freud and then revised by Lacan (who relates Freud's theories on dream formation to the language and the mechanisms at its basis) can be applied to architectural composition strategies. To demonstrate his hypothesis he examines seven architectural projects of different historical eras.

Freud (1941f, p. 299) writes: "Space may be the projection of the extension of the psychical apparatus. No other derivation is probable. Instead of Kant's *a priori* determinants of our psychic apparatus. Psyche is extended; knows nothing about it."

Renzo Piano argues that listening (in terms of understanding the feelings of a community and making them live inside you) is the fundamental step for doing architecture (Paternostro, 2004) and Libeskind (2004, p. 16) answers the question of how he knows how to design by saying: "I listen to the stones. I sense the faces around me. I try to build bridges to the future by staring clear-eyed into the past."

His answer comes to mind when the Italian psychoanalyst Cesare Musatti argues ironically and realistically that the only occupational disease of analysts is deafness and not muteness.[5]

CHAPTER TEN

The house

"Small is my humble roof."[1]

(Ludovico Ariosto, 1525)

The house as an organism

The word "house" immediately evokes a well-defined space, covered by a roof, constructed on solid foundations and surrounded by a material or symbolic barrier (Roux, 1976) that physically and emotionally protects us. The wall and the facade not only delimit a space, but also make an active division on the ground, drawing boundaries, distinguishing an inside from an outside. The wall and the facade are tools for differentially organising the space. They establish a hierarchy between outside and inside (Filoni, 2014).

In this sense, architecture can be conceived as a continuous elaboration of the areas that separate and link inner-private worlds from an outer-connected social world and organise the entrances and the exits from one space to another (Sperber, 2014b).

In the house all elements of basic construction and all symbolic values of earthly life can be found. The family finds protection under the roof, warmth near the hearth, happiness thanks to the wall decorations, and a sort of cohesion staying in the terrace. From these four basic functions found in the primitive house we can define the structure of a general theory of architecture (Semper, 1851).

I believe it is no coincidence that Pope Francis's 2015 encyclical letter is about the protection of our common home: he uses the expression "common home" metaphorically in order to describe the need to stop the deterioration of the environment by adopting the same attention we adopt for protecting our own home.

Many architecture experts, from Vitruvius to many others during the Renaissance, have sought to define the primitive house. Among the possible interpretations of this "house", we must not forget those found in mystic depictions. Clear examples of these are the many Nativity stables. These often look like simple cabins or, more suggestively, ruined houses or buildings in the educated paintings of Botticelli, Bronzino, Ghirlandaio, Joos van Cleve, Hans Baldung Grien, or Hugo van der Goes. Although these representations were often full of ruins and sometimes full of ephemeral features, they gave a comforting image of life's precarious and fleeting moments. In these moments, God or the man always had a central position closely connected to the mineral character of the walls holding many visitors in the night before Christmas (Tironi, 2007, p. 44).

In *Economic and Philosophic Manuscripts of 1844* the economist Karl Marx criticises material goods and points out how the house can become a cavern and an inhospitable home set in the subsoil. Further, in the first volume of *Capital* (1867) he describes the awful conditions of the British agricultural proletariat. He stresses the pathogenic aspects of these conditions and how the house is alienated from its dweller in so far as, once it loses its intrinsic value (usage value), it acquires an increasing trade value. Freud (1933a) was very critical of Marxism because of its aim at reducing everything to economics. He stressed that "(…) it cannot be assumed that economic motives are the only ones that determine the behaviour of human beings in society. (…) It is altogether incomprehensible how psychological factors can be overlooked where what is in question are reactions of living human beings; for not only were these reactions concerned in establishing the economic conditions, but even under the domination of those conditions men can only bring their original instinctual impulses into play—their self-preservative instinct, their aggressiveness, their need to be loved, their drive towards obtaining pleasure and avoiding unpleasure" (p. 178).

As Freud, Jung too argues that the house has an intra-psychic value because it is the place in which man lives; his relation with its surfaces and the objects with which he surrounds himself to represent his world, cannot be expressed by words. In this sense, the house can be a privileged way to discern the emotional world of its dweller and also a possible connection between the theoretical claims of architecture and psychoanalysis (Pesare, 2007). In his autobiography, Jung remembers a dream he has told Freud. In this dream, there is a two-storey house that he realises he has never seen before, in spite of it being his own house:

> It was plain to me that the house represented a kind of image of the psyche—that is to say, of my then state of consciousness, with hitherto unconscious additions. Consciousness was represented by the salon … The ground floor stood for the first level of the unconscious. The deeper I went, the more alien and the darker the scene became. (Jung, 1961, p. 160)

The philosopher Emmanuel Lévinas (1961) argues that the house is not the purpose of human existence, but it is its necessary condition and thus beginning. Both inside and outside himself, man starts from intimacy and then enters the external world.

The American psychiatrist Roy R. Grinker (1940) starts analysis with Freud in 1933 but has to interrupt it due to the health problems of the father of psychoanalysis. He restarts in 1934. About his analysis, he tells us that, when he refers to places, Freud goes to the library, asks him to show them on a map, and says that he wants to study them. This is because Freud wants to understand all details of these places, included the disposition of the houses and the rooms. For this reason he often asks his patients to draw floor plans and maps.

According to the psychoanalyst Alberto Eiguer:

> A house must be solid in order to contain us. This means that it must appear to be hard and having no noticeable weaknesses from the outside in order to reassure us by delimiting a space to make us feel comfortable. In this sense, it must appear to be also adaptable and open to help us with our activities and to adequately communicate with the external world. We want our house to be useful and satisfactory, as well as our body. Thus, we tend to reproduce the sketch

> of our body on the habitat we live, that is to say, to recreate the outline of our bodily figure and of our body's physiology. (2004, p. 12)

Eiguer also says (p. 17): "every individual has an internal image of the space in which he lives. He easily associates it with his body. It is a conscious and unconscious representation ... In this sense, the unconscious and the living space tend to work together."

In a family therapy context, the psychoanalyst Isidoro Berenstein (1976) makes use of the house plan. During sessions he asks all the family members to imagine this plan in order to stress the contradictions between the manifest content of their words and the unconscious representations emerging from their drawings.

Salomon Resnik (2006) depicts the analyst's mind as a house that the patient slowly inhabits, that is to say, a place where the patient can find shelter and be hosted.

Freud (1916–1917) assumes that the symbolic representation of the house in dreams is universal. He also argues that the house refers to the human body and that its parts make reference to parts of the body. He writes (p. 157): "It may happen in a dream that one finds oneself climbing down the façade of a house, enjoying it at one moment, frightened at another. The houses with smooth walls are men, the ones with projections and balconies that one can hold are women."

The psychoanalyst Sandor Ferenczi (1913) affirms that the first symbolisations through which the baby relates to his objects are about structures and their activities.

The psychoanalyst Gisela Pankow (1969) argues that a person with schizophrenia perceives every organ of his body as distinct from the totality of the body image. So, every room this person inhabits is not part of something, a house, but rather is a whole indistinguishable in parts (Stoppa, 1984).

From another point of view the linguist George Lakoff (1987) mentions that the body and its spatial coordinates are at the basis of many mental processes of metaphorisation and language acquisition. If we take a look at common language, we can find many metaphorical examples. The body, intended both as "body-structure" and "body-space", organises and articulates experience and reality in the way we perceive them.

The architect Harry Francis Mallgrave (2013, p. 9) writes: "our body and its emotional underpinnings, at all conscious and preconscious levels, shape how we think about or actively engage the world, and in our urban cultures this shaping generally takes place in the built environment that the architect or planner fashions." By proposing a perspective integrating history, philosophy, psychology, biology and neurosciences, Mallgrave points out that (p. 10) "we are continually evolving and self-organising organisms-within-environments, and that this dynamic mind/body/social field of relationships, rather than some static abstraction of our presumed human nature, shapes our pre-cognitive and cognitive understanding of the world." Then, he writes: (p. 88) "in recent years, we have more often than not regarded buildings as extravagant objects rather than as palpable environments into which our neurological systems and bodies are inextricably connected or woven. The idea of embodiment is no longer a philosophical abstraction; it is a biological reality."

In his *De Re Aedificatoria* (1452) the polymath Leon Battista Alberti expresses the poetics of organism, that is to say, the comparison between a building and a living body. Thus, if we cannot ignore any part of the body in order to maintain its functionality, we must assume that it is not a single part of a building that determines its beauty. In other world, beauty must pervade the building in its totality. In this sense, Alberti defines beauty as "that reasoned harmony of all the parts within a body, so that nothing may be added, taken away, or altered, but for the worse" (p. 420).

Tiziana Tuzi (1990, pp. 237–238) writes: "the anthropomorphism developed in the architecture of Renaissance is realised through the theory of proportions. In this sense, the human body becomes the ideal model of planning. The integration between macrocosm and microcosm the human figure in order to reach a balance between image and structure."

Late in the fifteenth century the architect known as Filarete conceives the human body as the first example of architecture. For him, the planning process is a procreative sexual act between client and architect, in which the architect becomes the mother of the building by giving birth to the plan.

Georges Bataille (1929) defines architecture as the expression of the way of being of societies just as physiognomy is the expression of the way of being of individuals.

The writer Curzio Malaparte (1940) skilfully describes buildings as bodies:

> Some buildings seem to be made of flesh and have a human figure with human limbs. Other buildings look like luxury furniture

> made of ancient wood or enormous jewels or immense amber tears. Other buildings look like animals: a building-horse, a building-fish, a building-bird. Others look like trees. Some are unexplainably feminine ... Other buildings will be deep-rooted in the earth, like insensible and static prisoners that cannot see, listen, or speak. On the other hand, there are other buildings walking under the moon and made of such stuff as dreams are made of. And some houses and buildings are made as us and of the same flesh. These buildings have blood flowing in their veins. They see, listen and speak, have a deep and human voice, full of human tones.

In *On Houses* (1923, p. 33) the poet Kahlil Gibran writes: "Your house is your larger body. It grows in the sun and sleeps in the stillness of the night; and it is not dreamless. Does not your house dream? And dreaming, leave the city for grove or hilltop?"

The architect Frank Lloyd Wright (1957) defines the human figure as the real basis of architecture.

In this context, professor of architecture Joseph Rykwert (2012) introduces the notion of empathy. He intends it not as a static projection, but as an activity that involves objectifying phenomena. He writes (p. 74): "The kern of empathy is the perhaps self-evident conception of the body as the experiential locus of the world, and the way in which we model experience is inevitably related back to the body, not just as a physical object, but as a psychophysical entity, with all the metaphorical implications of such a concept."

> The house has also been useful for interpreting the cosmos, that is to say, for understanding which forces are at work in the cosmos. Further, the house can be interpreted as a message, as a mean not only interacting with society but as an extension of the body. Thus, the house can be meaningful and become a topological presence only through the body. In this sense, architecture works as a sort of relay and means a sort of tool to be used in a complex set of conditions. (Tironi, 2007, p. 39).[2]

The introjection of the house and its fitness for habitation is a universal mechanism whose meaning can be understood in the words of the writer Natalia Ginzburg in her epistolary novel (1984, p. 166): "That house is still mine and it always will be. A man can sell his house or give it to someone else to his heart's content, but he always keeps it within himself nevertheless."

In his poem *Unknown Street* (1923, p. 11), Jorge Luis Borges describes the great existential meaning of the house: "every house is a branching candlestick/where the lives of men burn".

The house as a symbolic representation of the internal world

In his *Confessions*, Saint Augustine proposes a symbolic representation of memory:

> The next stage is memory, which is like a great field or a spacious palace, a storehouse for countless images of all kinds, which are conveyed to it by the senses. In it are stored away all the thoughts by which we enlarge upon or diminish or modify in any way the perceptions at which we arrive through the senses, and it also contains anything else that has been entrusted to it for safekeeping, until such time as these things are swallowed up and buried in forgetfulness. When I use my memory, I ask it to produce whatever it is that I wish to remember. Some things it produces immediately; some are forthcoming only after a delay, as though they were being brought out from some inner hiding place. (397 AD, p. 214)

Giovanna Rita Di Ceglie comments on Saint Augustine's proposal:

> I find that this view of the internal world is not very different from the modern psychoanalytic view of the internal world. The internal world is not a mirror image of the external one, nor is it in opposition to it; it is rather the result of an encounter between these two ... Freud's description of the unconscious has shown us ... that we are not even masters of our own home (using the same symbol of the home for the internal world used by St Augustine). He has give us, with the psychoanalytic method, an instrument to reach the "hiding places" of St Augustine's metaphor, so that we can inhabit our house with a certain degree of comfort, and desire to enrich it. (2005, pp. 95–96)

Although it is not the only symbolic representation of the internal world, the house in dreams is a basic and simple symbol often appearing in infinite versions and giving an idea of the internal reality and of the dreamer's personality structure. The house can be an effective synthesis of the way in which we perceive our bodies, our relationships, and ourselves with other people. The house in dreams can be old or new, rich or poor, luxurious or crumbling, warmly comfortable or unenthusiastically inhospitable, colourful or grey. A house that is going to crumble or be demolished can represent the dreamer's fear of a breakdown or a phase of emotional instability. The construction site of a house can represent a wish to change and to create new relational possibilities. In addition, the renovation of a ruined house can represent the attempt to make mental repairs to a damaged world during analysis. Dreaming of having been locked out of a house or having lost the keys to the front door can represent the patient's resistance in dealing with the difficult and painful complexity of her internal world. The childhood home can deal with the acknowledgment of certain aspects of personality strictly related to childhood. However, if in dreams the childhood home alternates with an unknown and mysterious house, a place of anxiety and disorientation, this can be related to the need to be reassured. This alternating in dreams between childhood home and unknown house can be typical of the first phases of the immigrant experience. Dreaming of an increasing number of home furnishings in an initially empty house can be correlated with relevant progresses in analysis and with the consequent emotional-affective enrichment. This can be also valid for those dreams about new or secret rooms whose existence has never been considered or whose doors have never been opened before.

The house in which we choose to live and the way in which we furnish it depend only partially on chance or the choices of others. Rather, they depend mainly on our internal world, on the deepest part of our mind, on the unconscious way we prefigure our container, and on the way in which this container takes shapes, features, or forms that we have not been able to think of before. These unexpected shapes, features, or forms force us to review the internal domestic images and the composition and disposition of the space. The psychoanalyst Masud Khan (1982) relates the home furnishing of an apartment to the reorganisation of the internal world of a patient in a mutually interdependent relationship. Victor Hugo (1843, p. 44) writes: "From the shell you can guess the mollusc, from the house the inhabitant."

When the writer Alice Munro won the Premio Flaiano (Flaiano Prize) in 2008, she talked about how literary creation comes from the writer's internal world: "A story is not a road we start to walk. Rather, it is a house. You enter into it, stay for a while, walk up and down, you sit whenever you like, discover the connections between the rooms and the corridor and how the world can be altered by looking it from its windows."

In her psychoanalytic study on the Glass House,[3] Adele Tutter (2011a, 2011b, 2012) compares architect Philip Johnson's masterpiece[4] to a dream and describes it as a container in which we can find encrypted and embedded representations of the self.

> Under this conjecture, the design of the Glass House contains an over-determined array of concealed or disguised representations of its architect—his memories, conflicts, and desires—transformed into design elements via processes similar to those that generate dreams, including condensation, displacement, symbolisation, and reversal. (Tutter, 2011a, p. 510)

Enrico Pinna (2013, p. 163) defines the house simply as "a place where you feel good ... It is the result of a composition of points of view, internal and external paths, proportions, the high, low, wide, or narrow rhythms of its location, and colours. The house is the totality of all these things." Pinna's considerations are reminiscent of those of Charles Darwin on the beauty of the female bowerbirds, which Domenico Chianese reconsiders:

> In order to court the female, the male bowerbird builds a nest and garnishes it with pieces of glass, delicious insects, and vanilla beans. Then the male invites the female into the nest to inspect the nest's architecture and construction. If she does not like the nest, she is free to leave;[5] she is not forced to accept the male's sexual advances. The female bowerbird has an almost human sense of beauty and her aesthetic judgement is free and impartial. (2015, pp. 4–5)

The writer Claudio Magris stresses the controversial features of the house:

> The house is not an idyll. It is a space of concrete existence and is thus full of conflicts, misunderstandings, errors, defeats, cold, failures. For this reason it is the main place in our life, with its strengths

> and weaknesses. It is the place where passion is strong and sometimes devastating for life partners and children. It is where passion fully engages. (2005, p. XIX)

Adolf Loos spent a lot of time listening to his clients and remained friends with them. He believed that people could learn how to construe their own home. In this sense, he thought that furniture could be transformed and adapted. He was firmly convinced that rooms contribute to human feelings.

Loos writes:

> Neither the archaeologist, nor the interior designer, nor the architect, nor the painter, nor the sculptor should furnish our apartments. Who should do it, then? The answer is quite simple: every person is their own interior designer ... If we lack taste, that's fine, then we will furnish our homes in a tasteless manner. If we have good taste, all the better. But we refuse to be tyrannised by our own rooms any longer. (1913, p. 57)

He continues to argue that we can furnish our homes only by ourselves and that this is the only way we can have our own home. In fact, if someone else, for example a painter or an upholster, did it for us, the home would never be ours. At best, it would look like a series of hotel rooms; at worst, a parody of a home. In his essay *Of Building* (1625, p. 427), the philosopher Francis Bacon writes: "Houses are built to live in, and not to look on."

Over time we have passed from a monolithic and closed archetypal house to a progressively disjointed, disunited, and even dematerialised and invisible (telematic) modern house (Tironi, 2007).

> Our own era, on the other hand, seems to be that of space. We are in the age of the simultaneous, of juxtaposition, the near and the far, the side by side and the scattered. A period in which, in my view, the world is putting itself to the test, not so much as a great way of life destined to grow in time but as a net that links points and creates its own muddle. (Foucault, 1997, p. 330)

New technologies allow us to create and dwell in new worlds of experience separated from material and concrete dimensions, defining new spaces between mind and reality, extending our mental and sensory capacities. In this sense, we can call this new space "technology of mind or psychotechnology" (de Kerckhove, 1995).

> These new technologies can be defined as "mental appendages" and allow unlimited extension of the dimensions of an experience at the same time virtual and realistic. This allows the opening of new fields of experiences and of mental functioning that must refer to the sciences of the mind. Virtual technology seems to blur the difference between objectivity, subjectivity, and illusion (in other words, between inside and outside) and thus to have an influence on our way of thinking. Virtual reality overturns our space-time categories and the connections and the conditions on which our subjectivity is based. As a consequence, our ideas about reality must be continually renewed: as Umberto Eco has pointed out, virtual reality pretends to be more real than reality itself. (Guerrini Degli Innocenti, 2011, p. 652)

The Möbius strip[6]

In mathematics, the Möbius strip (Figure 6) is a surface with only one side and only one boundary with the property of being non-orientable. Ordinary surfaces, those typical of architectural and structural elements,

Figure 6: The Möbius strip.

always have two sides or faces. Thus, we can colour one without touching the other, unless we cross a border or a corner. Even in the case of surfaces of more complex geometrical figures such as the sphere or the cylinder, we can conventionally establish an internal and an external side or a top and a bottom. That is to say, we can use at least two colours by avoiding having demarcation lines different from borders or angles. Such a condition does not occur in the Möbius strip, which is made by unifying the two short sides of a strip via a rotation of 180 degrees. In fact, we have only one surface with only one side and only one boundary. Thus, if we try to paint the strip with a brush by starting from a point taken at random, we arrive at the opposite side after one rotation. After two rotations, we arrive at the starting side and we notice that the painted portion occupies the entire surface of the strip. From there, we see that there is only one side or face and thus we cannot use another colour. In this way, we pass from the internal to the external surface without crossing the strip and avoiding the border, but simply by walking for a while. In 1961 the Dutch graphic designer and engraver Maurits Cornelis Escher used the Möbius strip in a woodcut in which a group of ants walk on the strip and pass through its surface (Figure 7).

I believe that this mathematical figure well defines the possible absence of doors, of transition spaces, of stops, of waits, of consumption, of elaboration, the uncertainty, the suspension, the lack of differentiation between inside and outside typical of the telematics house, and, more generally, part of the present culture in which it is difficult to define and

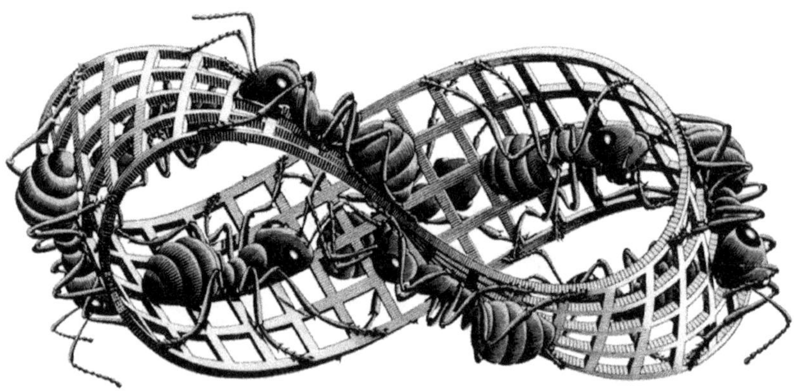

Figure 7. Maurits Cornelis Escher woodcut of the Möbius strip.

Figure 8. Swallow's Nest, new Gateway Park, Taiwan.

establish different passages and rites. The Möbius strip has inspired various contemporary architects, such as the Swallow's Nest (Figure 8), a spectacular project by the Belgian studio Vincent Callebaut Architectures, built in the new Gateway Park in place of the old airport of Taichung in Taiwan; and the bridge over Meixi Lake in Changsha in south-central China by Dutch studio Next Architects (Figure 9).

In his book *L'Intervallo Perduto* (The lost interval) (2006) the art critic Gillo Dorfles affirms the need for the interval in the architectural context,

Figure 9. Bridge over Meixi Lake, Changsha, China.

that is, for a space able to distinguish the outside from the inside. He refers to the distinction between the great external spatiality, characterised by the public and the masses, and the space of the family and of the hearth. He invites us to reconsider the value of a break between perceiving and existing. This break can give sense to the terms "inside" and "outside" and thus can be useful for understanding the meaning of architecture.

Between inside and outside

According to Hillman (2004), the first archetype is the refuge. The architect raises the first wall between people and the difficulties typical of our planet, such as perturbations, heat and cold, wind, water, and other dangerous natural forces. The architect builds a shell, a comfortable refuge, a niche, a receptacle that preserves and assembles. "The house gives an idea of border, of closure, and of security, perhaps of secrecy" (Perrot, 2009, p. 28).

Freud (1930, p. 87) writes: "The dwelling-house was a substitute for the mother's womb, the first lodging, for which in all likelihood man still longs, and in which he was safe and felt at ease."

The first refuge has been the maternal womb to which the architect refers by proposing technical solutions at both the aesthetical and functional level. On one hand, the house is an intimate place and, on the other, it is open to universal values. When the baby is born, although protected, he must start the distressing and liberating experience of meeting the external world (a wide, unknown, and probably dangerous place)[7] and suffer the loss of his house,[8] so the architect must prepare and modify the space around the refuge and create a transitional space able to protect but also to foster the future separation and autonomy.

The human being's "intra-uterine existence seems to be short in comparison with that of most animals, and it is sent into the world in a less finished state. As a result, the influence of the external world upon it is intensified." (Freud, 1926, p. 154) Freud's considerations seem to be confirmed by recent research. Eminent palaeontologists such as Stephen Jay Gould (2002) and Richard E. Leakey (1994) find that the human being shows a certain number of areas of delayed growth, that is to say, a certain number of morphofunctional features typical of its youth and lasting into adulthood. For example, because of the hypertrophy of skull volume and the presence of a well-defined anatomical constraint (the diameter of the birth canal), humans started to give birth prematurely. The skull volume of an infant is approximately one-fifth that of an adult, whereas that of a newborn primate such as a monkey or chimpanzee is approximately half. For this reason we can say that humans have a postponed brain development (Boncinelli, 2000).

Whether or not we agree with the theory of delayed growth (a possible reason for disagreeing with it is that it is not empirically confirmed), it is a matter of fact that *Homo sapiens* is more immature at birth than other species. For this reason, human babies demand much more parental care than do other anthropomorphic species. Further, humans take more time to grow and develop and, as a consequence, to socialise. This implies that adults show a tendency (perhaps a desire) to take care of children, whereas babies show a disjunction between the possibility of desire and the impossibility of satisfying it. According to this hypothesis, man is an expert at parental care and, as a consequence, very sensible to the immature form or, in other words, exposed to (and enthusiastic about) the baby's charm (Marchesini, 2001, 2002).[9]

> All of a sudden everything changes for the foetus. His lungs start to function, the surrounding environment is no longer liquid and the temperature is no longer uniform; the impact of air and the loss of continuous contact imply the loss of a constant limitation (the uterine wall) that until that time was for the foetus the natural border of his self. (Gaddini, 1976, p. 104)

As in the child, the distinction between self and non-self is still uncertain and the holding function of the mother (that is based on both genetic and socio-cultural aspects) is crucial, so the construction of a refuge and the passage to the outside are not only natural operations (also typical of other animals' use of nests and lairs, for example) but they require a continuous cultural contribution able to simplify the definition of the identity. The distinction between internal and external spaces is a fundamental regulatory polarity at the psychical, personal, and cultural level. It is learned throughout development, that is to say, from birth to babyhood and to the next phases of the self's development and the capacity to be distinguished from the non-self (Petrella, 2014).

The lack of regulation of the passage from the inside to the outside and vice versa can be a symptom of a serious disorder of space perception. In his novel *Fratelli* (brothers) Carmelo Samonà describes the experience of the outside of his schizophrenic brother:

> For him, the perception of the external world, of what is outside and open, is nothing but a limitless expansion of the house, of what is inside and closed. The city is nothing but the untidy, tossed-aside clothing in his apartment. His apartment is the centre, a privileged point from which to see the generating nucleus of the city, which is nothing but an evanescent and potential substitute or, at best, a possible development. (1978, pp. 49–50)

In his 1969 paper *Berlin Walls* Winnicott introduces a wider concept of environmental holding and its effects on the development of individuals. "The inherited maturational processes in the individual are potential and need for their realisation a facilitating environment of a certain kind and degree, and there are important variations in the social environment according to place and time." (Winnicott, 1969, p. 221)

The psychoanalyst and Winnicott biographer F. Robert Rodman focuses on the importance of Winnicott's theories for architecture. He asks how a building can promote the constitution of a true self, lead to the experience of being authentic, make us able to survive our strong fears of disintegration, hold together our conflicting needs of being alone, and be in relation with other people. He writes: "it is impossible to consider a building's capacity to nurture the true self without considering the interaction between the building and the people who use it" (Rodman, 2005, p. 59). He refers to an article entitled "There is no such thing as a building" to point to the simple fact that buildings and people go together and to Winnicott's famous statement, "There is no such thing as an infant". In fact, Winnicott argues that a baby cannot be thought of and literally cannot exist separate from the relationship with the holding environment: "It is the surroundings that makes it possible for each child to grow, and without an adequate environmental reliability the personal growth of a child cannot take place." (Winnicott, 1965, p. 44)

The psychoanalyst Esther Bick (1968) is probably the first to stress the importance of the experience of the skin in early object relations. An internal space of the self cannot take place without such an experience.

The psychoanalyst Didier Anzieu (1981) develops the notion of skin-ego, for which he defines three functions. First, it provides a unitary picture of ourselves; second, it defends us from external intrusions;

third, it allows us to relate to other people. He underlines the presence of a reciprocal fantasy of a "common skin" between mother and infant. This common skin works as an interface between them. At the beginning, it binds them together but later the progressive differentiation and separation causes fantasies of a violently torn-away skin.

Bion writes (1973, p. 91): "My skin is convenient as a method of saying what the boundaries are of my physical make-up, of my anatomy and my physiology. It is unlikely that that forms an adequate description of the boundaries of my mind." By referring to Bion's intuitions, the psychoanalyst Giovanni Hautmann (1999) proposes an evocative image of skin-tissue, a "film of thought" that he uses to define the most basic level of mental symbolic activity. It is the first sketch and it corresponds to "mental tissue" formed by a sensory-perceptive activity and an emotional-representative activity.

Giampaolo Visetti (2013) refers to recent architectural experiences[10] to propose a claustrophilic existence inside the house. In Chengdu, the provincial capital of Sichuan in Southwest China, the New Century Global Centre introduces a completely self-sufficient multipurpose building built of glass and cement. Its aim is to inaugurate the era of structures from which it is not necessary to exit to be happy, that is to say, a sort of architectural *Truman Show*. Rich Chinese seem to wish for the fantasy of being forever protected in the maternal womb.

Internal needs always inform and influence architectural solutions just as internal spaces justify external ones, as the following Emily Dickinson poem (1862, pp. 216–217) evocatively suggests:

> The Outer—from the Inner
> Derives its Magnitude—
> 'Tis Duke, or Dwarf, according
> As is the Central Mood
> …
> The Inner—paints the Outer
> The Brush without the Hand
> Its Picture publishes—precise
> As is the inner Brand

The magnificence of what appears to us always comes from what we have inside. Our being princes or dwarves comes from our most intimate feelings. It is what we have inside that, like a mould, models our internal aspect. Every building necessarily mediates between the person and his world.

However, it is also true that various architectural solutions can promote growth, development, wellbeing, communication, or, on the contrary, can obliterate freedom and creativity. Our unconscious and the living space are in a continuous inter-functioning. Freud is the first to be always interested in both the internal and the external worlds.[11] Every time one of the two worlds seems to be privileged, he is able to re-establish a dialectical balance between them. As evidence of this, he always criticises the position of his pupils, ex-students, or rivals if they consider only one of the two worlds.

Louis J. Kahn argues (1969, pp. 27–28): "Of course there are some spaces that should be flexible, but there are also some which should be completely inflexible. They should be just sheer inspiration, just the place to be, the place that does not change." Unfortunately, it is a matter of fact that many places cannot be changed or modified in any way. In Italy, the old mental hospitals are clear examples of this kind of places. Because they could not be changed or modified in any way, they had been closed.

However, in an uncertain way, the construction of the external space refers to our psychological home. Such a construction should promote the possibility of listening to the internal world and of emotional contact. In this sense, a planned external space may become a constitutive element of the analytic setting.[12] In other words, we are talking about "the relational analytic perspective that analysts must assume and preserve throughout treatment ... That is to say, analysts must provide a holding function and thus be able to comprehend, contain and elaborate the patient's anxieties until he has learnt how to provide such a function autonomously." (Saraval, 1988, p. 566)

CHAPTER ELEVEN

Therapy places

> The room had been square. I saw that two of its iron angles were now acute—two, consequently, obtuse. The fearful difference quickly increased with a low rumbling or moaning sound. In an instant the apartment had shifted its form into that of a lozenge. But the alteration stopped not here—I neither hoped nor desired it to stop. I could have clasped the red walls to my bosom as a garment of eternal peace. "Death," I said, "any death but that of the pit!
>
> (Edgar Allan Poe, 1842, p. 164)

Therapeutic architecture

In therapy places, the expression of pain and suffering is immediate, that is to say, many mediations that normally take place in socially accepted communications do not occur. Pain and suffering tend to produce identification, participation, and empathy only up to a certain threshold of patience. Beyond this threshold we witness an evacuation into the interlocutor's mind, which is unable to contain all the pain and suffering. As a consequence, certain defence mechanisms take place, such as emotional detachment, physical avoidance, and an extreme technicalisation and sanitisation of the meeting with the suffering person. Anxiety is experienced as overflowing and intolerable. Thus, a first response to it can be the creation of "enclaves" in which health professionals indulge in order to protect and defend themselves and to constrain and curb their empathy.

In psychiatric hospitals the division of space was very well defined. In one space were the crazy people, in another the psychiatrists who, shut in their rooms, talked about the crazy people. There was no possibility of meeting. If a meeting had to occur, it took place in medical spaces, not in the wings in which patients resided. Nurses entered these wings only for the time necessary to execute their functions; they found shelter in other, separate and protected interstitial spaces where they could avoid contact with the patients or, more precisely, being "infected" by mental disease. In today's hospitals the division of space is less defined but, at the same time, more differentiated. Near the wards we can find the nurses' and physicians' rooms, a small kitchen, etc. They can be seen as spaces for attenuating and suspending the anxiety over mental disease, spaces enabling one to feel part of the "healthy" group. In these spaces it is possible to avoid having a dangerous encounter with mental pain and disease.

The planning of new therapy spaces should first consider the needs (primary and secondary) of patients and health workers, of their mental balance and of their defensive necessities coming from extended and demanding contact with a high level of pain and suffering. The planning of intermediate places and of transition and mediation spaces should avoid the construction of hidden and seemingly comforting (but actually anti-relational) refuges similar to crypts in which anxiety cannot be avoided in any way.

In the fifteenth century, in the introduction of his *De Re Aedificatoria*, Leon Battista Alberti writes about the therapeutic function of architecture. In the Age of Enlightenment, Alberti's concept is considered again with the notion of personal hygiene. This notion attributes a therapeutic function to the space of healthcare architecture. According to Esquirol, the asylum cannot be considered a therapeutic aid like other kinds of instruments: it is the therapy itself. In the twentieth century the Modern Movement strongly supports the therapeutic possibilities of architecture. Hospitals, summer camps, kitchens, and sanatoriums are built on the basis of the principles of transparency and brightness. The *mens sana in corpore sano* (a sound mind in a sound body) is transferred from the human body to the environment hosting and taking care of this body. However, it is worth noting that here the central place of the psychophysical balance is far from being recognised. In fact, from the Age of Enlightenment onward we invented many "health machines" for saving people. Further, in the twentieth century, we introduced architectural solutions able to guarantee a transparent control via the disinfectant properties of sunlight and hygiene products.

Spaces conceived according to this view follow a therapeutic logic that does not consider a possible integration between a disease to be eradicated and the person to be treated. According to this logic, the emotional distance from the patient and his disease is a consequence. We can even say that emotional neutrality is a prescription or a necessary condition of the therapeutic organisation. The same features of neutrality can be found in the hospital, in which the use of colours (in general, the colours are white, grey, green, or azure), material (in general, the material is metal or synthetic), lights, and the finishing touches are in tune with hygiene and the quality of medical performance. The predominance of functional and hygienic dimensions obscures the possibility of the environment to promote interactive processes between individuals, therapeutic activities, and medical tools and thus does not allow for the recognition of the emotional influence of the space over the patients and health workers.

The Finnish architect Juhani Uolevi Pallasmaa (1994) opposes the notion of (supposed) neutrality of the environment and supports the need to "re-sensualise" architecture. He argues that the hegemony of sight (that he calls "oculocentrism", according to which sight has a leading role in Western culture)[1] has caused the loss of the tactile dimension of architecture and its consequent flattening and detachment from people. He refers to the French philosopher Henri Poincaré (1902–1908), who identifies a visual space, a tactile space, and a motor space, each defined by different parts of the sensory apparatus. In fact, in the preface of his book, he explains that the title *The Eyes of the Skin* (2012a) aims to evoke the relevance of touch[2] in our experience because touching is the sensory modality able to integrate the knowledge of the world and the knowledge of ourselves.[3] Thus, architecture must be able to hold together the image of ourselves and our experience of the world. Pallasmaa contrasts Le Corbusier's[4] perspective and its exclusive focus on sight and thus the overstated prevalence of the criteria proposed by formalism and the theory of pure visibility. He argues that only architecture able to foster a multi-sensorial experience can be meaningful.

Giuliana Bruno introduces the term "haptic" whose Greek etymology means "relating to the sense of touch".

> As a function of the skin, the haptic—the sense of touch—constitutes the reciprocal contact between the environment and us, both housing and extending a communicative interface. But the haptic is also related to kinesthesis, the ability of our bodies to sense their own movement in space. Developing this observational logic, we can consider the haptic to be an agent in the formation of space—both geographic and cultural ... Emphasising the cultural role of the haptic, we can develop a theory that connects sense to place. Here, the haptic realm is shown to play a tangible, tactical role in our communicative sense of spatiality and motility, thus shaping the texture of habitable space and, ultimately, mapping our ways of being in touch with the environment. (2002, p. 6)

The philosopher Walter Benjamin (1936, p. 240) anticipates this concept when he writes about the detached view people take when they approach an architectural work: "Buildings are appropriated in a twofold manner: by use and by perception—or rather, by touch and sight ... Tactile appropriation is accomplished not so much by attention as by habit."

The psychoanalyst Marion Milner (1952a) argues that the essential thing about our experience is what we add to what we see. Without such an addition coming from us, we could not see anything.

Calvino writes:

> Consider visual images, for example. We live in an unending rainfall of images. The most powerful media transform the world into images and multiply it by means of the phantasmagoric play of mirrors. These are images stripped of the inner inevitability that ought to mark every image as form and as meaning, as a claim on the attention and as a source of possible meanings. Much of this cloud of visual images fades at once, like the dreams that leave no trace in the memory, but what does not fade is a feeling of alienation and discomfort. (1988, p. 57)
>
> Will the power of evoking images of things that are not there continue to develop in a human race increasingly inundated by a flood of prefabricated images? ... The memory is littered with bits

> and pieces of images, like a rubbish dump, and it is more and more unlikely that any one form among so many will succeed in standing out. (ibid., pp. 91–92)

In his masterpiece *In Praise of Shadows* (1933) the Japanese author Jun'ichirō Tanizaki focuses on the charm of darkness and shadows. This charm is at the heart of Japanese and Asian cultures and is threatened by the diffusion of Western culture's way of life. Tanizaki praises the beauty of traditional toilets that, in Japanese culture, are far from home and in the shadow, thus in contrast with the modern need in Western culture for brightness and hygiene. He continues praising Japanese paper and ink, and silverware and copperware that, in contrast with Western culture, can gain aesthetic value thanks to the patina acquired over time. Tanizaki argues that Western culture values sight and underestimates the other senses. This has led to its typical geometrisation of experience. He argues against this lack of balance in sensorial experience by describing how our Western culture and its way of life (and, as a consequence, also our idea of pleasure) lead us to value certain senses and to weaken the other ones and never attempt to find harmony between them.

Giorgio Agamben (2008) argues that perceiving the dark is neither an inability nor an incapacity, but rather an action aiming at neutralising our age's lights in order to discover its darkness.

Through his amazing poetics of the indefinite, in a note of 20 September 1821 of his *Zibaldone*, Giacomo Leopardi provides us with a beautiful image of light:

> It is shown how objects half seen, or seen with certain impediments, etc., awaken indefinite ideas in use and may explain why the light of the sun or of the moon is pleasurable in a place where they cannot be seen and where the source of the light is not revealed; a place only partly illuminated by that light; the reflection of this same light, and the various material effects that derive from it; the penetrating of this same light into places where it becomes uncertain and blocked, and is not easily made out, as through a reed bed, in a wood, through half-closed shutters etc. etc.; this same light seen in a place, object, etc., where it does not enter and does not strike directly but is refracted on to them and diffused by some other place or object, etc., that it happens to hit; in a corridor seen from inside or from outside, and in a loggia likewise, etc., those places in

> which the light blends in, etc. etc., with the shadows, as beneath a portico, in a raised suspended loggia, between rocks and ravines, in a valley, on hills seen from the shade when their peaks are gilded; the reflection that, e.g., a coloured glass casts on those objects on to which are reflected the rays that pass through this same glass; all those objects, in short, that by means of different materials and slight changes in circumstance reach our sight, hearing, etc., in a manner that is uncertain, hard to distinguish, imperfect, incomplete, or out of the ordinary, etc. ... And for the reason identified above, the sight of a sky with a patchwork of little clouds, in which the sunlight or moonlight produces varied, and indistinct, and unusual, etc., effects, is also pleasurable. The same light is most pleasurable and very sentimental when it is seen in towns, dappled by shadows, where the dark contrasts in many places with the light, where the light in many parts fades gradually, as on roofs, where some secluded places hide the shining star from view, etc. etc. Variety, uncertainty, not seeing everything, and therefore being able to wander in one's imagination through things unseen, all contribute to this pleasure. The same goes for similar effects produced by lines of trees, hills, trellising, cottages, haystacks, uneven terrain, etc., in the countryside. (1821, pp. 1745–1746 & pp. 793–794)

These needs and demands are certainly basic, but their expression is strongly influenced by historical and cultural determinants. Thus, they need containers able to fit with changing ways of representation. In this sense, therapy places can be diversified and reshaped also according to these changes.

The architecture of psychiatric hospitals

The majority of architectural logic used for constructing mental institutions can be juxtaposed with that used for constructing general hospitals. Jeremy Bentham (1786) proposes the panopticon as the first and clearest model of prison architecture in the Age of Enlightenment. The panopticon is the prototype of the modern prison and consists of a circular structure that can be described in these terms:

> At the periphery, an annular building; at the centre, a tower; this tower is pierced with wide windows that open onto the inner

> side of the ring; the peripheric building is divided into cells, each of which extends the whole width of the building; they have two windows, one on the inside, corresponding to the windows of the tower; the other, on the outside, allows the light crossing the cell from one end to the other. All that is needed, then, is to place a supervisor in a central tower and to shut up in each cell a madman, a patient, a condemned man, a worker, or a schoolboy. By the effect of backlighting, one can observe the tower, standing out precisely against the light, the small captive shadows in the cells of the periphery ... The panoptic mechanism arranges spatial unities that make it possible to see constantly and to recognise immediately. (Foucault, 1975, p. 200)

As we can see, the principle at the basis of the dungeon is overturned here: full light is much more effective than shadows in order to have the best surveillance.

As an alternative to Esquirol's original idea of the mental institution (that is conceived as a monolithic structure characterised by a linear and magnificent geometry influenced by Neoclassicism) and to the idea of mental institution inspired by Bentham's panopticon (whose main features were the centralisation and a rigidly cloistered spatial subdivision), we find some isolated experiences whose common idea is that of a mental institution organised and structured like a small village. Examples include the experience of the town of Geel in Belgium, the "cottage" health system in England, and the "open doors" policy in Scotland (Maura & Peloso, 1999). After the decline of the (obsessive) idea of universal transparency and absolute visual control, of the possibility of total inspection, and of those features of mental institutions clearly aimed at segregating, the idea of an asylum architecture suggesting and planning defined spaces that are able to educate and act authoritatively on the emotional and affective disorder of psychiatric patients has taken place.

In the 1870s, the architect Francesco Azzurri (1877) proposed a fine-grained analysis of the various types of buildings housing mental institutions and emphasised the need to go beyond construction characterised by "geometrical and monumental forms [that] emphasise the fact that we are in a hospital. In other words, everything that brings to mind a place of imprisonment" (p. 427). He aimed at creating a kind of institution in which "the peace, the order and the family life (under the support of medical science)" (p. 428) acould be the main constituents of cure. The model proposed by Azzurri was a scattered system in the form of a village,[5] with wings of equal size and avenues able to give an idea of walking in an exclusive district. This model aims to create a micro-community, a small, autonomous and self-sufficient village based on the parameters of an ideal society of healthy people (De Peri, 1984). In this sense, we can see the constitution of an autarchic economy: new rural communities, livestock, bakeries, pasta factories, laundries, typographies, and carpenter and blacksmith shops are created in order to promote ergotherapeutic practices. In a few years these structures will appear as a deceptive humanisation of an anti-human institution.

In contrast to the state of abandon in which patients actually live, to the water stains and the peeling plaster clearly visible inside the stinking wings, the exteriors and the boardrooms of psychiatric hospitals are often characterised by vaults and by walls full of beautiful frescos and ornaments. The psychiatric department of the New Saint Mary's Hospital in Florence or the psychiatric hospitals of Quarto and Cogoleto in Genoa are clear examples of this phenomenon.

The patina is not the essence

Louis J. Kahn (quoted and criticised in Petrella, 1993b) argues that the distant walls of a wide room could feel less distant and thus the room could become more intimate if we were to approach someone who had a nice smile. This is certainly a naive and optimistic idea because in some places it is very difficult to smile or to get emotionally involved.

> A locked door is always a truly insurmountable barrier … If a door is the same as a wall, then there is a problem of communication, a modification of the meanings of spaces and uses, a semantic ambiguity that can have unexpectedly bad and destructive values. (Petrella, 1993b, p. 653)

I remember when parties or festivals were organised in the wards of old psychiatric hospitals. They were not parties or festivals at all, they were not unrestricted at all, and they were the antithesis of Freud's definition of festival: "A festival is a permitted, or rather an obligatory, excess, a solemn breach of a prohibition. It is not that men commit the excesses because they are feeling happy as a result of some injunction they have received. It is rather that excess is of the essence of a festival; the festive feeling is produced by the liberty to do what is as a rule prohibited." (1912–1913, p. 140)

A party is such when isolation is banned. Thus, if in a party the mental and physical spaces are closed and emotional involvement and enthusiasm are lacking, what we have is a miserable parody of a party.

In the parties organised in the wards of the psychiatric hospital, a certain degree of cynicism was evident. In fact, it was as if all were obliged to put aside their sufferance and estrangement in order to have fun at all costs. It was clearly an attempt at finding a solution to the lack of sociability in the institution by providing a spatial and temporal experience different to its usual rhythms. Unfortunately, such an attempt was substantially inauthentic or, in more precisely, based upon lies. In these parties, sociability was false because it was not based on the possibility of playing, laughing, and having fun together in a natural and collective manner. Further, in these parties, the common level of aggression towards the patients' individual identity, in general committed through the missed recognition of their basic needs, was partially denied. In this sense, the patients' basic needs could no longer be recognised as autonomous needs of care, protection, love, and amusement. There was no need for these parties: patients could neither benefit from them nor simply have fun at them. Rather, after the party, they had to go back to their dark rooms in which they would have experienced frustration for the vacuity of the party and the transience of a certain number of feelings and emotions substantially absent in their daily life. This means that, after the party, they would have withdrawn into themselves much more than before and continued to avoid relationships with others, experienced as unreliable and deceiving (Schinaia, 1998, pp. 13–14).

Segregation and separation cannot be masked or denied through despotic-paternalistic operations, as is shown in the painting of the "other nativity scene" at Cogoleto Mental Hospital in Genoa. This painting represents a party in a psychiatric hospital ward in the 1960s.

> The sad feeble lights, the absent and unhappy looks of dancers and their mechanic and disharmonic movements allow awareness of the deception and understanding of the impossibility of being happy without freedom. The couples dance sadly in an atmosphere of solitude and alienation: they have neither life nor rhythm.

> The dancers are like ghosts or dummies and seem to be in isolation and unable to communicate. Men and women seem to be forced to have fun only because the institution dictates they do so … The ornaments and decorations fail to make the ballroom less sad and miserable: on the contrary, they rather exaggerate its bleakness and are a sort of proof or announcement of the untruth of the mental institution. A party in a mental institution cannot have any resemblance to the indiscretions typical of carnival and cannot have any desperate collective joy that allows keeping on check the power, at least for one day in a year. The painting of the "other nativity scene" allows the observer to perceive the firm and conformist fiction of sociability, the repetitive space, and the uniform time. I believe it allows a stronger denunciation and unmasking than that written in an essay or a manifest. (Schinaia, 1997a, pp. 64–65)

The stanzas of *In Praise of Darkness* (1969, p. 299) by Jorge Luis Borges are moving:

> This growing dark is slow and brings no pain;
> It flows along an easy slope
> And is akin to eternity.

Planning new places for therapy

The history of mental institutions' architecture teaches us how external space can not only promote, but even determine, the onset or the chronicisation of mental suffering by denying or perverting communication needs, and by the closure of the way from the inside to the outside by creating abandoned areas. Thus, these areas lose their meaning and become "black holes" in the network of human relationships. I have personally conducted a research study on the so-called "square of the mental institution" (Schinaia, 1997a), a closed and fenced-in courtyard in which patients pass their time without any meaning or aim.

In general, the terms "closed" and "open" define a spatial and mental sequence from our home to the street and from the street to the square[6] through a series of potentially infinite possibilities of transformation. In this sense, Calvino writes (1972): "If you look into the square in successive moments, you hear how from act to act the dialogue changes." In the case of the mental institution's square[7] that I was observing, these successive moments and the possibility of dialogue did not take place and could not even exist. This is because there was no gradient, in the sense that there could not be a passage from the closed to the closed. Just as a closed door is always a contradiction in terms of its function, a square without any freedom and possibility of exchange is an expression of a set of rules that gives the space an ambiguous connotation. In fact, it is a space that simultaneously invites people to act while making acting impossible. Thus, the square of the mental institution is a sort of perversion of the very notion of square to which Calvino (1983a, p. 45) attributes the functions of freedom, openness, and exchange: "Many squares, streets, and flat spaces extend in front of me and seem very accessible. It is as if they are saying: 'Look, we are empty and clear, without any obstacle, you can go through us!'"

Today it is not completely clear how the connection between psychosis and environment is conceived (this is of course due to the complex interrelations and the many causal factors at the basis of mental diseases). In spite of this, we can say that there is a great lack of specific projects and plans (and also of appropriate economic investment) for places of therapy for mental disease. Few authors express interest in these issues. At the moment there is no model able to propose ways, trajectories, or highly functional specialised places connected to interstitial places,[8] that is to say, places open to less formalised forms of communication, with rooms of adequate size and brightness, or adequately painted walls, and so on. Rather, it is quite common to carelessly re-use spaces conceived, planned, and furnished for other health or social and administrative functions. In this sense, these spaces have no specific function. This lack of architectural thought relating to therapeutic thought often leads medical staff to receive patients in spaces that are anonymous, lifeless, and vague, and do not contain or promote socialisation. They are places in which suffering people become merely passive objects of therapy, restricted to partitioned spaces that prevent them reconstructing the split-off parts of their selves, but that are often able to promote their conservation.

The receiving environments cannot be based upon general, rationalising, or depersonalising models such as traditional hospitals and clinics. These models have their roots in strong cultural references such as Le Corbusier's *machine-à-habiter*. The rationale underlying the creation of this machine is the complete sanitisation of space and the predominant use of the colour white. Such spaces must be avoided because they can prevent if not outright censor conversation and can pose an insurmountable barrier to horizontal exchanges. These models do not allow the expression of emotions and feelings in any way. Of course, the aim of these models is not to completely and excessively reproduce the personalisation of a home environment in a new therapy environment, as when the bedrooms of senior citizens are exactly recreated in retirement homes. Doing so in a psychiatric setting would be impossible, confounding, and misleading.

The psychoanalyst Anna Ferruta writes:

> The culture of institutional psychiatric architecture must face a difficult issue in order to take care of its patients. It needs to create spatial-temporal constructions able to promote the development of lively relationships for both patients and mental institutions, and to integrate beauty, creativity, participation, and individuality. In the therapeutic relationship we can construe solid but strange buildings that … at last, can become a sort of prison in which the psychic life can languish and die … Even a very personal and not institutional (perhaps in contrast to the law of gravity) architectural structure can be a prison, a false movement, the ideology of a movement, a container that has become a content and that does not allow any dialogue, any match, any free meeting, any approach or any departure. (2009, p. 24)

It is objectively more difficult, but nonetheless more fascinating, to think about and then create avenues of real freedom able to promote the passage from the inside to the outside and vice versa. These avenues must also have rest stops or transitional spaces that permit one to become used to the new landscape. Such places must hold together public and domestic features through a continuous mixture of known and unknown elements and of areas in which it is possible to help patients to recognise their old identities and to foster their new ones inside the institution. Holding together public and domestic features involves removing conventional spatial distances and defining new ones. In these new spatial distances the contact must be at the same time warm and sufficiently formalised in order to respect the patients' suffering and to avoid that absence of space that often characterises intimate relationships between people. Thus, these spaces must be able to receive but not be intrusive and protect but not be peremptory. They must guarantee the patients' need to be both by themselves and with others when they are ready to do so. Hospital corridors are spaces that lead us, but I think that they could also be a way of seducing and making us move freely. Only architects can do this (Zumthor, 2006).

The anthropologist and inventor of proxemics Edward T. Hall (1959) deals with this issue by correlating it to other ethological and sociological issues.

The psychiatrist Humphry Osmond (1959) was the first to propose fan-shaped psychiatric wards and hospitals. These consist of a wide living room near medical and administrative services and some nuclei progressively moving away along the rays of a circle. These nuclei are initially larger in order to allow a small number of patients to gather, and then smaller in order to allow a single patient to isolate himself from excessive contact with the others.

The psychiatrist Paul Sivadon (1968, 1969; Sivadon & Gantheret, 1969) endorses Osmond's considerations and starts from the concept that space must be used in order to foster different ways of human communication and thus enable the suffering person to experience various forms of meeting and isolation. His models consider first meeting with oneself; second, small groups (approximately three to twelve people); then big groups (approximately thirty to 120 people); and lastly the crowd (more than 200). Sivadon criticises the organisation of space in concentric circles. For him, although it makes better sense economically, it gives a sense of unfamiliarity that, together with difficulty with orientation, does not promote a sense of security. His approach is based on the relevance of the role of mental functions between two contradictory demands, that of security (requiring human closeness) and that of autonomy (implying distance). Open spaces are more able to call to action and to assume responsibility than closed spaces, but they certainly provoke anxiety. In contrast, comforting spaces are quite small in size in order to be controlled by our glance and are characterised by protective walls and by exits. The point is to find good compromises and thus intermediate constructs of partial openness and closure of the space in order to reach an adequate level of arousal.

The architect Christopher Alexander (1964; see also Alexander et al., 1970) criticises the idea of a structure conceived as a tree (considering it an inhuman development of contemporary cities) for psychiatric institutions and suggests considering the hypothesis of an articulated series of spaces in which the particular merges with the general and the functional and specialist areas are connected with the others.

The art critic Gillo Dorfles (2006) focuses on the concept of the interval and its loss. The interval is not only a break during a job or during the process of an act but also an interruption able to remove a job or any creative act from its context. Dorfles focuses on the concept of *diastema*, which he defines as "a gap between two events, two objects, or two musical keys". The diastemic factor is the interval that allows us to pick out two discrete objects and thus makes the person who looks at them more aware of their differences. The lack of personal and individual areas, spaces, and stops in a place experienced as impersonal and shapeless can provoke sensory deprivation and thus seriously hinder physical healing.

In his book *Un Fossile Chiamato Carcere* (A Fossil Called Prison) (1993), the architect Giovanni Michelucci argues that space can make us free when it is conceived in order to consider man in his totality and vitality. In the opposite case, when it is conceived in order to enslave man and control his life and behaviour (this specifically occurs in prisons but also in institutions such as hospitals and schools), space becomes a tool of coercion and reduction of personality able to produce feelings of deprivation of freedom, segregation, and humiliation. In turn, these feelings can provoke devious or overt reactions against authority, power, and society.

We find the same sensations and confront the same anxieties when we look at *Carceri d'Invenzione* (Imaginary prisons) by the artist Giovanni Battista Piranesi. In his work Piranesi gives shape and an architectural visionary concreteness to the most hidden and cruel aspects of human experience.

There are many new examples of planning and constructing hospitals. In France, in the 1960s, a team of the World Health Organization led by Paul Sivadon planned the psychiatric hospital Marcel Rivière, whose main function was to create programmes for spatial rehabilitation. I remember the Oslo hospital *Riskospitalét* and its innovative and inventive solution (it is worth noting that this hospital is the main collector of artwork in all Norway after the national museums). In Italy we find the Ponticelli hospital planned by Renzo Piano in Naples and the European Institute of Oncology in Milan. I want to bring to mind also the centre for patients with Alzheimer's disease planned by the team of the architect Benedetta Spadolini (she was Dean of the Faculty of Architecture of the University of Genoa from 2003 to 2009) and the maternity ward in the Saint Martin Hospital in Genoa. After the 1960s we do not have many significant (that is to say, able to become a reference model) examples of architectural projects for mental institutions and therapeutic communities.

The way of the monks

I think that a possible reference model for a psychiatric rehabilitation community may be the architecture of the monastery. Such architecture is very well balanced and organised. First, we have the cell, an extremely private (and thus maternal) place intended for studying, concentrating, and sleeping. Second, there is the cloister, a place connecting the indoor with the outdoor, made for walking and resting and in which we can have whispered and intimate conversations and silent but collective meditation[9] which consists of "reading, writing or listening to words, sacred or profane, with the possibility of discovering themselves in them and renegotiating their meaning. We must not assimilate them and give up the doubt, the worry, and the discomfort they can provoke in us." (Demetrio, 2005, p. 211) Third, we have the chapter house, a public and paternal space in which most of the monks' meetings about the activities of the monastery and its community occur. Then there is the church, with the oratory and the choir,[10] perhaps the main place in which ritualised and organised oral communication takes place and in which the day ends with the compline, the final church office of the day. Fifth, there are corridors and the library, a place for reading and preserving books. Finally we have the refectory, the place in which to feed the body and the soul. In the refectory the exchanges are still ritualised but less formal and constrained, thus much freer. These exchanges are a prelude to a sociality that prefigures the outside, in other words, the exit from the monastery to the open square and thus to the world. "Different working activities occurring in purpose-built areas … having the aspect of small shops" (Marazzi, 2015, p. 103) accompany this exit.

I believe that we should be inspired by the Franciscan cloisters[11] that have removed the strong normativity and the rigid repetitiveness typical of monks' days[12] from the monastery's spaces in order to contain social needs in a creative way. This enables the flexible use of different spatial partitions and thus of adequately expressing different languages without an *a priori* excessively formalised manner, allowing multiple adequate functional expressions and communicative possibilities.[13] Monastery life is based not only on the laws of fraternity but also on those of hospitality: the community is so well grounded that it can receive foreign and unknown elements without changing its rhythms in any way.

> The door of hospitality allows external problems and life's tensions and unpredictable difficulties to enter the monastery. This is not in order to disrupt its stability, but to force the monastic community to test its balance between inside and outside, certainty and uncertainty, the expected and the unexpected. The open door of monasteries ... indicates that they are both peaceful and restless. They are able to maintain the difficult balance between themselves and what comes from meeting the new and the other (Boatti, 2012, p. 19).

The point is to access and confront dimensions in which the distinction between self and non-self is still uncertain (Winnicott, 1971) or lost. This means construing environments able to contain and receive this lack of distinction. In other words, we need specific and specialised settings.

> Perhaps we should create spaces able to adequately receive those imaginary constructs that have no place in the world, those ghosts we use to put in a hidden world full of the wishes, fears, hates, and needs that we find in our patients ... A feeling of being out of place, typical of psychosis, is created. Of course, this is also our feeling. (Petrella, 1993b, p. 657)

This is a feeling that we hope can be a prelude to us recovering ourselves, reorganising our daily life, and functionally using new and different communicative ways. The reflections of the therapy places are valuable not only for patients, inpatients, users, and citizens who become ill, but also for doctors, nurses, and all health workers. About the latter, we can say that an environment able to also recognise their suffering and to allow a form of elaboration of it can lead us to avoid the activation of strong defensive changes and thus communicative difficulties and high levels of anxiety. In fact, these distortions can result in occupational burnout and institutionalisation and, as a consequence, can create obstacles to efficiency in the entire health system.

A project of "chromatic urban renewal" of a centre for mental health

The Centre for Mental Health in the centre of Genoa is located in a sixteenth-century building that once served as the guesthouse of the ancient villa of the Peschiere. It is an apartment block on three floors (ground floor, first floor, and attic). It is a beautiful structure, full of luxurious architectural elements such as columns, stucco, and big doors made of precious wood. In the 1980s it was adapted for therapeutic functions even though its morphological and functional features do not fully allow them. In fact, the villa lacks an elevator connecting the first floor with the attic, accessible toilets, and various architectural configurations that would make it easy to access and pass through the internal areas. The villa is in the centre of the city and thus easy to reach, and the internal division of the space allows a good distribution of different therapeutic and support functions. Probably for these reasons, the users (who come from an area with a population of approximately 160.000 inhabitants) seem to appreciate it. But the old paint on the walls is a depressing beige and an anonymous white that time has faded and stained. I believe this paint cannot be good in a place where people with mental health problems are to stay and be cured.

In 2007 I was Director of the Centre for Mental Health and I asked the administration of the ASL (the *Azienda Sanitaria Locale*, the local health unit of the Italian national health system) to renovate the building. I proposed to the Dean of the Faculty of Architecture of the University of Genoa, and to the Director of the research centre at the Boero paint manufacturing organisation,[14] that some research be done concerning painting the building in a way that considered the peculiar features of the place and thus the demands of the users and the workers. The starting question for the project was what role the physical structure can play in the activities of a centre for mental health. How can the structure, the spaces, and the concrete opportunities have a positive influence on individual discomfort and on relationships often conditioned by old habits and by misinterpreted and inaccurate criteria for efficiency, cultural, and behavioural stereotypes? The aim of the research was not to indicate what the best colours to use should be but rather to try to individuate a "perceptive pattern" in that specific context. In fact, we know that it is not easy to isolate a single colour and that a single colour on its own probably does not exist. The perception of a colour is a complex process going from light to eyes and to hypothalamus and finally to the whole autonomic nervous system.

We also know how the same kind of paint can give rise to different perceptions under different kinds of illumination (natural and artificial light, various intensity of clarity, etc.) and how the same colour can assume different features on different surfaces (smooth, rough, etc.). In an internal location the effect of light on objects can provoke different chromatic changes at every hour of the day. The passage from light to dark creates a perceptive border in which the same colour assumes different tonalities. In the part of the project dedicated to the painting of the internal location, the first problem was the fact that the perception of colours changes also in terms of the relational context. To understand the role that colour has in personal experience, it is not sufficient to know the mechanisms of perception and the theories at the basis of their functioning. The history of art and science (and, of course, connections between the different disciplines) teaches us that man's relationship with colour changes according to the culture, the period, and the external reality and the various forms that this reality can take. In this sense, colour can be the means through which we read the reality of our souls (Carotenuto, 1995).

All these reflections provided the background for our study on colour.

Before the interior of the building was repainted, preliminary research in five stages was planned:

1. Individuation of the internal spaces and assessment of their dimensions and features through photographs.
2. Preparation of the planning proposal and simulation through virtual reality on the basis of the data gathered in stage 1.
3. Creation of a survey with a qualitative and quantitative questionnaire for a sample of patients and staff in order to assess the "chromatic necessities".
4. A small-scale trial of the painting on the basis of the data gathered in stage 3 and a discussion with all health workers involved.
5. A follow-up assessment of the painting (six months after stage 4) with a sample of users and workers.

Unfortunately, bureaucratic difficulties meant the project ended at stage 4. However, I believe that we reached some interesting results in the preliminary research.

In stage 3, users and workers were asked to associate a certain number of moods with a colour able to define them. Most participants associated yellow with acceptance and serenity, grey with worry and discomfort, red with anger and aggressiveness, lilac with anxiety, and beige with boredom.

Most described black as the colour of disease. On the one hand, most patients chose grey to mitigate black and thus to indicate an improvement, which can be interpreted as indicating worry and discomfort as feelings characterising patients' phases of transition; on the other hand, most workers chose green to mitigate black, which can be interpreted as indicating a need to have hope (and perhaps idealise) in the therapy. Patients chose white and workers blue to indicate their idea of healing. These results show that, probably more than users, workers needed to choose a colour reflecting openness. In contrast, users needed to choose white to define healing as the absolute absence of symptoms. In this sense, their choice can be interpreted as the progression from black (absolute presence of symptoms) through grey (partial presence of symptoms) to white (absolute absence of symptoms).

The second part of the questionnaire focused on the colour of locations. The responses indicated a general demand to use neither aseptic nor impersonal colours such as white, because they can prevent intimacy and communicative necessities, nor strong colours such as red, because they can be perceived as excessively stimulating, tiring, or discomforting.

Most users proposed painting the places of welcome such as the waiting room (that is to say, those places in which people tend to meet informally) in pale yellow because they associated it with the need for acceptance and tranquillity. Most workers also chose yellow but it is important to note that many of them chose green (again associated with hope).

Finally, users proposed painting the consulting rooms (rooms in which sessions between psychiatrists or psychologists and patients take place) in lilac to a greater extent and in green to a lesser extent, whereas workers proposed blue. It is worth noting that lilac has been associated with anxiety. Thus, users were probably aiming to emphasise their burden of anxious expectation coming from meeting with their therapists, whereas workers were probably aiming to emphasise the need for "open containment," in other words, a way of adequately containing users' anxieties in an manner.

As mentioned earlier, bureaucratic and administrative difficulties slowed down the execution of the project in the early stages before terminating it prematurely. These difficulties occurred just before realising an example of the painting (and thus also the painting of all locations) with the colours chosen by the research centre of the paint manufacture.

In spite of the end of our research project, I believe that the idea of thinking about and planning therapy places in which users, patients, and mental health workers can express their needs and thus influence architects' proposals is still alive and valid. I think that this idea allows us to avoid the wide gaps between needs and the responses to these needs that often characterise therapeutic spaces, in particular those dedicated to alleviating mental suffering.

CHAPTER TWELVE

The analyst's consulting room*

> I have undertaken and completed a forty-two day journey around my room. The interesting observations I have made, and the continual pleasure I experience en route, filled me with the desire to publish it … be so good as to accompany me on my journey … when I travel through my room I rarely follow a straight line: I go from my table towards a picture hanging in a corner; from there I set out obliquely towards the door; but … if I happen to meet my armchair en route, I don't think twice about it, and settle down in it without further ado. It's an excellent piece of furniture, an armchair; above all, it's highly useful for every man inclined to meditation … Once you've left my armchair, walking towards the north, you come into view of my bed, which is placed at the far end of my room: it's a most agreeable sight. It is situated in the most pleasant spot imaginable: the first rays of the sun come to disport themselves in my bed curtains.
>
> (Xavier de Maistre, 1794, pp. 1, 3, & 7–8)

*This chapter is an edited version of my 2008 article *Le Stanze dell'Analisi* (Analysts' consulting rooms).

The room

Because of the generality of needs they contain, rooms are atemporal but also very temporal and historical in both form and use. The historian Michelle Perrot argues that:

> From birth to agony, the room is the stage of life or, at least, the backstage of it. That is to say, it is the place where our body is naked and, once we take off our masks, can let go of emotion, pain, and sensual pleasure. We pass at least half of our life in a room, perhaps the most erotic, hidden, and nocturnal half. It is the half of our life full of insomnia, of wandering thoughts, of dreams. It is a window on the unconscious and perhaps on the afterlife, a contrast that continuously increases its force of attraction. (2009, pp. 23–24)

The architect Louis J. Kahn writes (1969, p. 253): "the room is the beginning of architecture. It is the place of the mind. In the room with its dimensions, its structure, its light, you respond to its character, its spiritual aura, recognising that whatever the human proposes and makes becomes a life."

Some writers skilfully describe the room and its furnishings. According to Virginia Woolf, having *A Room of One's Own* (1929) is a necessary metaphoric condition for recognising women's autonomy, self-determination, freedom, and potential to write about what they think and feel. Georges Perec writes:

> The resurrected space of the bedroom is enough to bring back to life, to recall, to revive memories, the most fleeting and anodyne along with the most essential. The coenesthetic certainty of my body in the bed, the topographical certainty of the bed in the room; these alone reactivate my memory and give it an acuity and a precision it hardly ever has otherwise ... The bed is thus individual space par excellence, the elementary space of the body (the bed-monad).[1] (1974, pp. 21–22 & p. 16)

Italo Calvino defines the pillow in these terms:

> It is the only shape in the world able to unify the stability of a square (or of a rectangle) and the fullness of a sphere (or of any body with a

> convex and curved shape over all its surface), the strength of an island and the ductility of a cloud … The pillow introduces the promise of the night—here intended, of course, as comfort, softness, laziness, and intimacy—and also of the light that will come. (1983b, p. 44)

We can't forget the verses of Homer's *Odyssey* (book XXIII, pp. 214–226) that emphasise the strong intimacy of the bed, the place of Odysseus and Penelope as a couple around which their bridal chamber is constructed:

> There was a branching olive tree inside our court,
> grown to its full prime, the bole like a column, thickset.
> Around it I built my bedroom, finished off the walls
> with good tight stonework, roofed it over soundly
> and added doors, hung well and snugly wedged.
> Then I lopped the leafy crown of the olive,
> clean-cutting the stump bare from roots up
> planing it round with a bronze smoothing-adze—
> I had the skill—I shaped it plumb to the line to make
> my bedpost, bored the holes it needed with an auger.
> Working from there I built my bed, start to finish.
> I gave it ivory inlays, gold and silver fittings,
> wove the straps across it, oxhide gleaming red.

Penelope tests Odysseus when she asks the nurse to move the bed he had construed. Of course, such a movement would have been impossible since Odysseus had built the bridal chamber up around the bed rooted in a branching olive tree and thus immovable.

Some notes on the analytic setting

The analytic setting is a physical and functional environment in which the analytic relationship takes place. It is characterised by a set of rules established by the so-called analytic contract (the schedule for sessions and their duration, the organisation of holidays, the form of payment, etc.) and a set of relational rules mediating the relationship between analyst and analysand and "making the setting possible in a defined spatiotemporal context" (Ferraro & Genovese, 1986, p. 96). These sets of rules allow us to construct a physical and mental scenario that is able to contain the unexpected and the different.

The function of the analytic setting is the transmission of the analytic knowledge and its rituality is the necessary condition for this function (Bleger, 1967; Quinodoz, 1992).

In this sense, the analytic setting is not a formless and neutral space. Rather, it is a living and dynamic space supporting all the vicissitudes of transference of the couple engaged in the analytic project. The quality of the analytic relationship and the space in which such a relationship occurs are not constituted only by the cognitive context but also by the immediate and pervasive physical context.

The room with an armchair and a couch can be the paradigm for that curious laboratory known as the consulting room. The architect Elizabeth A. Danze (2005) lists a series of specific necessary conditions in the construction of the analytic room, a space that must communicate and participate: the couch and the armchair, perhaps the common symbols of analytic treatment in the collective imagination; the relative position of the analysand to the analyst; the design of the room itself, especially with regard to objects, curtains, views, natural light, and the sequence of entering, including the peculiar transition across thresholds from one space to another. The typical position of the analyst and the analysand is for the former to be supine on the couch and for the latter to be seated in the armchair behind, out of sight. At the beginning of the analysis the lying position[2] causes confusion, disorientation, instability, and the need to reorganise the visual space. This is because the analysand goes from standing, moving, and having complete physical control to being passive, at rest, in a position in which one observes one's self. It does not matter where the couch is positioned, if it is next to or against the wall or in the middle of the room. The position on the couch always induces in the analysand a state of deep relaxation that, in turn, indirectly also allows feelings and emotions to arise in the analyst. The new position and point of view transform the consulting room from a passive spectator to a full participant of the analytic work or from a neutral film to a receptive container of actions and movements.

"The analytic room should have the capacity to evoke different kinds of associations and be able to accommodate richly variegated desires of the occupants. The effect of the architecture on the analytic relationship, and hence the analysis, in direct and indirect awareness, is profound." (Danze, 2005, p. 123)

The organisation and distribution of the external space (I mean, of the consulting room itself) is strongly influenced by the analyst's way of functioning, personality, technical assumptions, feelings and opinions about the relational space, degree of involvement in the analytic relationship (or, *mutatis mutandis*, how much he intends to be neutral), and how much his internal objects can be in contact with the analysand's internal objects in transference-countertransference dynamics.

In the same way, the architectural, aesthetic, and functional organisation of the physical space containing the psychoanalytic sessions' setting (the consulting room) cannot be immutable and repetitive. Rather, it must deal with the need for continuously contextualising tastes, communications, or habits and modifying building materials, furniture, forms, and uses of light, all things that continuously change. In spite of the fundamental need to consider all these socio-cultural and technological modifications, I believe we cannot ignore the foundations of the psychoanalytic theory and practice or the relevance of the demands of a deep level of communication that, after Freud, focus on the pre-Oedipal phases of the mind and the care of psychotic states. I think that we must consider the necessities of the analytic couple not according to already defined modalities, but according to creative ones.

Julie Leavitt focuses attention on the interactive interface between the physical field and the physical setting, that she calls "the thinking interface":

> In this interface the echoes of memories, the history, and the transference interact with the very physical dimension and make live and use again the visible features of the analytic room. Let's try to represent this "thinking surface" able to define the profile of the physical environment and envelop everything we can perceive. It is a sort of fluctuating shell waiting for a contact with our memories through the associations that the physical setting evokes in us. Thus, it is the border at which memory and physicality converge. (2013, p. 550)

The change and the evolution in psychoanalytic and architectural techniques cause a different construction and distribution of the space of the psychoanalytic setting. Using a metaphor of Maurice Merleau-Ponty, the psychoanalyst Federico Flegenheimer[3] compares the analytic setting to the dark (our perception of dark is due to the retina's peripheral cells that activate and allow this perception once light is absent. Thus, perceiving the dark is an action, not a disability or an inability) in a cinema: although we tend to take it for granted when we go to the cinema, it is a necessary condition for watching a film. We know that the dark, such a fundamental condition for the viewing of a film, has been created in different terms and forms from the early nineteenth century to today thanks to the architectural development of cinemas and cinematic techniques.

Also the silence has a different quality as a background for listening to music according to the personality of the musician who plays music, what kind of music he plays, which instrument he plays, and where he plays his music. For example, in a concert hall silence must be absolute so that it can give melody its rhythm because what cannot be heard is part of the composition. In contrast, we can hear brass instruments very well outdoors: perhaps the street is the best setting for them.

> We can think of the psychoanalytic encounter … in musical terms, with its specific melodic, harmonic, and rhythmical patterns, its crescendos and diminuendos of emotional tension; the tempo *largo* with some patients or a more hurried *allegro* with others. Some sessions may be described as presenting an initial theme followed by variations, others in terms of their chromatic or diatonic quality, in a confident major key or in a depressive minor one, and so on *ad lib*. (Sabbadini, 2014, p. 119)

Sigmund Freud points out that the peculiar arrangement of the consulting room:

> has its historical basis; it is the remnant of the hypnotic method out of which psychoanalysis was evolved. But it deserves to be maintained for many reasons. The first is a personal motive, but on which others may share with me. I cannot put up with being stared at by other people for eight hours a day (or more). Since, while I am listening to the patient, I, too, give myself over to the current of my unconscious thoughts, I do not wish my expressions of face to give the patient material for interpretations or to influence him in what he tells me. The patient usually regards being made to adopt this position as a hardship and rebels against it, especially if the instinct for looking (scopophilia) plays an important part in his neurosis. I insist on this procedure, however, for its purpose and result are to prevent the transference from mingling with the patient's association imperceptibly, to isolate the transference and to allow it to come forward in due course sharply defined as a resistance.[4] (1913, pp. 133–134)

The British psychoanalyst Donald Winnicott (1947, p. 199) writes that "for the neurotic the couch and warmth and comfort can be symbolic of the mother's love; for the psychotic it would be more true to say that these things are the analyst's physical expression of love. The couch is the analyst's lap or womb, and the warmth is the live warmth of the analyst's body."

> The frame marks off the different kind of reality that is within it from that which is outside it; but a temporal spatial frame also marks off the special kind of reality of a psycho-analytic session. And in psycho-analysis it is the existence of this frame that makes possible the full development of that creative illusion that analysts call transference. (Milner, 1952b, p. 183)

Casement writes:

> The space within the analytic frame is kept separate from the world outside, allowing that particular kind of relating to develop in which the transference can freely emerge ... To be healthy, every intimate relationship needs space and personal boundaries, and a corresponding respect by each person for the "otherness" of the other. Frequently, however, this space is either lacking or contaminated by intruding influences ... The analytic space ... acknowledges the need for boundaries between people, and therefore respects a patient's need for boundaries, including those that are still needed to protect the ego from whatever it is able to manage. (1990, pp. 158–160)

I think that we can find an architectural disposition for this aim and an architectural reason able to explain this disposition. The analyst's consulting room and the analyst's physical presence can become a sort of border allowing the patient to recognise the territory in which he moves and, as a consequence, the construction of his internal map.

> Especially when the experience and the meaning cannot be worked through at the representational level, they are brought back to their basic concreteness and physicality. In this sense, both are no longer decomposed and scattered but are grouped in a primary perceptual unity allowing the environment to be structured into a container

> through which the passage between conscious and unconscious is possible. (Preta, 2015, p. 77)

Elizabeth A. Danze (2005) argues that when two people sit and talk face to face, they create a defined and condensed space between them. This space is intimate and limited. When the analysand looks around and not at any particular focal point, a spatial openness and a spatial potential for infinity is created. This is true for the analyst as well. Thus, analysand and analyst have a relational opportunity. This opportunity is expanded, enhanced, limitless, and open-ended. This free-floating attention does not concern only the analyst but also the analysand. The walls of the room can contain the analysand and analyst together and independently at the same time.

Bion (1963, pp. 6–7) writes: "The patient is in analysis, in a family, or in the consulting room." In this sense, he proposes various possible emotional containers. As we can see, there is a particular spatial hierarchy as the analyst, sitting behind the analysand, can have a privileged perspective over his visual expressions. In spite of the fact that the analytic experience is shared, this asymmetrical spatial disposition accounts for a different and new distribution of power. In this sense, it is also a way that allows the working couple to understand each other through transference and countertransference.

Freud's consulting room

The bedroom is probably the stable and permanent place par excellence. For this reason and due to its attractiveness and its being a container of memories, Freud invents and construes his therapy place similar to a bedroom of his day. The bedroom allows understanding the whole of which we are part and represents the elementary particle of this whole by becoming the privileged place of emotional meetings and exchanges.

If we were able to go back in time and observe the consulting room (we know how it was thanks to some photographs that Freud transferred from Vienna to London—a few days before Freud's escape from Vienna, the photographer Edmund Engelmann (1976) was able to elude the Gestapo's surveillance and photograph Freud's consulting room before it was dismantled), we would see a narrow space, interconnected with domestic spaces and thus with their smells and noises (Figures 10 and 11). It was neither a neutral nor an institutional space

Figure 10. Freud's consulting room, London, England.

Figure 11. Freud's consulting room, London, England.

but rather a common place in everyday life. It was full of furnishings, carpets, decorative objects, and relics able to give clear indications of the taste and cultural interests of the analyst. Because all these objects were familiar in the analyst's everyday life, we can say that they functioned to reduce his solitude (we can say that this solitude was often emphasised by the continuous contact with the uncanny). Further, because these furnishings highlighted some aspects of the analyst's privacy, they were able to "organise this place of intimacy" (Eiguer, 2004, p. 6) and certainly to become part of the contents of the analysand's fantasies. Thus by exhibiting his collections, Freud was literally able to reveal things about himself. That is to say, he was able to disclose himself and thus to permit to ideally put together the past of the single person and that of civilisation.

The German psychoanalyst Ernst Blum argues that, during his analysis, Freud would put a significant object in the centre of the table for the entire day. He adds that Freud would also speak to this object. In Freud's consulting room, analyst and analysand were allowed to talk about Freud's cultural interests and to assess in psychoanalytic terms which cultural and historical interests could direct the patient (Pohlen, 2006).

In his description of his analysis with Freud, the psychiatrist Smiley Blanton (1971) writes that the founder of psychoanalysis used to loan and donate his books to his analysands. He also adds that Freud and the analysand tended to move around in the room and did not only use the couch and armchair during the session.

The anthropologist Abram Kardiner (1977) remembers that one day, Freud took him to the room near his study to show him his eucalyptus trees. He explained to him that their colour was faded because they were the product of a dig similar to those relics coming from the unconscious.

The philosophical writer Maryse Choisy recalls being enchanted by all those satyrs and divinities one could find in Freud's *sanctum sanctorum* (1973, quoted in Albano, 2014).

In his memoirs, the Wolf-Man says:

> The rooms themselves must have been a surprise to any patient, for they in no way reminded one of a doctor's office but rather of an archaeologist's study. Here were all kinds of statuettes and other unusual objects, which even a layman recognised as archaeological findings from ancient Egypt. Here and there on the walls were stone

> plaques representing various scenes of long-vanished epochs … Everything here contributed to one's feeling of leaving the haste of modern life behind, of being sheltered from one's daily cares. (Gardiner, 1972, p. 139)

In the magazine *Domus* the architect Italo Rota writes:

> If we observe Freud's consulting room from the couch and from the perspective of an architect, it looks wide, with a distant and almost blinding source of light coming from the near room of Freud's house. It is a fascinating world, threatened by gods of many different forms, materials, and cults. His patients lie down on precious carpets like uncomfortable paramours and observe this apparently chaotic but actually rigidly organised mise-en-scène. This represents nothing but the mental organisation of the owner of these places. (2010, p. 60)

The psychologist Rita Ransohoff (in Engelman, 1976, p. 111) writes: "The silent yet somehow eloquent figurines of the past confronted the patient who came here to discover his own origins and buried history."

The psychoanalyst Domenico Chianese writes:

> As soon as the patient entered Freud's consulting room, full of statuettes in every part of it, she was under a sensorial attack moved by the ancients: the invitation to the patient was explicit and the direction was mandatory. The patient entered a sacred place in which the particular and the universal, the past of the individual and the past of civilisation, the millennial memories and the individual memory were juxtaposed and confounded. (2015, p. 34)

Lynn Gamwell, former Director of the Art Museum at the State University of New York at Binghamton, connects the fact that Freud's consulting room was full of ancient and precious small sculptures (that have a bigger physical presence than paintings) to the sense of solitude he experienced after his father's death in 1890, which, in turn, corresponded to his longest time of scientific and professional isolation. "Several accounts reveal that Freud treated these figures as his companions." (1989, p. 27) Bolognini (2008) argues that these figures not simple surrogates of his colleagues and disciples (it is worth noting that, in 1890, there were no psychoanalysts yet). In fact, even after psychoanalysis's great diffusion, the continuous conflicts inside it saddened Freud so much that he "always returned to his writing desk and loyal audience (the figures) that he considered as representing the wisdom of ancient times" (Gamwell, 1989, p. 35). Throughout his life, Freud was surrounded by a big collection (about 2000 pieces) of objects and relics in his consulting room. All these things symbolised his continuous and mute questions about the past. "This was a world made up of external and internal objects, then, a source of comfort and of inspiration at the same time, in an illusional, intermediate area of potential creativity." (Bolognini, 2008, p. 7)

The psychoanalysts Chianese and Fontana remark on Freud's research and construction of an invisible space (one in which to listen and not to look) and his need to be surrounded by ancient objects and statuettes (whose function should be that of comforting him in those moments in which things did not appear so clear). "When Freud begins to construe 'the invisible' of mental life, his need of the presence of his collection in the consulting room shows that, to be true life, mental life must find its nourishment in the perceptions and images of the visible." (2000, p. 105)

The analyst's consulting room transmits a sense of security and familiarity. For this reason, it is the sublime protected centre of the intimacy of the patient and, of course, of her sexuality. It is the centre of the transferral and counter-transferral vicissitudes of the analyst-analysand couple and it is away from prying eyes. Thus, it assumes the role that has been typical of the bedroom in history.

Winnicott describes Freud's clinical setting with these words:

> This work was to be done in a room, not a passage, a room that was quiet and not liable to sudden unpredictable sounds, yet not dead quiet and not free from ordinary house noises. This room would be lit properly, but not by a light staring in the face, and not by a variable light. The room would certainly not be dark and it would be comfortably warm. The patient would be lying on a couch, that is to say, comfortable, if able to be comfortable, and probably a rug and some water would be available. (1954, p. 285)

In speaking of her analysis with Freud, the poet Hilda Doolittle (1944) remembers that in the room there was an ancient porcelain stove at the foot of the couch and many books. She has slightly different thoughts from Winnicott's about the atmosphere in Freud's room: "It is quiet here, anyway. There is no sound of traffic from the street, no familiar household sounds from the Freud family side of the house. We are quite alone here in this room." (1944, p. 523)

When Freud was forced into exile after the Nazis came to power, he was able to bring along his antiquities. He could do this thanks to a ransom that the Princess Marie Bonaparte paid to the Nazis. He met the princess when he was invited to her house in Paris when he made the journey from Vienna to England. In a letter to the psychoanalyst Jeanne Lampl-de Groot dated 8 October, 1938, he writes: "all the Egyptians, Chinese, and Greeks have arrived, have stood up to the journey with very little damage, and look more impressive here than in Berggasse". As we can see, here Freud heaves a sigh of relief when he can see his collection saved in his new home at Maresfield Gardens in London. In this home, Paula Fichtl, the Freud family maid, and Ernst, the son of Sigmund Freud, carefully arranged all the pieces of the collection in the same way in which they were placed in the rooms in Bergasse 19 in Vienna (where Freud had lived and worked for 47 years).

The analyst's consulting room after Freud

For some years now, we have seen an increasing number of published photographs of consulting rooms. This is curious because it contrasts with the well-known discretion of psychoanalysts about their personal life and therapy places. From 2000 to 2004 the magazine *International Psychoanalysis* published colour photos, submitted by members themselves, of the consulting rooms of the members of the International Psychoanalytic Association. The German photographer Claudia Guderian's 2004 book *Magie der Couch* (The magic of the couch) can be considered the first exploration of contemporary consulting rooms with a camera. She visited approximately 100 psychoanalytic settings and assessed their visual and aesthetic impact and their hidden meanings. In the same year her photographs were exhibited in Freud's house-museum at Maresfield Gardens.

The exhibition "The couch as the symbol of psychoanalysis" at the 2008 national conference of the Italian Psychoanalytic Society included a section called "Where the words stretch out: today's psychoanalytic couches". Curated by the psychoanalyst and photographer Roberto Basile, the section consisted of pictures of Italian analysts' consulting rooms. Basile aimed to represent the dialogue between the analyst's armchair and the analysand's couch, the ways in which such a dialogue can take form, and the results that can emerge. In this sense, the subject of the photographs is not simply the couch as an object.

The photographer Dan Welldon's[5] series "50 minutes" at the showcase of the 2012 International Architecture Exhibition in Venice, showed psychoanalysts from throughout the world in their rooms. Each photograph is accompanied by the analyst's comments about the emotional impact the picture had on them. About Welldon's work, Basile writes: "The studies look very similar and very different at the same time. All the studies are very personal. Looking at these studies makes me think about how we present our interior architecture to our patients. Some of these studies are full of furnishings ... Others look like a home, sometimes with a fireplace, and promote a sort of desire to live there." (2012, p. 914)

The pictures draw attention to those modifications of space and furniture over time not only by virtue of scientific and ideological assumptions, but also of socio-cultural changes in the environment.

I have chosen to mostly show pictures from *International Psychoanalysis* (some of Claudia Guderian's photographs are also found in her *Magie der Couch*, from which other photographs are taken) because they have been submitted and taken by the analysts.

After the "too full spaces" of Freud's and first Freudian analysts' rooms (Figures 12 and 13) of which traces can also be found in some contemporary analysts from Vienna and London (Figures 14 and 15), we attend to the idea of reduction, simplification, and deprivation (this idea is based on the German architect Ludwig Mies van der Rohe's maxim *less is more* and his *skin and bone* architecture) and thus to the "too empty spaces" of the subsequent analysts' rooms (Figures 16, 17, and 18).

These studies are generally furnished in Franciscan style, being simple, frugal, essential, cold, and almost anonymous. On the one hand, these studies are affected by American puritanism of the 1940s with its tendency toward uniformity and stability so that, for many decades, nothing could be changed in the analyst's study or clothes (Guderian, 2004); on the other, by the minimalist claims of modern architecture. There is only an armchair, a couch, sometimes a writing desk and closet. No books, no paintings on the walls, and no decorative objects are allowed: they could give indications of the analyst's personality and

Figure 12. Early Freudian analyst's consulting room: "too full space".

Figure 13. Early Freudian analyst's consulting room: "too full space".

Figure 14. Contemporary Freudian analyst's consulting room: "too full space".

Figure 15. Contemporary Freudian analyst's consulting room: "too full space".

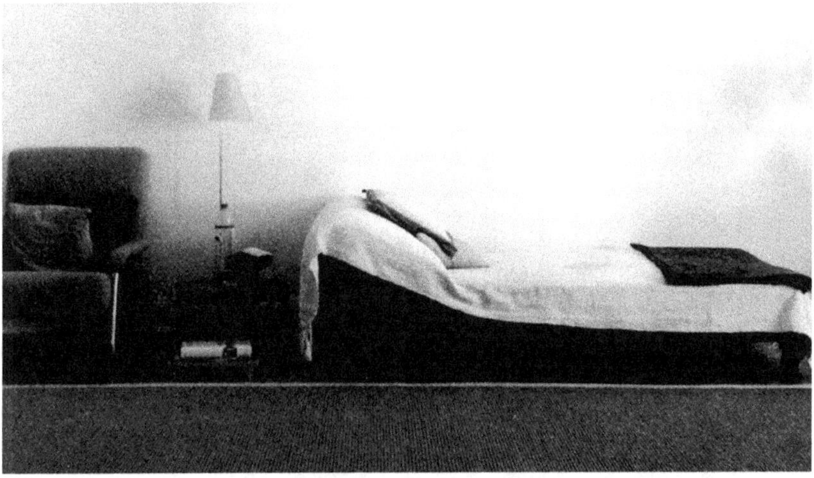

Figure 16. Contemporary analyst's consulting room: "too empty space".

Figure 17. Contemporary analyst's consulting room: "too empty space".

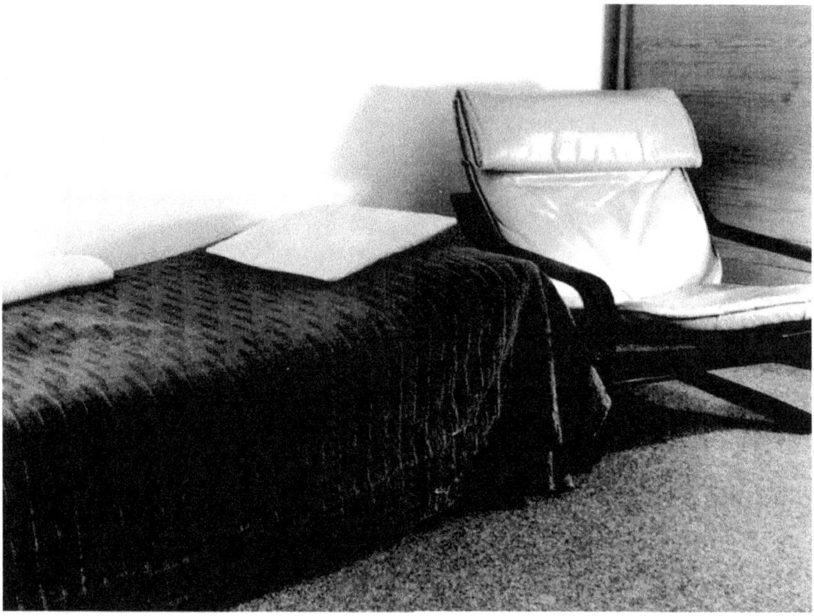

Figure 18. Contemporary analyst's consulting room: "too empty space".

interfere with the analysand's phantasmatic and associative freedom. The basic idea is to reduce as much as possible the analysand's projections to objects that belongs to the analyst and, in a certain sense, to foster the analysand's expression of dreams, fantasies, and experiences without any supporting material provided by the analyst.

The psychoanalyst Christopher Bollas writes:

> In English culture ... psychoanalysts tend to have consulting rooms that are dimly lit and yet luminous. The rooms are comfortable, with few paintings or physical distractions, so that the self is able to recline into interiority. Rather than using couches most analysts provide an ordinary bed covered with soft quilting and a pillow. Analysts sit behind the patient, out of sight, thus sustaining an illusory sense that both are inside the same object. (2013, p. 53)

Thus, the neutrality of the room allows mediating between physical and psychical and fostering a safe separation, that is to say, a safe passage from the centre of the world (represented in the analytic relationship) to the external world for both analyst and analysand. Bolognini writes that he visits many studies of colleagues in different cities and countries and tries to imagine them at work in his personal thoughts during sessions. Only very rarely he has discovered in these studies:

> The characteristics of the indecipherable and spartan neutrality that were recommended until a few decades ago as a guarantee of the "blank slate". Today's analysts—in their exterior settings as well—seem to have in part renounced the pretext of an ideal undetectability of the analyst's self in the professional relationship. If anything, judging by the distinctive language of their office furnishings, they appear inclined to officially admit to their existence as individuals, in addition to their identities as those who merely fulfil a function. (2008, p. 8)

In general, the latest generations of analysts deal with the issue of the emergence of the presence of the analyst as something fundamental for the analytic relationship (Figures 19, 20, 21, and 22).

Figure 19. Analyst's consulting room: individually furnished.

Figure 20. Analyst's consulting room: individually furnished.

It is clear that there are different degrees to which the analyst can reveal herself as a person. The definition of the setting is between two polarities, one in which the analyst has the function of a "blank screen" or "hanger" and one in which she makes excessive use of intersubjectivity. This use can lead one to excessively define the setting on the basis of the analyst's personal tastes and of her self-disclosure. (I mean, the analyst's act of consciously and deliberately revealing personal information to the analysand. It is completely different from the accidental and "unconscious" revealing of personal information. It can strongly interfere with the analysand's tastes and experiences and with the freedom of expressing them.)

Thus, on the one hand, we should avoid being rigid and mechanising the external factors of the setting: thus, the analyst's role must not be limited to the elimination of those obstacle that can stop the rhythm of

Figure 21. Analyst's consulting room: individually furnished.

the session (conceived as a sort of machinery) (Fachinelli, 1983). On the other, we should avoid giving rise to an internal setting consisting of attitudes that are vague, indefinite, ineffable, and useless at the psychoanalytic level (Correale, 2003). We should think of a third way that avoids the excesses of these two polarities.

I think that today the presence of a plain interior design able to communicate the analyst's aesthetic–cultural interests is no longer something to avoid.

As Roberto Basile (2009) points out in his comments on his photographs: "As well as those toys that children carry from home to kindergarten, in their studies analysts often have objects that allow mediation between their feelings and those of their patients. Perhaps it is a painting, an African mask, an Indian doll, a spiny cactus, or only a strange ceiling." (p. 1)

Figure 22. Analyst's consulting room: individually furnished.

I think that it is necessary that analysts maintain "their good sense and good taste in limiting themselves to a perceptible but usually sober personalisation of the environment, avoiding a narcissistic invasion of the working field with the exhibition of their private iconography" (Bolognini, 2008, p. 8).

The inside and the outside in the analytic relationship

Other notes about various photographs of analysts' studies comment on the spatial dimensions of the rooms, the height of their ceilings, and the size of their doors and windows that, together with the spatial subdivision and the position of the pieces of furniture and decorative objects, define the horizontal and vertical position between two bodies by measuring and defining their architectural scale.

"Understanding architectural scale implies the unconscious measuring of an object or a building with one's body, and projecting one's bodily scheme on the space in question. We feel pleasure and protection when the body discovers its resonance in space." (Pallasmaa, 1994, p. 36)[6]

In general the spaces of the European analysts' consulting rooms are smaller than those of the Americans. This means that the distances between the analyst's armchair and the analysand's couch and between the analysand's perspective and the room's different furnished parts are smaller, too. In this sense, the room seems to hark back to a primitive refuge. This implies a change at the perceptual level, that is to say, a different mutual way of listening, of visual observation, and of proprioception in relation to proximity and separation but also to material, acoustics, lights, and all the physical elements we must consider. Rooms of different forms and material reverberate in a different way (Rasmussen, 1962, p. 224). The sound can be hard or soft, reflected or absorbed, depending on the different features of form and material. In this sense, these features can define in many different ways the issues of proximity, security, and fear that the presence or absence of sound near the consulting room (from the street or the waiting room) can provoke. Further, it would be beneficial that there be between analyst and analysand "a sensible listening and a continuous dialogue, similar to what happens in the execution of a piano piece for four hands … This requires of the piano players continuous critical attention, good taste, and a shared capacity to reveal emotion." (Petrella, 2010, pp. 33–34).

Every time Franca spoke of her repressed and coerced sexuality, she did it with a subtle and feeble voice, a sort of whisper. This forced me to get close to her by moving my neck and my head in order to better my hearing through an improbable enlargement of my ears. So, she forced me to get close to her and thus make a further effort to comprehend words that could not be completely said. Her fear that I could not listen to her was projected onto me. I was not able to listen adequately. Her childhood need to be listened to came along with her narcissistic demand of having me close to her, as if she was asking whether I would really listen to her words.

The change of my posture in the armchair due to Franca's whispers helped me feel how she desired to be understood by me. I felt like a mother who is able to individuate her child's needs without attempting to make them felt to her. Perhaps in a wider place and with a bigger distance between the couch and the armchair I could have not felt at the countertransference level that she needed to maintain her privacy and that I could receive and understand only a faint message from her. Perhaps, in a bigger room, I would have felt the urgency of an interpretation about her narcissism, I would not have been able to listen to her, and I would have not understood her need to be listened to. Thus, my later interpretation about her need to be understood has been favoured by this possibility of acoustic intimacy.

In the consulting room, sometimes we hear faint voices that force us to stand still in order to not make any noise when we focus our attention on the analysand, like a mother who goes close to her child's cradle to be sure that he breathes. Sometimes we hear strongly dissenting voices; sometimes we hear voices that look similar to foreign bodies. Sometimes we hear insistent and inexpressive voices … The analyst's work is that of containing and harmonising all these sounds and voices: it is a sort of bodily adaptation of what the analysand's body expresses. (Monterosa, 2013, p. 585)

The experience of intimacy is reinforced by the presence of a window that marks the distinction between the unmeasurability of the outside and the intimacy of the inside. If this experience can be called into question by the distraction provoked by too big windows, a vision of the horizon or of distant places can give a concrete idea of the infinite. Rather, the sense of closure of the interiors reminds us of something finite and tangible. Every polarity needs the other for its fulfilment (Danze, 2005).

The quantity and the quality of natural light into a consulting room is very important because, in architecture, all the things that the eyes see and the other senses perceive are determined by conditions of light and shadow (Holl, 1994).

The studies of American analysts seem to have much more light than the ones of European analysts not only because of the size of the windows, the colour of the walls, or the use of material, but because of the combination of these three elements. All these elements influence the perception of natural light, which can be excessive for an intimate and private place such as a consulting room.

On beautiful and sunny days, before starting the session, Giovanna would put on a pair of sunglasses to protect herself from what she felt as an excess of brightness in the room. This brightness could blind her and prevent her from looking at herself. This is because she had the sensation that brightness did not leave space for this need for privacy and intimacy, unlike semi-darkness. Using sunglasses was a clear indication of her degree of tolerance of my interpretations. When she wore them, it was as if she said to me that she would have experienced my interpretation as if I were turning on a very intense light in dark place. This is more or less like the actions of an inspector who questions someone under investigation for a crime. When she did not wear her sunglasses, it was as if she took my interpretations as flashes in the dark, more or less as fireflies in the countryside at night.

Also in such a case, the presence of wide and luminous windows should have invalidated my possibility of perceiving certain indications. Perhaps Giovanna would have had more difficulties in representing her degree of tolerance of my interpretations without her sunglasses.

I received positive comments from patients when I substituted in my consulting room a chaise longue designed by Le Corbusier for a wider and softer couch. This is probably because the shape of the former put an objective spatial constraint, a lack of comfort, and a difficult in the bodily movements of the patients, whereas the shape of the latter fostered relaxation in their bodily movements and thus helped them remember their dreams and fantasies.

I remember the experience of temporariness and promiscuity of a patient who, before asking to start analysis with me, had been in treatment with an analyst who made him lie down on a common living-room sofa. The patient fantasised that his analyst used to drink coffee with his guests on this sofa. In this sense, he fantasised that no place, that sofa included, could be a non-promiscuous place and unique for him. That is to say, he thought he could not have an intimate place only for him and with a well-specified function.

I believe that we cannot speak of consulting rooms without considering the spaces near them. The sequence of arrival contains many thresholds and subtle and powerful elements in establishing territory and the dialectic between inside and outside (Malnar & Vodvarka, 2004).

The reception desk of a building, its hall, its stairs, its elevator, its anteroom, its waiting room, and also its toilets are examples of the spatial sequence we must cross from a public space to a private home. "As one enters the building's precinct and proceeds towards the analytic room, layers of space are penetrated slowly, at walking pace, preparing for the inner sanctum, while insulating the analysand and the analyst from the outside world." (Danze, 2005, pp. 120–121)

> Architecture could be viewed as a series of suggestions and experiments on the nature of internal and external relations, a machine programmed to manipulate and regulate these links. Therefore, one can see architecture as a sublimation in which we bind our experiences of being connected to nature and society while maintaining sophisticated levels of differentiations from those same ever-present larger unities. (Sperber, 2014b, p. 514)[7]

Architecture is a reflection on entering and exiting able to define the frames containing our lives (Sperber, 2015).

After an interpretation of mine about his methods of only allowing the expression of his childhood needs through clandestine transgressions, Andrea looks very worried. He says that the entrance to the lift in the building where my study is located opens when the lift moves and does not stop at a certain floor, so that the lift can be very risky to take. Because this is so serious a communication, I verify it and I exclude the possibility of real danger. This means that my act of verifying is a proper countertransference enactment demonstrating that my anxiety and urgency in verifying has been a response to his intense sense of danger. The signal of serious danger and the fear of death by falling seem to indicate his terror of passing through an entrance that does not lead to a containing lift but directly and dramatically to a lifeless and distressing void. I have felt such a strong fear that I have had to test its truth. This entrance open to the abyss and unable to give neither maternal containment nor paternal protection has been the signal that going through the painful conflicts of his internal world could have been a mortal danger not only for him but also for me.

Entrance, exit, and greetings are fundamental parts of the analytic experience. The borders are certainly physical and concrete but can occur in many different ways. Some are clearly visible, others are invisible, and others still are only implicitly suggested but nonetheless are strongly felt at the physical and emotional level. The real or imaginary borders of the room refer to the real or imaginary borders of the analytic relationship also at the spatial level. The quality of such a curious relationship between analyst, analysand, and the space in which the analysis takes place does not depend only on the cognitive context but also on the immediate and pervading physical context. "The analytic room should have the capacity to evoke different kinds of associations and be able to accommodate the richly variegated desires of the occupants." (Danze, 2005, p. 123)

In his last session before summer vacation, Andrea points out that I have left the door of the consulting room ajar. I stand up and I go to close it. After my excuses for my lack of attention, I say that he may fear that the half-open door can also indicate my lack of attention towards his need for privacy. In this sense, my lack of attention can foster intrusion from the external world just when he feels that his place inside me is threatened by the forthcoming holiday. At first, Andrea proudly denies the validity of my interpretation because he says he does not fear an open door, as he has nothing to hide from anybody. Then he tries to justify my inattention by arguing that I was probably thinking of the patient who preceded him, a man who limps. Before parting ways with Andrea and starting to think of my holidays and my loved ones, which would exclude him, Andrea neither expresses jealousy nor stresses my unkind lack of attention in a paranoid way. Rather, he expresses a defensive comprehension of the fact that another person, the previous patient who limps and thus needs more attention than him, occupies my mind. Andrea uses this defensive comprehension in the same way he did when he was a child and his mother was far away from him, teaching, and thus thinking of her students. The interpretation of this defensive false self allows Andrea to talk about his weaknesses, his fear that his mother cannot give him adequate attention because of his insignificance, and his incapacity to attract her attention.

The role of connective architectural space, as well as that of interstitial space, is to connect the inside with the outside and to mediate conjunction and separation. Before entering the analytic space you must pass through many doors that represent parts of the space indicating (at least to a certain degree) intermediate or transitive situations. These situations do not necessarily indicate exclusions but can be experienced as crossings, passages, or filters that can prepare you to meet the other or that can be inaccessible barriers. In his *Arcades Project* (1972), written between 1927 and 1940, Benjamin shows how inadequate thresholds are. He also calls them transitions and he relates them to the rites of passage that in turn have evident consequences on the articulation and the organisation of space.

> The threshold is a place where two identities certify, wait for, confront, reflect on, and defend themselves in the space. It is necessary to stress the differences ... Without this solution of spatial continuity the density differences around different presences could not express and adequately make a comparison between them. (La Cecla, 2000, pp. 110–111)

Last night, before sleeping, I watched a TV programme about the Red Brigades in Genoa. It showed the street in which your study is located and also in which one of their terrorist attacks occurred. A man was killed. (It is true that an armed commando of the Red Brigades committed a murder near the building in which my study is located.) It was a very dark and gloomy street. Genoa had been described as the most extended in length of any European city and above all as the best refuge because of its narrow and steep streets. I think of all the people who were killed by the Red Brigades and all the people who chose to stay at home because of fear of terrorist attacks. The dark and frightened city of the TV programme does not correspond with the hospitable and colourful place that Genoa is for me. I look forward to coming to your study but, before that, I like to have a rest in the small park near here or to enjoy window-shopping in the city centre.

Here the patient seems to compare his internal Genoa before the beginning of his analysis (a dark, distressing, frightening, frightened, full of closed places, and dead city) and his internal Genoa at the end of his analysis (a hospitable and coloured city). In this new internal Genoa my study can be found in a wide panorama full of open green spaces, of places to sit in the sun, and of objects that can be found in the beautiful shops in the city centre.

Of course, I have no intention of proposing an architectural model for a consulting room. I am aware of the risk of having excessive simplifications and reductions that make us pay less attention to the unique and original features of every consulting room, as well as to the integration between the spatial and perceptual spaces, the patient's internal world, and the specifics of the analysand-analyst relationship.

In spite of this, I believe it is useful to stress certain historical aspects. For example, it is a matter of fact that, unlike American analysts, European analysts tend to have their consulting rooms inside their homes. Geographically, external spaces are greater in America than in Europe, which means the population density is less and thus also the possibility of having places to live. In terms of architecture, it is a historical fact that American analysts give more relevance to interior lighting than do European ones. The interiors of European studies are less illuminated than the American ones probably due to the old age of the buildings and to the historical necessity of having reduced spaces and little communication with the external world in order to conserve heat. Sociologically, we can see the increase of professionalisation of psychoanalytic work and its consequent display of certificates as trophies; and technically there are the various theoretical models in psychoanalysis that I discussed earlier.

All these aspects can have a non-neutral role in the constitution of the analytic setting and also in the experience and interpretation of transference and countertransference. I think that knowing and scrutinising the effects of consulting rooms' architectural aspects and furniture on the analytic relationship's dynamics can promote an assessment of the different components of the rooms themselves. The same applies to the assessment of the consulting room. This room can be conceived as a place in which to project "shadows of memories and association through a presence that can be shared between analyst and analysand and put on a surface. In this sense, we must not forget to see, hear, and touch how this surface thinks and responds." (Leavitt, 2013, p. 569)

The architect Peter Zumthor (1999, p. 24) writes: "In my buildings I try to enhance what seems to be valuable, to correct what is disturbing, and to create anew what we feel is missing."

I believe that this can be a source of inspiration for architects, psychoanalysts, and all creative talents.

CHAPTER THIRTEEN

Some notes and suggestions on a possible partnership between architects and psychoanalysts

> Writing can give us the illusion that ... we have the possibility to give something essentially erratic a home.
>
> (Agostino Racalbuto, 2005, p. 288)

Between certainty and responsibility

The word "building" indicates a progressive activity. Houses are not definitively construed but are always in construction (Hillman, 2004). They change over time; sometimes they get better, sometimes worse. In every case, they have significant consequences for their inhabitants' experiences and behaviours. This does not depend only on the architect and the material used for the construction, but also on the point of view of the generations inhabiting the houses and on their continuously changing interests. In turn, the points of view construct and deconstruct what architects have prepared and thus are influenced by environment, culture, and history. The same can be said about all theoretical models and therapeutic techniques, including those of psychoanalysis, which must be continuously tested and, when necessary, reformulated and modified according to the different historical and social contexts.

For example, one of Freud's last papers (*Constructions in Analysis*, 1937d) abandons the archaeological metaphor and introduces construction features in the analytic relationship.

The literary critic Mario Lavagetto (1985) points out that Freud uses the German term *Konstruction* every time the subject is the analyst. But when, for example, Freud compares a neurosis with a building constructed with different sorts of materials to which the builder has tried to give coherence and solidity, he uses different German terms: *der Bau* (the building), *der Vorbau* (the front extension), *der Aufbau* (the structure), *die Bildung* (the development), *die Fabrikation* (the production), *die Herstellung* (the manufacture).

The psychologist Giancarlo Ricci writes:

> In general, the German term Bau refers to the construction of a house or a street, whereas Konstruction can have different meanings since it can be a construction in a logical, geometrical, grammatical, and graphic sense. As we can see, the construction of the psychoanalytic city (or, in other words, the analyst's work) has a strong and specific meaning: it is distinct from the idea of restoration, remake, rebuilding, correction, or adjustment. (1995, p. 164)

The continuous exchange between identity and change, the osmosis between the natural needs and the social and cultural expression of these needs, and the strong relationship between genotype and phenotype (to use a metaphor from biology) have an effect on our capacity to have a good life.

The continuous exchanges and the juxtapositions between the internal and external world are well described by Calvino (1972): "Perhaps all that is left of the world is a wasteland covered with rubbish heaps, and the hanging garden of the Great Khan's palace. It is our eyelids that separate them, but we cannot know which is inside and which outside." (p. 94)

From another point of view, neurobiologist and winner of the 1981 Nobel Prize in Physiology and Medicine, Roger Sperry (1965), argues that ideas cause other ideas and help the new ideas to grow. Ideas interact with each other and with other mental forces in the same brain, in different but nearby brains and, through international communication, in unfamiliar and distant brains. Ideas also interact with the external environment to produce great advances in evolution.

The Italian jurist Gustavo Zagrebelsky (2014) is inspired by Jorge Luis Borges' *Funes, His Memory* (1944). In this story, Ireneo is a character able to remember every thing and every detail, even the most forgettable ones, but he is unable to think of defined concepts, for criticising hyper-specialised knowledge. He defines this knowledge as subdivided in different and increasingly fragmented competences and criticises the lack of a common container able to hold them together.

So, it is crucial to pay attention to the complexity of the symbolic system linking together the houses and the cities and their inhabitants. This can be done through discussion between architectural and psychoanalytic knowledge that is able to have an intimate relationship with the individual and social history.

> We must think to those conditions allowing a meeting and a common way between subject and object. This meeting must allow a connection between different mental functions, a transition able to free from certain mental prisons and to offer generative solutions able to give a meaning to our projects and so on. (Ferruta, 2009, p. 25)

The point of view of an expert should focus upon the features of the research field, the territorial phenomenology, the concreteness of settlements, and the assessment of the different contexts. This can be done by flexibly and carefully considering all the functional, aesthetic, symbolic, and anthropological features, going between tradition and innovation, avoiding looking for something extraordinary or magnificent at all costs, and creatively dealing with the ordinary, the useful, and the moderate.

The ethics of conviction require dedication and hard work in respect to a work intended as a search for a formal and beautiful harmony. However, the ethics of conviction cannot be separated from the ethics of responsibility, which require attention to the social meaning of a work. In this sense, the ethics of responsibility demand that a work should be useful for the entire community, respectful of the available resources, and adequate in both spatial dimension and environmental sustainability (Emery, 2010).

By starting from this principle, Emery (2011, p. 286) argues that an ethical alternative to "building *ex novo*" should be "a more modest work of recovery and transformation or of re-work when necessary. Further, it is important that there be a constant taking care of the building that does not mean a simplistic technical re-using."[1]

As a consequence, it is necessary to study the environmental impact of architectural work and the construction or restoration techniques able to reduce energy consumption and the level of pollution.

Failures

In an interview with the anthropologist Paul Rabinow, Foucault argues:

> Men have dreamed of liberating machines. But there are no machines of freedom, by definition. This is not to say that the exercise of freedom is completely indifferent to spatial distribution, but it can only function when there is a certain convergence; in the case of divergence or distortion, it immediately becomes the opposite of that which had been intended. (1984, p. 247)

In this sense, during the 2014 Venice Biennale in Architecture, the architect Stefano Boeri invites his colleagues to reflect together on architectural failures. It is worth noting that, before Boeri's proposal, in his *Scientific Autobiography* (1981, p. 48) the architect Aldo Rossi has written about his unsuccessful projects: "My most beautiful designs for competitions have always regularly been rejected. It would be easy but dishonest for me to blame inadequate support, factions, or friendships. My projects have been rejected … because of their incomprehensibility or, more precisely, their impracticality."

Boeri asks himself why architects do not openly speak of their failures, for example those coming from contingent professional mistakes or inadequate or technically erroneous planning. It is as if any failure did not exist or never depends on architects themselves. Boeri seems to not tolerate architecture populated by legendary heroes who show only their sequence of victories and make sure to hide their fiascos, frustrations, humiliations, and wrecks.

Thus, Boeri invites us to learn from failures and mistakes, to view them as useful experiences, and to teach young architects to do the same. He provocatively proposes organising a Venice Biennale on failure.

Of course, architects are free to fail and make errors, especially when they aim at developing their design in an innovative and original way.

For example, they can make errors in the use of some new materials (of which they ignore the features, the weaknesses, the durability) or in the realisation of certain constructions that, once realised, are not as good as someone expected or even are terrible. I think that the point is to recognise a construction's problems and faults, the lack of attention to clients' and users' demands, flaws in choosing materials, wrong economic evaluations, and unexpected changes in social and political conditions that require some modification of the original plan according to these new and sudden demands.

We know that sometimes the rejection of a certain generation can be the gold of the next one. A clear example of this is the controversial realisation of the Tour Eiffel (Bollas, 2000). However, Daniel Libeskind (2004) stresses that there is only one Tour Eiffel in the world, whereas "a Mies building is a Mies building in Berlin as well as in Havana". In this sense, an error can be the repetition through which a certain model or style is proposed: such a repetition means to not consider the distinctive and particular features of the place in which a certain construction will be installed.

In the Cartesian system and, more generally, in all the rationalist and empiricist paradigms, error occurs only if data is gathered and assessed or interpreted incorrectly. However, human perception is not linear but depends on the internal world or, cognitively speaking, on an already acquired and learned knowledge.

I think that, in both architecture and psychoanalysis, the possibility of error or even an obvious error can be the basis for a creative process of transforming the original idea.[2] In this sense, an error can be a sign able to reflect at the same time difficulty and dynamism.

In *Beyond the Pleasure Principle* (1920, p. 56), Freud quotes the following: "What we cannot reach flying we must reach limping ... The Book tells us it is no sin to limp."[3] In order to remind us to always deal with the omnipotence that resides in every analyst's mind, Freud (1937a, pp. 228–229) proposes this of the nineteenth-century satirist Johann Nestroy: "Every step forward is only half as a big as it looks at first." Then, in order to invite analysts to abandon every therapeutic triumph and to be cautious, rigorous, modest, and aware of their limitations, he writes: "What has once come to life clings tenaciously to its existence."

In the case of psychoanalysis, the analyst's acknowledgment of his error and not the accusation against the patient of resisting interpretations (Casement, 1985) can provide useful indications for understanding the clinical material, more or less as manure makes a field fertile. On the contrary, the continuous repetition of an error and its lack of recognition can lead to blindness and thus to situations in which the analyst is unable to comprehend anything about the patient. These situations often arrive at therapeutic impasses that can precede the interruption of psychoanalytic treatment. The analyst's capacity to recognise his errors allows the analysand to recognise his errors too and thus learn to renounce his omnipotence and limit his narcissism (Schinaia, 1997c).

If the exercise of humility (this word comes from the Latin *humus*, meaning soil or earth) is interpreted as something concrete, referring to a soil in which we roam, wander, and construe our meeting with the other, with his needs and wishes, so the profession of the analyst as well as that of the architect cannot be based upon a previously defined strict model of relationship but on an open one that is still being constructed.

In his autobiography (1985, p. 52), Bion writes: "it is not the successful building of the Tower of Babel but the failure, which gives life and initiates and nourishes the energy to live, to grow, to flourish".

In human affairs to err is not only essential, but also unavoidable. The psychoanalyst Elliott Jacques (1970) argues that the growth of our ego comes from our capacity to deal with uncertainties, lost opportunities, and errors. Such a capacity is the basis of that constructive self-criticism that allows us to learn from our mistakes and to conceive our projects or experiences as incomplete rather than definitively interrupted. In this sense, we should be able to feel frustration or disillusion for having been able to finish something rather than failure, humiliation, and anger (Schinaia, 2012).

In favour of critical town planning

In *Civilization and its Discontents* (1930a, p. 92) Freud asserts the importance of beauty, cleanliness, and order. He gives much importance to the fact that "the green spaces necessary in a town as playgrounds and as reservoirs of fresh air are also laid out with flower-beds ... We require civilised man to reverence beauty wherever he sees it in nature and to create it in the objects of his handiwork so far as he is able."

Jung (1950, p. 200) argues "we all need nourishment for our psyche. It is impossible to find such nourishment in urban tenements without a patch of green or a blossoming tree. We need a relationship with nature."

In *Truth and Method* the philosopher Hans-Georg Gadamer writes about a medium, a filter, and an optical instrument:

> Architecture involves a twofold mediation. As the art that creates space, it both shapes it and leaves it free. It not only embraces all decorative shaping of space, including ornament, but also is itself decorative in nature. The nature of decoration consists in performing that two-sided mediation: namely to draw the viewer's attention to itself, to satisfy his taste, and then to redirect it away from itself to the greater whole of the life context that it accompanies. This is true of the whole span of the decorative, from municipal architecture to the individual ornament. A building should certainly be the solution to an artistic problem and thus attract the viewer's wonder and admiration. At the same time it should fit into a way of life and not be an end in itself. It tries to fit into this way of life by providing ornament, a background of mood, or a framework. (1960, p. 151)

By arguing for a new relationship between artefacts and natural things, Lloyd Wright (1957) posits that the building and the environment are the same and that planting trees around the building and furnishing or decorating the building itself acquire new relevance, as they become features in harmony with the internal space in which we live.

The American philosopher Henry David Thoreau (1860) writes: "What is the use of a fine house if you haven't got a tolerable planet to put it on?"

However, in their designs, architects should not consider only the need to respect the environment, the balance between their work and the context in which it will be construed, and all the different demands at play: they should also propose true and concrete cooperation with those who will use their work, whether single clients or more generally the inhabitants of a neighbourhood or a city.

It often happens that questions impose their language and their internal structure onto answers (Augé, 1994). The direct questions of the inhabitants (or of those who will occupy the built environment) are able to avoid the excess of subjectivity that can strongly influence the interpretation of people's needs that the architect makes. In this sense, the active participation of the building's users seems absolutely necessary. In this sense, asking questions is an indispensable democratic act.

In the 1994 Italian film *Il Postino* (The postman),[4] directed by Michael Radford, the poet Pablo Neruda says: "When you explain poetry, it becomes banal. Better than any explanation is the experience of feelings that poetry can reveal to a nature open enough to understand it." The simple-minded postman Mario Ruoppolo translates Neruda's words in this way: "Poetry does not belong to those who write it, but those who need it."

I think that some of Derrida's considerations can represent a good transposition of this dialogue in the field of architecture:

> Architecture is not only a field limited to buildings, houses, and offices. It is not like painting or creating objects that people use; it deals with buildings in which all we live. In a certain way, we are all experts in architecture ... The citizen must have the right to ask questions (good and adequate questions) of the architects and to share with the architect a certain degree of professional competence. This is the reason why I think architecture must be taught from primary school. (2008, p. 171)

By paraphrasing Bion's words, Casement (1985) argues that psychoanalysts need to learn from patients and he reminds us that some gifted analysts such as Freud and Winnicott had a natural disposition in this sense.

Pope Francis writes:

> Given the interrelationship between living space and human behaviour, those who design buildings, neighbourhoods, public spaces, and cities ought to draw on the various disciplines that help us to understand people's thought processes, symbolic language, and ways of acting. It is not enough to seek the beauty of design. More precious still is the service we offer to another kind of beauty: people's quality of life, their adaptation to the environment, encounters, and mutual assistance. Here, too, we see how important it is that urban planning always take into consideration the views of those who will live in these areas. (2015, p. 85)

In his pamphlet *Contro l'Urbanistica* (Against town planning), Franco La Cecla focuses on the prescriptive or normative aspects of town planning. He argues that town planning has not become a discipline able to observe, listen to, and interpret urban realities.

> Town planning is not able to know what happens in the cities because it is locked into numerical and statistical parameters and lists of things and has thought that social reality can be understood through maps, percentages, and the probability theory. It is clear that town planning cannot understand the real movements and motivations, in other words, what people living in a city think and feel about it and what sort of motivations people give themselves for living in it. (2015, p. 13)

It often happens that hurried, populist, or insufficient solutions are proposed under the mask of a form of environmentalism. These solutions are actually false and avoid really dealing with the difficulties. So, these difficulties are not confronted and are likely to increase in the future.

However, the philosopher Duccio Demetrio (2005, p. 282) tells us to focus on falsifications and thus proposes radical city planning rather than simple, pseudo-reparative, urban decoration: "We must head … towards a new polis [city] in which to walk. We can do it only by recomposing all our split parts and learning to be here and elsewhere at the same time. This is not only for a better pedestrian area, of course."

The issue of the false and of the pseudo-reparation in a bourgeois society can be found in the writer Alberto Moravia's 1937 short story *The Architect* (L'architetto). Moravia has his character optimistically say that the modern house (which should rise from the restoration of an ancient monastery) should be open to nature in order to be rational. In this sense, it is a necessary reconciliation between the house and nature after many centuries of separation. Unfortunately, the acknowledgment of the indissoluble union of life inside of the house and the possibility of seeing outside the house in Moravia's story is inauthentic and illusory because reality is an obstacle to planning. In fact, this planning only serves as an overturned perspective that can oppose an optimistic and idealised image of the material construction as a symbol of moral and ethical construction: the dirt and the kitsch of real homes are the visual paradigms of an indifferent society without any moral and ethical points of reference.

It is worth noting that Pope Francis stigmatises those urban solutions that can be conceived as partial and (in a certain sense) class-conscious by stressing the right to beauty for every person:

> In some places, rural and urban alike, the privatisation of certain spaces has restricted people's access to places of particular beauty. In others, ecological neighbourhoods have been created that are closed to outsiders in order to ensure an artificial tranquillity. Frequently, we find beautiful and carefully manicured green spaces in so-called safer areas of cities, but not in the more hidden areas where the disposable of society live. (2015, p. 32)

However, it is true that some important town planners started to deal with the issue of sustainable urban planning some time ago. They have proposed town planning able to focus on the women and the men, all the women and men, the city's inhabitants, their identities, their interiorities, their feelings, their memories, their imagination, their relationships, the relation between the places and the people's unconscious minds, and between internal and external topographies.

In a crystal clear essay originally published in 1972 by the Royal Australian Institute of Architects titled *An Architecture of Participation*, the architect Giancarlo De Carlo aims at demonstrating that the idea of participatory design or architecture[5] can be a realistic utopia, in the sense that I can be completely realisable.[6] The process of participation does not imply the denial of the role of the town planner at all, but rather expands it.

Giancarlo De Carlo (1966) also argues "town planning is an interdisciplinary or trans-disciplinary social science. This is because it involves architects, sociologists, economists, psychologists, geographers … painters, sculptors, poets."

The town planner Bernardo Secchi seems to share De Carlo's position and supports the need to transform the scientific status of town planning in order to guarantee exchanges and accessibility to nature, to people, to everyone without distinction. According to Secchi, town planning must deal with the history and the definition of attitudes and urban collective consciousness:

> The town planner, but also the economists and the sociologists,[7] should return to the discussion with geographers, botanists,

> hydraulic engineers. They should immerse themselves into the individual and collective imagination much more than they have done in the recent past … I believe we should deal with the questions of the majority of people and not only with small social and technological niches. (2013, p. 78)

There is also a need to protect those common areas, visual landmarks and urban landscapes which increase our sense of belonging, of rootedness, of "feeling at home" within a city, which include us and bring us together. It is important that the different parts of a city be well integrated and that those who live there have a sense of the whole, rather than being confined to one neighbourhood and failing to see the larger city as space that they share with others. Interventions that affect the urban or rural landscape should take into account how various elements combine to form a whole that is perceived by its inhabitants as a coherent and meaningful framework for their lives. In his encyclical letter *Laudato Si'* Pope Francis writes:

> How beautiful are those cities that overcome paralysing mistrust, integrate those who are different, and make this very integration a new factor of development! How attractive are those cities that, even in their architectural design, are full of spaces that connect,[8] relate, and favour the recognition of others! (2015, p. 102)

In *The Interpretation of Dreams* (1900, p. 486) Freud alerts the analyst to the apparent coherence of a dream's connections and writes "a dream is a conglomerate which, for the purposes of investigation, must be broken up once more into fragments". Esther da Costa Meyer, a professor of the history of art, refers to Freud's words when she writes: "A city as a coherent totality is unconceivable … No one can avoid the tough opacity of the urban space and its many levels of meaning … [The cities] are places in which the meaning is always relational and continuously changing, in which only temporariness is unscathed." (2012, p. 107)

The philosopher Jean-Luc Nancy (2002) first considers and then gives great value to terms like mixture and juxtaposition. He does it when he argues that a way of thinking aiming at dealing with globalisation cannot assume the Greek city-state (*polis*) as a political model. He thinks that today a city cannot be the ideal city. Globalisation consists in a mutual and reciprocal creation of the world, in sharing, in singular-plural existences. He writes (p. 42): "A world is the common place of a totality of places: of presences and dispositions for possible events."

In a 2004 essay the architect Stefano Boeri describes how photography was able to register the urban changes of Italian cities. Until a few decades ago, this change took place gradually and with small variations and moved from the centre to outside. It was a sort of journey, in which:

> First, you could see the network of medieval alleyways sometimes interrupted by Roman archaeological ruins; second, some traces of growth of the Renaissance; third, the great, extended and powerful nineteenth-century city, characterised by regular blocks, boulevards, circles, and by its great public services (such as the fruit and vegetable market, the prison, the hospital, the cemetery, the stations); fourth, the big manufacturers, directly connected to suburbs and the first working-class villages ... Today these gradual changes have been substituted by fragmented and molecular change. It is as if the old partitioning of the city in big homogenous areas had crumbled and the differences between the single individualities of its body were prevailing ... The city is a sort of urban nebula that hosts portions of antiquity in a context of contemporary growth and niches grown up in developed areas of the city. (2004, p. 417)

Finding a balance in architectonic design and town planning means also putting together new and old things, respecting certain old demands and, at the same time, paying attention to certain new ones. This can be reached only by avoiding conceiving cities as museums because they could suspend the urban landscape and distort those (sometimes controversial and contradictory) features of contamination that give energy and colour to social and cultural life.

When Frank Gehry (in the 2006 documentary film *Sketches of Frank Gehry* directed by Sidney Pollack) contends that the past to which his work refers is neither Ancient Greece nor its architectural models, but more distant ancient times, perhaps the dawn of mankind, he gives great relevance to the force of the past. He does not deny history in an omnipotent way but rather he paves the way for us to consider the past. According to him, the past does not belong to a defined historical era and to its way of providing a model of the space. This is very similar to Freud's comparison between the dawn of mankind and the early phases of human development in order to increase his knowledge.

"All things keep the life of the people who have conceived them but their souls have something in common that comes from the origins of the universe, of mankind, and of cultures and this is continuously revived every morning of each new day." (Marc, 1972, p. 12)

I think it is important to remember some impressions about city life, a life full of conflicts, contradictions, and contrasts, that Sigmund Freud reported in order to try to anticipate some aspects of the discontent of metropolitan existence and, more in general, of contemporary civilisation.

About Paris, in a letter to Minna Bernays dated 3 December, 1885 (pp. 187–188) Freud writes: "the city and its inhabitants strike me as uncanny ... I don't think that they know the meaning of shame and fear; the women no less than men crowd round nudities as much as they do round corpses in the morgue or the ghastly posters in the streets." However, quite soon in the same letter, he focuses on the attractive features of Paris: "the brilliant exterior, the swarming crowds, the infinite variety of attractively displayed good, the streets stretching for miles, the flood of light in the evening, the over-all gaiety and politeness of the people; but to bring all this into harmony with the rest one has to know a great deal."

About the USA, this how Jones reports some of Freud's considerations (1957, p. 60): "America is a mistake, admittedly a gigantic mistake, but a mistake nevertheless." After a visit to Coney Island in New York, he says: "A magnified Prater" (p. 55). Then, after a visit to Niagara Falls, Jones writes that for Freud, "it was grander and larger than he had expected" (p. 57).

About Freud's visit in New York, Giancarlo Ricci writes (1995, p. 121): "Freud does not seem to be attracted by New York as the city of freedom and progress, as the urban jungle, as the city full of exhibitions and shows." However, in order to appreciate the sensitivity of Freud's judgements, I think it is important to stress that he was attracted by Niagara Falls' greatness and by the force of nature.

About Genoa, Freud makes some comments in a postcard to his wife dated 13 September, 1905 (Freud, 1905b). In it he focuses on the lack of green areas in the urban landscape and argues that there are some similarities with Vienna's town planning: "It is all made of stones, there are only streets like the Herrengasse and squares with buildings, then the harbour, some fortifications, the sea, the cemetery. Everything is extremely elegant, impressive, solid, almost defiant."

So, for Freud the urban anonymity of Paris is reconsidered in the light of Parisians' gaiety and politeness, the USA's tendency towards the gigantic in the light of the wonder provoked by the untamed exuberance of nature, the elegance of Vienna and Genoa in the light of their lack of green areas. I think that these comments have a great value in terms of a critical perspective about town planning even today. Freud's remarks are not unidirectional and unprejudiced, unlike the words of Pope Francis when he notes:

The disproportionate and unruly growth of many cities, which have become unhealthy to live in, not only because of pollution caused by toxic emissions but also as a result of urban chaos, poor transportation, and visual pollution and noise. … Neighbourhoods, even those recently built, are congested, chaotic, and lacking in sufficient green space. We were not meant to be inundated by cement, asphalt, glass, and metal, and deprived of physical contact with nature. (2015, pp. 31–32)

CONCLUDING REMARKS

> I view psychoanalysis and literature as holding in common a profound love and respect for language as a vehicle not simply for the expression of thoughts and feelings, but, more importantly, a medium for the creation of thoughts and feelings, (Thomas H. Ogden, 2013, p. 630)

Freud (1907a, p. 92) argues that psychoanalysts must necessarily know literature: "We probably … draw from the same source and work upon the same object, each of us by another method. And the agreement of our results seems to guarantee that we have both worked correctly." Of course, by extension, this can be applied equally well to architecture and town planning.

Loos likes to quote Leon Battista Alberti (1452) when he writes that an architect is a builder who has studied Latin. According to this great mind of European Modernism, architects need to learn to be aware not only of construction and composition techniques but also of the historical and relational context in which they work.

Celant writes:

> Architecture and the architect grow together. They are tied together in a basically altruistic relationship. The focus of this relationship is the construction of a narration that is not self-referential but aims at concretely and politically interacting with reality for a long time. This functional and useful assumption belongs to the ethics of planning and does not deny an indirect recognition of the author and of his existential and historical features ... The personality of the author is reflected in his plans and thus in the external world and also in a deep internal and hidden world. Thus, it can realise itself in his relational and contextual path. (2013b, p. 25)

Celant's considerations about the identity of the architect are very similar to some contemporary considerations on the identity of the psychoanalyst and of the analyst as a person. If the question of who goes to an analyst is often about the analysand's solitude and confusion, desire to find someone able to listen and then to talk with, or find a container able of reverie, the psychoanalyst can answer only by being intimate and in touch with the patient and by improving his self-analytic capacities. Once the analyst has perfected these capacities, she can get close to the patient through words able to touch and to cure, that is to say, words able to make the patient grow wiser and to promote internal elaborations and transformations. In this sense, I think that the analyst can give adequate answers to the patient only through new and original narrative ways that depend on the analyst's history, on the way in which society and culture have influence her growth as a person and a psychoanalyst, and on the interesting and passionate meeting with the patient's narrations.

By making reference to Bion's psychoanalytic function of the mind, Di Chiara et al. (1985) write about how psychoanalysis uses a natural and spontaneous human attitude. This attitude is a disposition at birth and it is the capacity to function in a three-dimensional space whose references are the ego, the internal objects, and the external object. The way and the style of using this capacity and the presence of the analyst as a person can provide an original and unique narrative co-construction of the analytic relationship.

I hope that the way in which psychoanalysts take care of mental suffering and the way in which architects and city planners assess the environment and take care of it can find a common view on dwelling. It is a matter of fact that dwelling remains in an articulated and complex context of biological need and symbolic function that determines a defined disposition to deal with spaces in an environment built in a sustainable manner. We do not need architects as "engineers of the human soul" and psychoanalysts able only to comfort people as new confessors Rather, we need experts in both fields who are able to enrich their competencies with the contribution of other points of view. We need also critical intellectuals who support both psychological and environmental sustainability and thus a new general perspective of the relationships between resources, people, and territories.

In this sense, psychoanalysis and architecture can come together to consider and design not only our homes but also the analyst's consulting room and, more generally, therapy places. I think that this can be possible only if they renounce a narrow and limited model and propose a model able to resolve the questions posed by clients. This can be a way through which psychoanalysis and architecture can enhance and increase the chances of mental containment and exchange between the inside and the outside.

I think that creating harmonious and not disturbing relationships with those buildings in which we live every day[1] (these buildings can be our houses, public buildings such as schools, prisons, therapy places for mind and body, hospitals, clinics, etc. And, of course, consulting rooms) can be a measure of the degree of advancement of a society and of the quality of its institutions. Further, it can represent a positive way of conceiving our existence and of building the common good or, in other words, of having an ethical focus on solidarity and social cohesion. I think also that this ambitious task is not only for psychoanalysts and architects but also for teachers and politicians. Teachers should aim to educate their students to aspire to wellbeing and the common good, and politicians ought to promote policies of harmonious dwelling and living, and, consequently, propose that the public practise a respectful and active civic life at the local level.

I believe the best conclusion to this book is in Freud's words (1930, p. 95): "The essence [of civilisation] lies in the fact that the members of the community restrict themselves in their scope for satisfaction; whereas the individual knew no such restriction."

AFTERWORD TO THE ENGLISH EDITION

Stephen M. Sonnenberg

In 2012 my colleague Elizabeth Danze[1] and I were asked to write a critique of an article by Adele Tutter on the work of the architect Philip Johnson (Danze & Sonnenberg, 2012). Tutter's central thesis was that Johnson's Glass House, an architectural masterpiece, was a self-representation that had dream-like qualities. In our critique we looked at the design process, and in one section of our essay Danze self-reflectively shared her own experience as a designer and teacher. She wrote:

> Architectural design projects ... are extraordinarily complex; they involve the resolution of myriad conflicting agendas ... Solutions are inevitably complex, involving a visual creative process that results in three-dimensional, spatial, and volumetric propositions often created out of patterns and organisations outside of anyone's awareness. Projects are imagined, drawn, and completely "built" before they are actually constructed. They are "dreams" that are both created and experienced by the designer before any construction on the site has begun.
>
> It has been my experience that solutions present themselves, not in a purely logical, linear process, but often while in a state much like dreaming. I find idea generation to be most productive when

> I am able to suspend reality and respond to vague cues, memory impressions, subjective evaluations, and stimuli, all with some degree of structure but also lacking clarity. Time after time my solutions seem to emerge from nowhere, as if attributable to a muse. The best of these solutions then appear logical and inevitable, as if the result of keen, linear intellect. But I know better.
>
> I believe that a part of what accomplishes this resides deep into what is active in me while dreaming, and it is complex, spatial, and visual. Reinforcing these views of mine is that as a teacher working with a student I have often experienced the sudden inability to continue speaking, in mid-sentence, and I seem to be relying on a nonverbal dream state while very much awake and designing through drawing.
>
> My teaching technique has evolved in relation to this kind of experience. To encourage inner orientation in my students I ask them to recall very specific moments of their past and to put the sensations or sensual qualities of their remembrances into a drawing or three-dimensional model. They are then compelled to make physical connections to the forgotten, the obscured, the essential, and the intuitive. The memory and the object become the same by distilling, abstracting, and overlapping. This involves the moving in and out of abstraction and concretisation, encouraged by what I think of as a process of daydreaming, reverie … I am aware that while designing, my consciousness changes, and I believe processes are at work that have much in common with what happens when I'm asleep and creating dream images. (2012, pp. 539–540)

Also in that essay we wrote:

> We have explored ideas about the … visual … pointing out that the visual attracts the unconscious, that the unconscious stimulates the visual, and that there is a psychodynamic feedback loop that operates over time during the work of designing. This loop has a power of its own, as it operates as a self-stimulating system impelling the architect to design and build. (ibid., p. 547)

I think it is important to emphasise these ideas, because they help me understand, and explain to a reader, what Cosimo Schinaia has done in this book. Like the anthropologist who is caught up in the culture he investigates, and "goes native", Schinaia has been cognitively and emotionally kidnapped by the architects and designers he studies, and in this book the demarcation within him between a state of dreaming and waking while writing has often been obscured, if not obliterated. In order to read Schinaia effectively, at times one must read like the analyst listens: with freely hovering attention, in reverie, not trying to dissect every sentence and paragraph, but letting the words embrace and bathe, stimulating associations and imaginings, visual, musical, verbal. I have never been there, but I imagine that is how I'd feel were I to find myself in reverie, pleasurably immersed in Peter Zumthor's Therme Vals spa baths.

Let us examine Schinaia's text, using an example from Chapter Two—Fruitful contaminations. Schinaia writes:

> According to the architect Renzo Piano (2000), architecture is a frontier profession. It can exist only in so far as it accepts the challenge of being contaminated. If it does not accept this challenge, it is an armchair and rhetorical discipline. Piano also points out that "to live in a frontier means to avoid the borders. I chose to work through muddling and confusing different disciplines. I have not got any interest in the differences between arts and sciences, but in their similarities." (2004, p. 123)
>
> Martin Heidegger (1954) used to say to himself that it is the bridge that gives the meaning to the scene.
>
> The philosopher Michel Serres (1977, p. 28) writes: "The bridge is a way connecting two banks or gives continuity to a discontinuity or mends a tear."
>
> The philosopher and sociologist Georg Simmel (1909, pp. 3–4) describes the bridge as a symbol of the expansion of our will over the space. He argues that only the human beings can connect and divide. The action of connecting is always the condition of the action of dividing and vice versa. "Immediately and symbolically, bodily and spiritually, in every moment we are who divide what is connected and connect what is divided."

The writer and 1961 Nobel Prize in Literature winner Ivo Andrić writes:

> Of all the things created and built by humankind as a part of life's effort, nothing in my mind is better or worthier than bridges. They are more important than houses, more sacred, and more universal

> than temples. They belong to all and treat all alike; they are useful, always built for a purpose, at a spot where most human needs entwine; they are more durable than other buildings and serve no secret or evil purpose … They are all essentially one, they are equally worthy of our attention, because they show the place where humankind encountered an obstacle and did not stop before it, but overcame and bridged it the way humankind could, according to understanding, taste, and circumstances … Thus, everywhere in the world, wherever my thoughts wander or stop, they encounter faithful and silent bridges like an eternal and ever insatiable human desire, to connect, to reconcile, and to join everything that challenges our spirit, eyes and feet, to stop division, contradiction, or parting … Finally, everything that this life reveals itself by—thoughts, efforts, looks, smiles, words, sighs—they all sway toward the other shore, to which they are directed, as if toward a target, and once reaching it, they gain their true meaning. They all have to overcome and bridge something—disorder, death, or the lack of meaning. For everything is a transition, a bridge whose ends fade away into the infinity and toward which all earthly bridges are nothing but mere playthings, pale symbols. And all our hopes are on the other side. (1963, pp. 156–157)

For me, the paragraphs quoted are the written equivalent of a set of dream images, and the words themselves force me to listen as they take shape in my mind's ear, and then conjure up, create the images they demand in my mind's eye. First I encounter Renzo Piano, and the idea that to be an architect is to be contaminated, then to be a frontiersman, then to avoid borders, then to muddle, disinterested in similarities, focused on differences. I meet Serres, who tells me that bridges mend what is torn, followed by Simmel who informs me that human beings bodily and spiritually divide what is connected and connect what is divided. Finally I meet Andrić, and the idea that bridges are sacred, that when they are encountered they have an eternal and insatiable quality akin to desire, and that smiles, and words, and sighs must bridge disorder, death, and lack of meaning.

Of course, I can try to force myself to reconfigure and interpret these words as part of a coherent whole, but I find myself flooded with visual images, as I experience Schinaia inviting me into his dream experience. First, I see a contaminated man, alone on a frontier, muddling, focused on differences and avoiding borders. While a more literal translation of the text might suggest that the architect embraces similarities, I have conjured up in my imagination an image of a frightened person, dirty, foul, poisoned, avoiding confrontations with authorities that demand compliance with artificially constructed boundaries. Then, the idea of healing what is damaged comes before me, not in a bodily form, but as an idea, a possibility, an affective experience. Then that state of mind takes on a bodily dimension, and I imagine a person who has the capacity to divide and connect. I feel hopeful that someone, maybe another architect, will reach out to the frontiersman and embrace him, welcome him. This is followed by a notion of the insatiable sacred, a benevolent force of nature that will counter death, disorder, and meaninglessness. Then, in the spirit of self-analysis about which I have been writing and thinking for decades (Sonnenberg, 1990, 1991, 1993a, 1993b, 1995, 2005) I associate to these images and affects, and come up with an idea.

I believe Schinaia, in choosing to overwhelm me with a series of loosely connected descriptions of images, has conveyed a very respectful view of the heroic role of the architect: to bring order and equilibrium to a world in which manmade structures threaten to destroy the advantages offered us by our natural world. When I find myself arriving at that point, this book makes a lot of sense to me. Had Schinaia simply insisted on the noble mission of architecture I might have dismissed his assertion. Writing the way he has, encouraging me to share a dream-like state of reverie with him, the mission of the architect becomes a shared co-construction between author and reader. I can own it; I do not feel lectured into submission.

Now let's look at Schinaia's final Chapter Thirteen—Some concluding notes on a possible partnership between architects and psychoanalysts. Here, Schinaia more directly uses words to invite me to share his dream, as his written words come alive as auditory images in their own right, as words similar to the spoken ones I hear when I dream. He quotes Agostino Racalbuto (2005, p. 288): "Writing deceives … we have the possibility to give something essentially erratic a home … The words of cure and the cure of words." We heard in the introduction from Laurent Beaudouin (2007, p. 8): "The words of architecture do not explain everything: they translate some images that maintain something inexpressible … they are travel companions that can lead us through the dark side of soul." Then Schinaia embraces Thomas Ogden (2013, p. 630), who says: "I view psychoanalysis and literature as holding in common a profound love and respect for language as a vehicle not simply for the expression of thoughts and feelings, but, more importantly, a medium for the creation of thoughts and feelings…" Finally, Schinaia turns to Franco La Cecla (2008, p. 13), who says:

> Writing is the most honest form of expression of the thoughts about the city and the space. This is because writing does not reduce the complexity of the present and does not want to invent or completely understand it. Writing goes with and caresses the houses and the people inhabiting them and describes the process through which houses and people confuse [one] with another.

Schinaia has bombarded me with extremely complicated words, as he shares with me manifest content that defies my efforts to literally and easily understand what I have just encountered. My experience, then, begs first for reverie, and later for self-reflection and interpretation. What gradually emerges as I contemplate is that if I am insensitive to them, words can confuse me, and if I casually dismiss them, they can deceive me because I will not respect and embrace their power to create in me meaningful thoughts and feelings. But, I realise, if I embrace words thoughtfully and respectfully they have the power to caress me, reassure me, and translate for me otherwise inexpressible images of the relationship of the inanimate and the human. And it is then that I think about the relationship of words (the tool of the psychoanalyst) and design (the tool of the architect): together, better than either alone, these disciplines can lead us through the dark side of our souls and heal us. And we must appreciate that potential synergy, and foster it.

Once again I am struck by the way Schinaia has engaged with me in deriving a critical dream-based co-constructed lesson from his book: psychoanalysts and architects have much more of a common professional foundation and heritage than might be initially appreciated. While one seems to think more in words and the other more in images, while the analyst writes and the architect draws, upon closer inspection their ways of creating overlap.

It seems fitting then, to close this appreciative commentary on Schinaia's book with the observation that the author's wish for a closer collaboration between these two fields, for the benefit of humankind, will be facilitated by those who have the experience of reading his book. And it is further in that spirit that I share what I have learned from colleagues at the University of Texas at Austin School of Architecture, about the architect Louis Kahn, who is sometimes referred to as the "brick whisperer". Supposedly, Kahn would tell students:

> If you are ever stuck for inspiration, ask your materials for advice … You say to a brick, "What do you want, brick?" And brick says to you, "I like an arch." And you say to brick, "Look, I want one, too, but arches are expensive and I can use a concrete lintel." And then you say: "What do you think of that, brick?" Brick says: "I like an arch."[2] (27 June 2015)

So, you see, Schinaia is in good company when he gently teaches us that a fuller appreciation of the relationship of architecture and psychoanalysis is consistent with his view of their potential for closer collaboration. We come away from this book understanding that Schinaia's idea about collaboration is based on an accurate appreciation of the synergy between words and the material elements of the built environment, and the fundamental similarity between those who use words and those who draw images.

Stephen M. Sonnenberg
Psychoanalyst and Adjunct Professor, School of Architecture, University of Texas at Austin

NOTES

Preface to the Italian edition

1. As pointed out by the architect Giordano Tironi in a lecture titled *D'où viennent les idées et que deviennent-elles* (From where ideas come and what they become) that took place at the Haute Ecole de Paysage, d'Ingénierie et d'Architecture of Geneva, 19 March, 2013, the architect's slate cannot be blank any more because our contemporary culture has already put a lot of images and signs upon it.

Introduction

1. Later in the seminar Bion appeared to soften his stance: "You may not have decided what sort of artist to be, but as you see what you are fairly good at, you may have to 'make the best out of a bad job', as we say, and decide to find out what you can do with what you have in your atelier." (p. 198)
2. The process of analogy permits the importing of qualities from one system into another.

3. These theories can be traced back to Alberti's *De Re Aedificatoria* (circa 1452).
4. Writers, poets, and, of course, psychoanalysts.

Chapter One

1. The journalist Sergio Zavoli (2011, p. 253) writes: "Ithaca is everywhere and every day. It is the journey itself, what is known and what is wished for: it lies just before and just after what you cross. From time to time, Ithaca is the reason for the journey and its soul, an escape and a haven: it is the reason why it's always worthwhile to leave again, whether with the wind or against it, led by something waiting for you inevitably."
2. I think that this is a risk we must run during the process of structuring a new identity.

Chapter Two

1. In other words, Lacan refers to a hidden reality aiming at containing nothing.
2. Of course, this can be done only by respecting and paying attention to the frameworks and the "realities" at the basis of these points of view.
3. Santiago Calatrava is the most important architect specialising in bridges. In his work he continually tries to connect structure and movement and to create a unique synthesis that can make the forms surprising and graceful. Calatrava conceives the architectural project not as a combination of static spaces, but as a sort of well-structured organism composed of different and interacting flow lines. His poetry of movement consists of the incorporation of social and cultural aspects. Calatrava is able to move through art, engineering, and architecture. Thus he goes beyond the various fields of knowledge. "Calatrava invites us into a dream, in a sort of Buñuelian atmosphere. He introduces us to structures free from the yoke of statics in favour of a movement directed towards the generation of other possible worlds." (Lefaivre & Tzonis, 2009, p. 25)
4. He argues that much of architecture's critical literature and the decodification of architectural figurations is full of these analogies and metaphors.

Chapter Three

1. Chianese and Fontana (2010, p. 12) comment on this point: "The image grafts inorganic forms to the inorganic, death to death … Beneath the surface, the image has depth and profundity. The image opens the space, what can be depicted produces objects and spaces."
2. Freud's quotation continues (1937b, p. 260): "It is not, however, a preliminary labour in the sense that the whole thing must be completed before the next piece of work can be begun, as, for instance, is the case with house building, where all the walls must be erected and all the windows inserted before the internal decoration of the rooms can be taken in hand. Every analyst knows that things happen differently in an analytic treatment and that both kinds of work are carried on side by side, the one kind being always a little ahead and the other following upon it."
3. "There are some aspects of the theory that assume the conclusive form of a probable account. A clear example is the story, a just-so story, of the primitive horde told in *Totem and Taboo* (Freud, 1912–1913). Such a story is a genuine myth of the origins built up arbitrarily on the basis of different sources of material. In *Totem and Taboo*, fantasy and storytelling are the crucial ingredients of Freud's theoretical construct." (Petrella, 1988, p. 102)
4. In other words, Freud here admits to having deliberately added parts to what appeared incomplete to him.
5. Probably, Freud here refers to Lucano. In a famous passage from a 1896 conference he made the comparison (outlined in his *Studies on Hysteria*, 1895) between his analytic work with his patients and the archaeologist's work, that is to say, his "procedure … of clearing away the pathogenic psychical material layer by layer [and] … the technique of excavating a buried city".
6. It is worth noting that the physicist Albert Einstein, a member of the Goethe Prize committee, was against awarding Freud the prize. He justified his opinion by arguing that the father of psychoanalysis was actually a psychologist and not a writer.

Chapter Four

1. In his work, Freud uses the term "topic" (whose meaning "theory of places" has been used in philosophical language since time immemorial). According to ancient philosophers (in particular Aristotle), places

can be conceived as arguments with logical and rhetorical features and as premises of argumentation. It is worth noting that the term topic can be found also in the philosopher Immanuel Kant's *Critique of Pure Reason* (1781, p. 269). According to him, the transcendental topic is "for determining that place for all concepts … (it should permit to assess) to which cognitive ability every concept properly pertains to".

Chapter Five

1. The expression "International style" comes from Walter Gropius' 1925 book *International Architecture*. The architectural historian Henry-Russell Hitchcock and the architect Philip Johnson used it as a title for the catalogue of a modernist exhibition in New York (1932). In the catalogue the authors did not mention Frank Lloyd Wright or Adolf Loos. In fact, although they must be considered modernists, they expressed different positions from those of Le Corbusier, Gropius, and van der Rohe. Further, it is worth noting that the architectonical and existential views of Lloyd Wright and Loos were quite different. "Loos embraced modernity's physical and intellectual restlessness, enthusiastically participating in a broad swathe of urban activities, including those of the demi-monde. For him, the new was natural and normal. Wright believed modernity to be socially and psychologically destructive, precisely because of its restlessness—lack of rootedness, he might have said—rejecting the city as a place to live for himself and for his clients. For him, modernity was unnatural and abnormal." (Twombly, 2005, p. 205) According to the architect Joseph Hudnut (1940, quoted in Stipe, 2004, p. 58), "[International style's] buildings and its modernity's claims do not exist in a modern world, in our time, and according to our lifestyle. They are not weaved together with industry and social experiments, but with the earth upon which they are based; sometimes it seems that the transcendental spirit living in prairies, hills, rivers, or trees inhabits them."
2. All these things are assessed as ugly, bad, or useless.
3. In this sense, the Spanish architect Rafael Moneo argues that his projects are based on the particular features of materials. He points out that the materials are the substance of architecture, that is to say, "the material substance of a building very much represents its conceptual meaning" (Moneo, in Casamonti, 2007, p. 24). This point of view contrasts with that of the American architect Peter Eisenman, who conceives a conceptual architecture not based on the particular features of materials.

Because of it, this architecture could find a meaning in the abstractness of a formal structure uninfluenced by external factors.

4. In other words, we can speak of politics of surveillance and visibility or of "universal transparency".
5. In Aristotle's *Physics* (II, 8, 199–215) we can find something similar: "Thus if a house, for example, had been a thing made by nature, it would have been made in the same way as it is now by art; and if things made by nature were made also by art, they would come to be in the same way as by nature." According to philosopher Silvana Borutti (2006, p. XXXIX): "[For Aristotle] the doing (*poiein*) of a human being building a house would be the same as the dung, if nature could give birth to houses: in fact, it is to show something through a skill, a fictional detour, a surplus of technique and imagination."
6. At least as this work was usually conceived in his time, with the copy as a substitute for the original.
7. For example, replacing a broken tile or a single stone.
8. Or, we can say, between the fetishists of sacred stone and the fanatics of innovation at all costs.
9. At a young age, the architect Louis Kahn writes (1950, quoted in Brownlee & De Long 1991, p. 50): "I firmly realise that the architecture of Italy will remain as the inspirational source of the works of the future. Those who don't see it that way ought to look again. Our stuff looks tiny compared to it and all the pure forms have been tried in all its variations. What is necessary is the interpretation of the architecture of Italy as it relates to our knowledge of building and needs … I see great personal value in reading one's own approaches to the creation of space modified by the buildings around as the points of departure."

   In Sebald's novel *Austerlitz* (2001b), the protagonist fiercely criticises the overall plan and the illogical internal regulation of the new Bibliotheque Nationale (National Library of France) as features that lead to excluding the reader or to seeing him as a possible enemy. In fact, he defines these features "as the official manifestation of the increasingly importunate urge to break with everything which still has some living connection to the past" (p. 286).
10. It must be said that probably Venturi continues and completes the work of renewing the link to the totality of our past that Louis Kahn proposed and started in his later works (Scully, 1966).
11. According to Aldo Rossi (1981) the Abbey of San Galgano in Tuscany (Italy) is perhaps the clearest example of architecture's return to nature, where abandonment is identifiable with hope.

12. Loos makes a neat distinction between outside (which must be "silent," non-interfering, unable to cause any modification of the environment because the home's external shape belongs to the public) and inside (which is characterised by a distributive and dimensional perspective and by abundance of materials) (Coppa, 2013). The philosopher and politician Massimo Cacciari calls Loos's method an "establishment of places" (2002, p. 40): "[The space] is not the pure, uniform, and equivalent extension of a technical project any more, but the game of a set of places. Every place is a collection of things, a bunch of events. A place is an 'abode' of things and a dwelling of the human being within them."
13. According to the writer Claudio Magris (1997), we should number churches and pubs among the disappeared or outdated places. Magris believes that they are the main places of every respectful human settlement thanks to their liberal character. In fact, when you enter a church or a pub, no one asks you where you come from or what your political views are.
14. It is interesting to note the resemblance between the title of Gregotti's 2010 book and that of Binswanger's (1956) book, *Tre Forme di Esistenza Mancata* (Three forms of failed existence).
15. Paul Valéry (1928) writes about his own writing style and stresses the importance of the "remains of the future", that is to say, those covert elements triggering unexpected paths.
16. The architect Filippo Juvara defines them as "thoughts of architecture".
17. "The apprehension of beauty implies the premonition of its destruction. In Bion's terms, the present object contains the shadow of the absent-but-present-as-persecutor object." (Meltzer, 1973, p. 322)

    The psychoanalyst Hanna Segal (1952, p. 404) argues that, in order to make a full aesthetic experience, both the beautiful and the ugly are necessary. The ugly can be defined as the expression of the bad object and of death instincts; beauty can be defined as the need for harmonious rhythms and unity (completeness, entirety, etc.) and thus as an expression of sexual or life instincts. "The achievement of the artist is in giving the fullest expression to the conflict and the union between those two [instincts]."

    Gaburri and De Simone (1982) argue that the emergence of beauty often corresponds to a harmonic reformulation of the relationships between internal objects. However, in spite of this, they warn against those cases in which "an aesthetically complete image has the function of a container of idealised and split parts" (pp. 132–133).

Chapter Six

1. Pier Paolo Pasolini introduced the idea of anthropological mutation in 1974, in articles published in the newspaper *Corriere della Sera* (re-published in 1977 in *Lettere Luterane*).
2. The cultural theorist and urbanist Paul Virilio (2005) argues that today we cannot make a clear distinction between natural and industrial (caused by technical progress) disasters. He argues: "The twenty-first century starts the era of integral accident on a planetary scale. For example, the 2004 tsunami has had a global dimension because many tourists were involved in it. The case of the US World Trade Center in 2001 had dramatic implications for the world economy. The media has had a crucial role in both these cases: it flooded the whole world with catastrophic images in real time. Unknown emotions have echoed throughout the world." (Virilio, 2005, p. 28)
3. For further criticisms of postmodernity, see also Eagle, 2003; Frie, 2004; Schinaia, 2005b.
4. "Was du erebt von deinen Vätern hast, erwirb es, um es zu besitzen", from *Faust*, part I, night. Freud quotes it in *Totem and Taboo* (1912–1913, p. 158), in *Introductory Lectures on Psycho-Analysis* (1916–1917, p. 355) and on the last page (p. 208) of *An Outline of Psycho-Analysis* (1940). The *Outline* is an unfinished work that Freud started writing during his exile in London.
5. I think of participants in the protests of 1968 and their slogan "Be realistic, demand the impossible!" or of hippy communes and their use of drugs.
6. The psychoanalyst Morris N. Eagle (2003) rebuts the positions of four contemporary authors (Stephen A. Mitchell, Owen Renik, Roy Schafer, and Donald P. Spence), influenced in different ways by postmodernism. He defines these positions as "new paradigms" and argues that they cannot be a basis for comprehending the analytic situation, the patient's mind, or the future development of psychoanalytic theory.

Chapter Seven

1. That is to say, in the era of the myth of speed (Virilio, 1984).
2. This is nothing but infamous obsolescence.
3. In his lecture on quickness (1988, p. 45) Calvino writes: "The motor age has forced speed on us as a measurable quantity, the records of which

are milestones in the history of the progress of both men and machines. But mental speed cannot be measured and does not allow comparisons or competitions; nor can it display its results in a historical perspective. Mental speed is valuable for its own sake, for the pleasure it gives to anyone who is sensitive to such a thing, and not for the practical use that can be made of it."

4. Free time is the only luxury good that, in terms of personal income, has strongly decreased since World War II. Further, many statistics show that this is more relevant in Italy than in other industrialised countries. This is probably due to inefficiencies in the Italian production system (Tarantelli, 2013).
5. However, it must be said that, because of the global economic crisis, retirement has become more difficult.
6. I want to stress the many similarities between the things listed here and the futuristic illusion born under fascism.
7. The aberration of fast food also concerns baby food. "All baby foods, from chamomile tea to semolina soup, are instantaneous. This means that they do not require a preparation time that allows the forming of a dream state that can permit, as Ferenczi pointed out, step-by-step access to reality." (Goretti, 2002, p. 48)
8. Street food is food that can be bought at temporary stands and stalls close to open-air markets. Generally, it is cheap but well-cooked ethnic food. In this case the good quality of this non-globalised food is connected with an uncomfortable way of eating it (for example, by standing or by sitting on a park bench, by using fingers or plastic cutlery).
9. Giorgio Agamben (1977) reminds us that thirteenth-century European poets assumed the *stanza* (room) ("capacious dwelling" or "receptacle") as the essential nucleus of their poetry.
10. In his lecture on "lightness", Italo Calvino (1988, p. 12) makes a comparison between "the sudden agile leap of [the person] who raises himself above the weight of the world, showing that with all his gravity he has the secret of lightness, and that what many consider to be the vitality of the times (noisy, aggressive, revving, and roaring) belongs to the realm of death, like a cemetery for rusty old cars."
11. It seems that in China (where rapid economic growth is a matter of fact) clients are becoming increasingly impatient and are forcing architects to quickly produce projects and buildings. For this reason, two famous Chinese architects, Lyndon Neri and Rossana Hu, have

proposed a "manifesto for slowness", for a new Chinese cultural revolution to recapture time for understanding, thinking, projecting, and proposing.

12. "In order to obtain a *dérive*, let's take a walk without any destination or timetable. Let's choose the route little by little, not on the basis of what you know but on what you see around you. You must be a stranger and see everything as if for the first time. A way to foster this state of mind is to march in time and to direct your gaze slightly upwards: this allows your field of vision to focus on the architecture and puts the street in the background. You must perceive the space as something unitary and unique and be provoked by the details." (Debord, 1956, p. 103).
13. André Green (1975) speaks of *le temps mort de l'analyse* (the dead time of analysis). I prefer to speak of "the living time of analysis".
14. That is to say, not reducible or restrictable in any way.
15. In the case of mechanisation, the analyst's intervention is limited to the elimination of those hindrances that can slow down or even block the evolution of the analytic session (conceived as a machine).

Chapter Eight

1. Freud starts to write this brief essay in 1911 but then he stops. There is no trace of his reflections or of his correspondence during this period. At the end of the First World War, Freud is writing one of his masterpieces, *Beyond the Pleasure Principle*, which he interrupts to return to *The "Uncanny"* and publishes it in the journal *Imago*. It is worth noting that in 1922 Freud discusses the issue of the "disturbing double" in a letter to the writer Arthur Schnitzler, in which he expresses his admiration (Freud, 1922, pp. 282–283).
2. Heidegger (1966) uses the German expression *das Unheimliche* to translate the Greek term *deinon* from the first chorus of Sophocles's *Antigone*.
3. Silvana Borutti (2006, p. 151) believes that the *Unheimliche* is actually a genuine ontological condition of disorientation. This is because it indicates both an origin (*Heimat*) and its denial (*Un-*). She conceives it in terms of "non-experience of μετάβασις (metábasis) or of passage to something unpronounceable: it is the experience of looking into an abyss, of an *Ab-grund*, of a radical lack. It is an unclear experience that can be expressed only by paradoxes and oxymorons."

4. The Romanian sculptor Constantin Brâncuşi argues that "what is real is not the external form, but the essence of things" (Stoullig, 1995, p. 5).

Chapter Nine

1. At the beginning of September 1904 Sigmund Freud and his younger brother Alexander visited Athens and went to the Acropolis in order to see the ruins of the temples and the ancient sculptures. Freud wrote about this visit many years later in *A Disturbance of Memory on the Acropolis* (1936b, p. 2). "When, finally, on the afternoon after our arrival, I stood on the Acropolis and cast my eyes around upon the landscape, a surprising thought suddenly entered my mind: so all this really does exist, just as we learnt at school!" Freud thought the feeling of disorientation he felt over the Acropolis was probably due to his feeling of guilt for having succeeded more than his father. His father was only a businessman and not a scholar and had never travelled outside Central Europe.
2. Libeskind (quoted in Terragni, 2013, p. 22) argues: "In a moment music can set the mood. The important buildings do the same, that is to say, they induce certain emotions in the exact moment you enter into them. As well as a song, the space has a structure, a voice, a tone."
3. The American psychoanalyst Stephen Sonnenberg (2012, p. 120) describes his personal experience of visiting this museum with the following words: "In the here and now and the past simultaneously, again experiencing a merging of inner space and outer physical space, again realising that I was interacting in both passive and active ways with the space I saw, entered, and experienced with all my various senses."
4. In Calvino's work, architecture is a means through which man can paint the world and give a form and a shape to the space in which he lives. In many of his texts the space described is characterised by verticality. Calvino thinks of verticality as a (probably utopian) architectural ideal, along with other qualities such as lightness, geometry, symmetry, and also an idea of multifaceted and various crystal structures. He contrasts verticality with horizontality, which produces disorientation and confusion. It is easy to get lost in a horizontal city: this kind of city is chaotic and denies the concept of city itself. It is a matter of fact that Calvino's architectural descriptions and visions are characterised

by vividness and visibility. However, the literary critic Ulla Musarra Schrøder (2012) argues that, although it is true that these descriptions and visions are based upon sight, the possibility of imagining them is actually based on synesthesia or on the contaminations of all five senses.

5. This is what Musatti said during his lessons at the SPI (Italian Psychoanalytic Society). In my personal opinion, Musatti has probably been inspired here by Plutarch of Chaeronea's famous aphorism: "Nature has given us two ears, two eyes, and but one tongue—to the end that we should hear and see more than we speak." (c. 100 AD, p. 396)

Chapter Ten

1. This is the beginning of the elegiac Latin couplet Ludovico Ariosto put on the door of his house in 1525, when he transferred from the Garfagnana (where he served as governor) to the city of Ferrara in which he settled permanently: *Parva, sed apta mihi, sed nulli obnoxia, sed non sordida: parta meo sed tamen aere domus*. It may be translated as: Small is my humble roof, but well designed/To suit the temper of the master's mind;/Hurtful to none, it boasts a decent pride,/That my poor purse the modest cost supplied.
2. An amazing image of a petite bourgeoisie modern house in Paris can be found in Georges Perec's *Life: A User's Manual* (1978). The author describes a Parisian building whose facade has been removed so that all rooms of the anterior part, from the ground floor to the attic, are immediately and simultaneously visible. All the rooms are connected like pieces of a jigsaw puzzle. It is the same for the lives of the apartments' inhabitants. Thus, these lives can be seen as an amazing concatenation and cross-section of existences and experiences.
3. The Glass House was built in 1949 in New Canaan, Connecticut. The rectangular one-room house has a single floor and is 56 feet (17 metres) long and 32 feet (9.8 metres) wide. It is a sort of steel and glass cage sitting on a brick base. Every facade has a biaxial symmetry and its opposite sides are identical. Inside, the space is subdivided asymmetrically into areas of different heights and a cylindrical bathroom. The bathroom is made with the same bricks as the basement from where it seems to come and can be considered the centre of the house, a sort of anchor point.

4. Philip Johnson (1979, p. 73) quotes Gaston Bachelard when he writes, "the simpler the image, the greater the dream".
5. The construction has both an entrance and an exit.
6. The name of this object comes from the mathematician and astronomer August Ferdinand Möbius (1790–1868). In an 1858 treatise on polyhedrons, he introduced a geometric figure consisting of an extended surface rotated 180 degrees with only one side and one border.
7. The theory of the trauma of birth (Rank, 1924) is the main cause of the end of the relationship between the psychoanalyst Otto Rank and Sigmund Freud. Rank considers birth as the first experience and the paradigm of anxiety, in particular, of separation anxiety. Conversely, Freud argues that the trauma of birth is biological and not psychological and that we do not know anything about the foetus's mental state and how it perceives pain. At birth, no object exists, thus no object can be lost. The psychoanalysts Melanie Klein, Donald Winnicott, and Eugenio Gaddini, and the results of studies on infant observation, seem to find an intermediate position between Rank and Freud by stressing the biological character of the primary emotional experiences and their differences with the adult experience of anxiety. In this sense, this intermediate position avoids the adultomorphic fallacy. Winnicott (1958) proposes three kinds of birth experience. The first is theorised but not empirically demonstrated and is a kind of normal and healthy experience. It is a good and positive experience but very limited and uncommon. In this case, the experience of birth is one of the factors promoting the person's self-confidence, his sense of continuity, his stability, his security, etc. The second is the common traumatic experience that can be associated with and thus strengthened by other environmental traumatic factors. The third is the most extreme traumatic experience that cannot be repaired by subsequent care.
8. That he probably thinks to be irreparable for a while.
9. The psychoanalyst Jean Laplanche (2002) argues that the asymmetry between adult and baby is one of the main elements of the "founding situation of human identity" (according to him, the fundamental anthropological situation).
10. I believe these experiences are quite perverse because they avoid contact with an outside world experienced as bad and dangerous.
11. It is worth noting that, in spite of the many revisions to his work and to his approach, he always has a privileged outlook on the intra-psychic and internal world.

12. I believe that here it is crucial to avoid loose analogies and similarities between psychoanalysis and architecture.

Chapter Eleven

1. Aristotle defined sight as the most important of the human senses since he considered it the best possible approximation of mental activities.
2. The psychoanalyst Glauco Carloni argues that the term "tact" can metaphorically be intended as: "the art of dealing with the others. It is an art made of perspicacity, rapidity, convenience, prudence, politeness, and moderation. It requires intelligence and flexibility, invention and adaptability in order to understand and solve every new problem … As we touch […] so we observe, feel, and study the others' dispositions that are always dependent on the individual vulnerability with something we can call 'mental touch' [that always makes use of all senses and also of that 'sixth sense' known as empathy]. The fact that touch is especially sensitive in the hands explains the origin of the use of certain words at both figurative and concrete levels. In particular, I refer to those words like handling, handy, or handful." (1984, pp. 196–197)
3. By referring to the texts of Merleau-Ponty, Sartre, and Lévinas, the philosopher and psychoanalyst Luce Irigaray (2011) notes that, in spite of the fact that touch is part of all our existential relationships, the prevalent sense in our culture is sight. She argues that we "look at" and we do it by following a logic of possession rather than contemplation. She supports a new form of relation with knowledge in which touch is fundamental in constituting our individuation and our relationships with the others.
4. "It is worth noting that in the second half of his life, especially in his *Poème de l'angle droit* (poem of the right angle), by drawing a hand mediating between nature and humanity, Le Corbusier … emphasises the synthesis, the reconciliation of the mind that can recognise the deep order of the world thanks to touch and sight. In this sense, the sense of touch and the hand stop having a mere subordinate role and become the privileged mediating element." (Calatrava, 2007, p. 182)
5. I want to quote here part of the technical report for the new project of Genoa's psychiatric hospital in 1878: "The main conditions that a psychiatric hospital must satisfy are the following ones: excellent position and location, that is to say, the future building should be construed in open country, on very high ground, in an area without any fog, with

excellent air, with an open and wide horizon in order to benefit from the pure air and from the lively rays of sunshine, sufficiently defended from the cold and violent winds and so near to a town that it could benefit from all possible advantages and not be affected by any disadvantages. In terms of the disposition and distribution of the building, it must be organised in scattered districts or distinct groups of buildings separated one from another by wide and suitable courtyards or gardens; each building must consist of only two floors (one of which must be the ground floor) in order to respect the prescribed norms of hygiene according to which maximum fresh air must be guaranteed in all areas of the building. This is in order to accommodate the smallest number of people in the same space and to avoid contagious diseases" (Timosci, 1878, p. 485).

6. The architect Paolo Portoghesi (1990) uses sociologist Alberto Abruzzese's definition of "square" as the place in which people exchange looks and thus can memorise the presence of others. In other words, it is a place in which a simple snapshot can become a perfect image.
7. The square is probably one of the most typical architectural elements of a mental institution. In general it consists of a wide courtyard placed opposite the ward's main entrance. You can enter the square from the living room. For this reason, when the weather is fine, the square is considered to be the obvious continuation of the living room. Rather, during housekeeping, patients seem to be alternatively obliged to pass from the living room to the square. In general, it is a very wide space in which you can find trees, flowerbeds, benches, tables, and foul-smelling open-air toilets. Very high metal fencing surrounds it and prevents direct communication with the street. In this sense, an external observer may think of a zoo. One of the attending male nurses is in the square. He is in a strategic position allowing him to constantly control the patients (Schinaia, 1997a). All is the opposite of what happens in a monastery. "Don't stare at someone else. According to this rule, we must avoid making anyone else aware of talking, asking, communicating, questioning, assessing, criticising, disapproving, or supporting words or looks. This is an implicit rule that you very soon learn to respect in a monastery. A monk sees without looking." (Boatti, 2012, pp. 24–25)
8. The term *interstice* comes from the Latin *interstitium* and means "to stay between", in other words, to be located, to be in an undefined

situation, a situation that is an anomic for certain aspects or, at least, that does not follow a set of formal rules of order and organisation. Cianconi (2013, p. 2) says: "The interstice is not necessarily a defined place, is not necessarily stable over time, it is not necessarily functional, it is not necessarily on balance."

9. The philosopher Demetrio (2005, p. 214) writes: "Without any ritual or smell of incense, meditation begins every time we pass from practical problems connected to our physical survival, to the solution of a question about the status of our place in the flow of time. Of course, this flow of time cannot return but has always a beginning and an end."
10. Every monk takes sits in his standing seat and leans his elbows on the lateral arms of the seat.
11. Cloisters differ from monasteries: the former are poorer and smaller than the latter; they have no land tenure and are very close to the city walls (if not inside them) (Scaraffia, 2015).
12. We must remember that they are established by ancient treatises, by the *Regulae* (the rules).
13. The settlements of the Order of Preachers and the mendicant orders did not only consider places inhabited by monks and thus closed to other people (*clausurae*). Rather, these settlements provided a new concept of the spaces of the church as completely open to all believers (Marazzi, 2015).
14. The results of the research were presented at the congress "Colour for cure. Effects of colour and frail users" (*Il colore per la cura. Effetti del colore e utenza debole*) during the Eurocoat Expo in Genoa in November 2007. Contributing to this research project were head physician and psychiatrist Cosimo Schinaia and psychologists Giovanna Sommariva and Daniela Ratti of the Department of Mental Health at ASL 3, Genoa; professors Maria Benedetta Spadolini and Raffaella Fagnoni; psychologist Marilena Chirivì and architect Michele Lagomarsino of the Department of Architectural Science of the University of Genoa; Olga Bottaro, Paola Baldoni, Giampaolo Pasino, and architect Manuela Costa of the Boero research centre.

Chapter Twelve

1. In French it is *lit-monade*, which sounds like lemonade.
2. This position should lead to partial sensorial deprivation.
3. Personal communication.

4. *The Wolf-Man and Sigmund Freud* (Gardiner, 1972, p. 142) recalls how Freud described how the so-called psychoanalytic position was created: "Freud told me that he had originally sat at the opposite end of the couch so that the analyst could look at each other. One female patient, exploiting this situation, made all possible—or rather all impossible—attempts to seduce him. To rule out anything similar, once and for all, Freud moved from his earlier position to the opposite end of the couch." The psychoanalyst Andrea Sabbadini (2014) casts many doubts on the truthfulness of this statement, which comes from an unreliable source and has never been confirmed. Further, it seems at odds with the main function of the couch.
5. He is the son of the psychoanalyst Estela Welldon.
6. Between 1942 and 1946 Le Corbusier developed the so-called "Modulor", a system of measurement in which every single unit is mathematically linked to the proportions of the human body. He writes: "[The Modulor is] a range of harmonious measurements to suit the human scale, universally applicable to architecture and to mechanical things." The Modulor aims to establish a direct relationship between the proportions of buildings, objects, and living beings.
7. In her article Sperber refers to Loewald's concept of sublimation (Loewald, 1988). According to this concept, there is a link between a mature mental organisation of differentiated reality and an original experience of primary narcissistic unity. In his revision of the psychoanalytic concept of sublimation, Loewald argues that symbols always have a twofold meaning, referring to what is symbolised while maintaining the symbol's primary affective meaning.

Chapter Thirteen

1. Piano (2000) proposes building over what has been already built. He defines this planning operation as the patching of urban suburbs.
2. Of course, this can be done only as long as we are able to recognise an error and to look at it in a moralistic way.
3. This is a quotation from *Die beiden Gulden* by Friedrich Rückert, based on a makãmãt (sermon) of al-Hariri. Freud also quoted these verses in a letter to Fliess (1899).
4. This film is an adaptation of the Chilean writer Antonio Skármeta's (1986) novel *Ardiente Paciencia* (Ardent patience). In Latin-American

countries this novel is better known as *El Cartero de Neruda* (The postman of Neruda).

5. It is "when everyone equally takes part in the power management or, perhaps more precisely, when the power does not exist anymore because everyone is directly and equally involved in the decision-making".
6. In this sense, De Carlo refers to Le Corbusier and his proposal of achieving realistic utopias.
7. In my opinion, also the psychoanalysts.
8. "When we talk about a neighbourhood we have in mind a relatively small area that we can explore entirely by walking. A neighbourhood is populated by people we know, or about whom we know something, and, *mutatis mutandis*, these people know us or are aware of our existence … The neighbourhood is a grey area able to separate and link the space of anonymity and that of familiarity … It is the space of contrast, opposition, and reconciliation between 'I' and 'me'. It is the setting in which the dramas of self-identification and the search for recognition are played out." (Bauman, 2015, p. 45)

Concluding remarks

1. I think the way in which these buildings are perceived and felt is also important.

Afterword to the English edition

1. Elizabeth Danze has been my teacher and partner in a ten-year exploration of the relationship of architecture and psychoanalysis. She is an accomplished professor of architecture at the University of Texas at Austin, a superb designer, and has achieved a capacity for self-reflection that as a psychoanalyst I encounter rarely in colleagues within my own discipline.
2. Available at: www.theguardian.com/artanddesign/2013/feb/26/louis-kahn-brick-whisperer-architect.

REFERENCES

Adorno, T. W. (1951). *Minima Moralia: Reflections from Damaged Life*. E. F. N. Jephcott (Trans.). London: NLB, 1974.

Agamben, G. (1977). *Stanzas. Word and Phantasm in the Western Culture*. R. L. Martinez (Trans.). Minneapolis: University of Minnesota Press, 1993.

Agamben, G. (2008). *What is an Apparatus?* D. Kishik, & S. Pedatella (Trans.). Stanford: Stanford University Press, 2009.

Albano, L. (2014). *Il Divano di Freud*. Milan: Il Saggiatore.

Alberti, L. B. (1452). *On the Art of Building in Ten Books*. J. Rykwert, R. Tavernor, & N. Leach (Trans.). Washington: Library of the Congress, 1988.

Alexander, C. (1964). *Notes on the Synthesis of Form*. Harvard: Harvard University Press.

Alexander, C., Hirshen, S., Ishikawa, S., Coffin, C., & Angel, S. (1970). *Houses Generated by Patterns*. Berkeley, CA: Center for Environmental Structure.

Algini, M. L., & Lugones, M. (1999). Emigrare. *Quaderni di psicoterapia infantile. 40*: 5–13.

Amati Sas, S. (2010). Which unconscious for the transcultural? *EATGA-AEATG, Newsletter*, pp. 38–45, 2013.

Ambrosiano, L., & Gaburri, E. (2013). *Pensare con Freud*. Milan: Cortina.

Andrić, I. (1945). *The Bridge on the Drina*. L. F. Edwards (Trans.). Chicago: University of Chicago Press, 1977.

Andrić, I. (1963). Bridges. In: I. Andrić & R. Gorup (Eds.), *The Slave Girl and Other Stories* (pp. 69–91). Budapest: CEU Press.
Angel, V. T. (2000). Trans-subjectivity: the space where psychoanalysis and architecture meet. *International Forum of Psychoanalysis, 9*: 76–83.
Arendt, H. (1961). *Between Past and Future: Six Exercises in Political Thought.* New York: Viking.
Argentieri, S. (2013). Tramandare la psicoanalisi. In: S. Argentieri, S. Bolognini, A. Di Ciaccia, & L. Zoja (Eds.), *In Difesa della Psicoanalisi* (pp. 5–29). Turin: Einaudi.
Arieti, S. (1976). *Creativity: The Magic Synthesis.* New York: Basic.
Aristotle. *Physics.* R. Waterfield, & D. Bostock (Trans.). Oxford: Oxford University Press, 2008.
Assoun, P.-L. (1993). *Freud e le Scienze Sociali.* Rome: Borla, 1999.
Assunto, R. (1984). *La Città di Anfione e la Città di Prometeo. Idea e Poetiche della Città.* Milan: Jaka Book.
Augé, M. (1992). *Non-Places: An Introduction to Supermodernity.* J. Howe (Trans.). London: Verso, 1995.
Augé, M. (1994). *Il Senso degli Altri. Attualità dell'Antropologia.* Turin: Bollati Boringhieri, 2000.
Augé, M. (1997). *Disneyland e Altri Nonluoghi.* Turin: Bollati Boringhieri, 1999.
Augé, M. (2003). *Rovine e Macerie. Il Senso del Tempo.* Turin: Bollati Boringhieri, 2004.
Augé, M. (2006). Una scommessa sull'avvenire (Dialogo con Mimmo Pesare). *Quaderno di comunicazione, Fiducia/Sicurezza, 6*: 75–82.
Augustine (397 AD). *Confessions.* R. S. Pine-Coffin (Trans.). London: Penguin, 1961.
Azzurri, F. (1877). Intervento al II° Congresso della Società Freniatrica Italiana (Aversa). *Archivio Italiano per le Malattie Nervose e più particolarmente per le Alienazioni Mentali*, pp. 427–428.
Bachelard, G. (1958). *The Poetics of Space. The Classic Look at How We Experience Intimate Places.* J. R. Stilgoe (Trans.). Boston: Beacon Street, 1994.
Bacon, F. (1625). Of building. In: *Francis Bacon: The Major Works.* (pp. 427–430) Oxford: Oxford University Press, 2008.
Balint, M. (1959). Philobatism and ocnophilia. In: *Thrills and Regressions.* (pp. 14–37) London: Karnac, 1987.
Balsamo, M. (2014). Che cos'è il presente? Editoriale. *Psiche, 1*: 1–4.
Barale, F. (2001). Prefazione. In: C. Schinaia, *Pedofilia Pedofilie. La Psicoanalisi e il Mondo del Pedofilo* (pp. 13–20). Turin: Bollati Boringhieri.
Barale, F. (2003). Normale caos dell'amore: corpo, Edipo e sexualtheorie all'epoca della modernità liquida. *Psiche, 1*: 19–32.

Baranger, W., & Baranger, M. (1990). *La Situazione Psicoanalitica come Campo Bipersonale.* Milan: Cortina.

Barthes, R. (1977). Inauguration lecture of the Chair of Literary Semiology, Collège de France, January 7. *October,* Vol. 8. R. Howard (Trans.), pp. 3–16, 1979.

Basile, R. (2009). *Where the Words Stretch Out.* Rome-Milan: Cromografica.

Basile, R. (2012). Dan Welldon, 50 minutes. *Rivista di Psicoanalisi, LVIII,* 4: 914.

Bataille, G. (1929). Architecture, Dictionnaire Critique. P. Hegarty (Trans.). In: N. Leach (Ed.), *Rethinking Architecture* (pp. 21–22). London: Routledge, 1997.

Bataille, G. (1936). The sacred conspiracy. In: A. Stoekl (Ed.), *Vision of Excess. Selected Writings 1927–1939* (A. Stoekl, C. R. Loevitt, & D. M. Leslie, Jr., Trans.) (pp. 178–81). Minneapolis: University of Minnesota Press, 1985.

Bateson, G. (1972). *Steps to an Ecology of Mind.* Chicago: University of Chicago Press.

Baudelaire, C. (1869). The stranger. In: L. Varese (Trans.) *Paris Spleen* (p. 1). New York: New Directions, 1947.

Baudrillard, J. (1990). *The Transparency of Evil. Essays on Extreme Phenomena.* London: Verso, 1993.

Bauman, Z. (1993). *Alone Again. Ethics After Certainty.* London: Demos, 1994.

Bauman, Z. (2000). *Liquid Modernity.* Cambridge: Polity.

Bauman, Z. (2003). *Identity: Conversations with Benedetto Vecchi.* Cambridge: Polity.

Bauman, Z. (2015, September 18). Ci sentiamo tutti Napoleoni digitali. *La Repubblica.* Retrieved from http://ricerca.repubblica.it/repubblica/archivio/repubblica/2015/09/18/ci-sentiamo-tutti-napoleoni-digitali45.html [last accessed 3 February 2015].

Bauman, Z., & Mauro, E. (2015). *Babel.* Rome-Bari: Laterza.

Bauman, Z., & Tester, K. (2001). *Conversations with Zygmunt Bauman.* Cambridge: Polity.

Beaudouin, L. (2007). *Pour une Architecture Lente.* Montrouge: Quintette.

Benjamin, W. (1936). *The Work of Art in the Age of Mechanical Reproduction.* In: *Illuminations* (pp. 217–252). New York: Harcourt Brace.

Benjamin, W. (1972). *The Arcade Projects.* R. Tiedemann (Ed.). H. Eiland, & K. McLaughlin (Trans.). New York: Belknap, 2002.

Benjamin, W. (1986). *Parigi, Capitale del XIX Secolo. Progetti, Appunti e Materiali 1927–1940.* G. Agamben (Ed.). Turin: Einaudi.

Bentham, J. (1786). *The Panopticon Writings.* M. Bozovic (Ed.). London: Verso, 1995.

Berenstein, I. (1976). *Familia y Enfermedad Mental.* Buenos Aires: Païdos.

Bernardi, R. (2003). What kind of evidence makes the analyst change his or her theoretical and technical ideas? In: M. Leuzinger-Bohleber, A. U. Dreher, & J. Canestri (Eds.), *Pluralism and Unity? Methods of Research in Psychoanalysis* (pp. 125–36). London: International Psychoanalysis.

Berry, N. (1982). La maison passée, presente. *Nouvelle Revue de Psychanalyse, 26*: 179–194.

Bick, E. (1968). The experience of the skin in early object relations. *International Journal of Psychoanalysis, 49*(2–3): 484–486.

Binswanger, L. (1946). L'indirizzo antropoanalitico in psichiatria. In: *Il Caso Ellen West e Altri Saggi (1944–1946)* (pp. 17–51). Milan: Bompiani, 1973.

Binswanger, L. (1956). *Tre Forme di Esistenza Mancata. Esaltazione Fissata, Stramberia, Manierismo*. Milan: Garzanti, 1978.

Bion, W. R. (1959). Attacks on linking. In: *Second Thoughts: Selected Papers on Psychoanalysis* (pp. 93–109). London: Heinemann, 1967.

Bion, W. R. (1963). *Elements of Psycho-analysis*. London: Heinemann.

Bion, W. R. (1965). *Transformations*. London: Heinemann.

Bion, W. R. (1973). *Brazilian Lectures. 1973 São Paulo. 1974 Rio de Janeiro/São Paulo*. London: Karnac.

Bion, W. R. (1978). Visibilità attraverso una vetrata. Seminario di Bion a Parigi. In: S. Resnik, *Biografie dell'inconscio*. R. Clemenzi Ghisi & M. Dailati (Trans.) (pp. 176–199). Rome: Borla, 2007.

Bion, W. R. (1980). *Bion in New York and São Paulo*. F. Bion (Ed.). Strath Tay: Clunie.

Bion, W. R. (1985). *All My Sins Remembered. Another Part of a Life and the Other Side of Genius: Family Letters*. London: Karnac, 1991.

Bion, W. R. (1992). *Cogitations*. F. Bion (Ed.). London: Karnac.

Blanton, S. (1971). *Diary of My Analysis with Freud*. New York: Hawthorn.

Bleger, J. (1967). Psychoanalysis of the psychoanalytic frame. *International Journal of Psychoanalysis, 48*: 511–519.

Bloch, M. (1945). *The Historian's Craft: Reflections on the Nature and Uses of History and the Techniques and Methods of Those Who Write It*. P. Putnam (Trans.). Toronto: Alfred A. Knopf, 1954.

Boatti, G. (2012). *Sulle Strade del Silenzio. Viaggio per Monasteri d'Italia e Spaesati Dintorni*. Rome-Bari: Laterza.

Bodei, R. (2001). *Il Dottor Freud e i Nervi dell'Anima. Filosofia e Società a un Secolo dalla Nascita della Psicoanalisi. Conversazioni con Cecilia Albarella*. Rome: Donzelli.

Bodei, R. (2009). *La Vita delle Cose*. Rome-Bari: Laterza.

Boeri, S. (2004). Movimenti dello sguardo. In: U. Lucas (Ed.), *Storia d'Italia. Annali 20. L'Immagine Fotografica 1945–2000* (pp. 403–419). Turin: Einaudi.

Bollas, C. (2000). Architecture and the unconscious. *International Forum of Psychoanalysis, 9*: 28–42.

Bollas, C. (2013). *China on the Mind.* Hove: Routledge.

Bolognini, S. (2003). *Intervento nella giornata scientifica del training SPI,* Milan, May 31. *Notiziario Società Psicoanalitica Italiana,* 2: 72–73.

Bolognini, S. (2008). *Secret Passages. The Theory and Technique of Interpsychic Relationships.* G. Atkinson (Trans.). Hove: Routledge, 2011.

Bolognini, S. (2010). Passaggi segreti verso l'inconscio: stili e tecniche di esplorazione. *Rivista di Psicoanalisi, LVI,* 3: 599–613.

Boncinelli, E. (2000). *Le Forme della Vita. L'Evoluzione e l'Origine dell'Uomo.* Turin: Einaudi.

Bonfanti, E. (2001). *Nuovo e Moderno in Architettura.* Milan: Bruno Mondadori.

Borges, J. L. (1923). Unknown street. In: *Selected Poems. Vol. 2* (pp. 11–12). A. Coleman (Trans.). London: Penguin, 2000.

Borges, J. L. (1944). *Funes, His Memory.* In: *Fictions* (p. 91–99). A. Hurley (Trans.). London: Penguin, 2000.

Borges, J. L. (1969). In praise of darkness. In: *Selected Poems. Vol. 2* (p. 299). A. Coleman (Trans.). London: Penguin, 2000.

Borges, J. L. (1970). The end of the duel. In: *Dr. Brodie's Report* (pp. 45–50). N. T. di Giovanni (Trans.). New York: Bantam, 1973.

Borutti, S. (2006). *Filosofia dei Sensi. Estetica del Pensiero tra Filosofia, Arte e Letteratura.* Milan: Cortina.

Botta, M. (2013, March 29). Archistar io? Andiamoci piano con gli insulti. Interview with M. Romani. *Il Venerdì di Repubblica* (pp. 88–91).

Botta, M., & Crepet, P. (2007). *Dove Abitano le Emozioni. La Felicità e i Luoghi in cui Viviamo.* Turin: Einaudi.

Braghieri, N. (2005). *Buoni Edifici, Meravigliose Rovine. Louis J. Kahn e il Mestiere dell'architettura.* Milan: Feltrinelli.

Braghieri, N. (2013). *Architettura, Arte Retorica.* Genoa: Sagep.

Brownlee, D. B., & De Long, D. G. (Eds.) (1991). *Louis I. Khan: In the Realm of Architecture.* New York: Universe.

Bruno, G. (2002). *Atlas of Emotion: Journeys in Art, Architecture, and Film.* London: Verso.

Bruno, G. (2007). *Public Intimacy: Architecture and the Visual Arts.* Boston: MIT.

Bruzzone, M. (2007). *Frank Gehry. Architetture, Testimonianze.* Milan: Feltrinelli.

Cacciari, M. (2002). *Adolf Loos e il Suo Angelo.* Milan: Electa.

Calatrava, J. (2007). Le Corbusier e Le poème de l'angle droit: un poema abitabile, una casa poetica. In: *Le Corbusier, Le poème de l'angle droit.* (pp. 166–185) Milan: Mondadori Electa.

Calvino, I. (1972). *The Invisible Cities*. W. Weaver (Trans.). Orlando, FL: Harcourt, 1974.

Calvino, I. (1983a). Accanto a una mostra. *FMR, 15*: 44–51.

Calvino, I. (1983b). Il guanciale. *FMR, 13*: 44.

Calvino, I. (1983c). *Mr Palomar*. W. Weaver (Trans.). Orlando, FL: Harcourt, 1985.

Calvino, I. (1988). *Six Memos for the Next Millennium*. Cambridge, MA: Harvard University Press.

Capozzi, P. (2003). Ermeneutica e psicoanalisi. In: M. Bezoari & F. Palombi (Eds.), *Epistemologia e Psicoanalisi: Attualità di un Confronto* (pp. 85–106). Milan: Centro di Psicoanalisi Cesare Musatti.

Capuano, M. (2006). Introduzione. In: M. Capuano (Ed.), *Architettonicamente. Contaminazioni tra Architettura e Psicoanalisi* (special issue of *Architetture Pisane*) *5*: 9–12.

Capuano, M. (2010). Psicoanalisi e architettura. Una visione d'insieme sul Darwinismo architettonico. Retrieved from www.spiweb.it/index.php?option=com_content&view=article&id=1226:psicoanalisi-e-architettura-una-visione-dinsieme-su-darwinismo-architettonico&catid=322&Itemid=614 [last accessed 20 August 2015].

Careri, F. (2002). *Walkscapes. Walking as an Aesthetic Practice*. Barcelona: Gustavo Gili.

Carloni, G. (1984). Tatto, contatto e tattica. *Rivista di Psicoanalisi, XXX*(2): 191–205.

Carotenuto, A. (1995). Il colore delle emozioni. In: *I Colori della Vita. Atti del Convegno internazionale. Torino, 27–28 Agosto 1995 Promosso da Fiat* (pp. 71–84). Turin: La Stampa.

Casamonti, M. (2007). *Rafael Moneo. L'Architettura. I Protagonisti*. Rome: L'Espresso.

Casement, P. (1985). *On Learning from the Patient*. Hove: Routledge.

Casement, P. (1990). *Further Learning from the Patient: The Analytic Space and Process*. Hove: Routledge.

Castoriadis, C. (1989). Logique, imagination, réflexion. In: R. Dorey (Ed.), *L'Incoscient et la Science* (pp. 9–36). Paris: Dunod, 1991.

Celant, G. (2013a). *Frank O. Gehry. L'Architettura. I Protagonisti*. Rome: L'Espresso.

Celant, G. (2013b). *Rem Koolhaas. Oma Amo. L'Architettura. I Protagonisti*. Rome: L'Espresso.

Cesarani, R. (1998). Forme del postmoderno. *Psiche, VI*(1): 19–25.

Cesarani, R. (2001). Freud di fronte all'individuo postmoderno. In: F. Borrelli (Ed.), *Pensare l'Inconscio. La Rivoluzione Psicoanalitica tra Ermeneutica e Scienza* (pp. 177–181). Rome: Manifestolibri.

Char, R. (1946). *Leaves of Hypnos*. C. Corman (Trans.). New York: Grossman, 1973.

Chasseguet-Smirgel, J. (1975). *The Ego Ideal: A Psychoanalytic Essay on the Malady of the Ideal*. P. Barrows (Trans.). New York: Norton, 1985.

Chianese, D. (2005). L'infelicità nella civiltà. *Psiche, 2*: 11–17.

Chianese, D. (2015). *Come le Pietre e gli Alberi. Psicoanalisi ed Estetica del Vivere*. Rome: Alpes.

Chianese, D., & Fontana, A. (2010). *Immaginando*. Milan: Franco Angeli.

Chodorow, N. (1995). Multiplicities and uncertainties of gender: commentary on Ruth Stein's "Analysis of a case of transsexualism". *Psychoanalytic Dialogues, 5*: 291–299.

Choisy, M. (1973). Memories of my visits with Freud. In: H. M. Ruitenbeek (Ed.), *Freud as We Knew Him* (pp. 291–295). Detroit: State University Press.

Cianconi, P. (2013). Teoria dell'interstizio e psicopatologia. *Psichiatri Oggi, XV*(4): 1–3.

Claude, R. (1944). Auguste Perret et la demeure. *Formes et Couleurs, 4*: 26.

Coppa, A. (2013). *Adolf Loos. L'architettura. I protagonisti*. Rome: L'Espresso.

Correale, A. (2003). Percorsi pubblici dell'interiorità: psicoanalisi e istituzioni psichiatriche. *Rivista di Psicoanalisi, XLIX*(2): 341–352.

Curi, U. (2010). *Straniero*. Milan: Cortina.

da Costa Meyer, E. (2012). The city within. In: E. A. Danze & S. Sonnenberg (Eds.), *Center 17: Space & Psyche* (pp. 89–107). Austin, TX: University of Texas.

Danze, E. A. (2005). An architect's view of introspective space: the analytic vessel. *Annals of Psychoanalysis, 33*: 109–124.

Danze, E. A., & Sonnenberg, S. (2012). Commentary on Adele Tutter's "Design as dream and self-representation: Philip Johnson and the Glass House of Atreus". *Journal of the American Psychoanalytic Association, 60*(3): 533–549.

De Carlo, G. (1966). Urbanistica e architettura sono la medesima cosa. Lettera inedita a Giorgio Pecorini. Retrieved from www.laconfederazioneitaliana.it [last accessed 12 July 2015].

De Carlo, G. (1972). *An Architecture of Participation*. Melbourne: Royal Australian Institute of Architects.

De Certeau, M. (1987). *Storia e psicoanalisi. Tra scienza e finzione*. Turin: Bollati Boringhieri, 2006.

de Kerckhove, D. (1995). *The Skin of Culture: Investigating the New Electronic Reality*. London: Kogan Page.

de Maistre, X. (1794). *A Journey Around My Room*. A. Brown (Trans.). London: Alma Classics, 2004.

De Martino, E. (1952). Angoscia territoriale e riscatto culturale nel mito Achilpa delle origini. In: *Il Mondo Magico* (pp. 261–276). Turin: Bollati Boringhieri, 2007.

De Micco, V. (2012, May 25–27). La radice mancante. Il narcisismo ferito dei migranti di seconda generazione. In: *Realtà Psichiche e Regole Sociali. Denaro, Potere e Lavoro tra Etica e Narcisismo. Proceedings of the 16th National Conference of the Italian Psychoanalytical Society (SPI). Rome.*

De Micco, V. (2014a, May 22–25). Radicamenti e sradicamenti della soggettività. In: *All'Origine dell'Esperienza Psichica. Divenire Soggetti. Proceedings of the 17th National Conference of the Italian Psychoanalytical Society (SPI). Milan.*

De Micco, V. (2014b). Soggettività e transiti migratori. Retrieved from www.spiweb.it/antropologia/5694-soggettivita-e-transiti-migratori [last accessed 20 November 2015].

de Mijolla-Mellor, S. (2013). Archéologique (methaphore-). In: A. de Mijolla (Ed.), *Dictionnaire International de la Psychanalyse* (p. 132). Paris: Fayard/Pluriel.

De Peri, F. (1984). Il medico e il folle: Istituzione psichiatrica, sapere scientifico e pensiero medico fra Otto e Novecento. In: *Storia d'Italia. Annali 7. Malattia e Medicina.* (pp. 1057–1140) Turin: Einaudi.

de Saint-Exupéry, A. (1943). *The Little Prince.* I. Testot-Ferry (Trans.). London: Wordsworth.

de Tocqueville, A. (1835–1840). *Democracy in America.* H. Mainsfield, & D. Winthrop (Eds. & Trans.) Chicago: University of Chicago Press, 2000.

Debord, G. E. (1956). Introduction à une critique de la geographie urbaine. In: *Les Lèvres Nues*, 6, Bruxelles. Retrieved from www.larevuedesressources.org/theorie-de-la-derive,038.html [last accessed 2 September 2015].

Delaunay, A. (1978). Emozione/motivazione. In: *Enciclopedia, Vol. 5* (pp. 339–370). Turin: Einaudi.

Deleuze, G. (1988). *The Fold, Leibniz and the Baroque.* T. Conley (Trans.). Minneapolis, MN: University of Minnesota Press.

Demetrio, D. (2005). *Filosofia del Camminare. Esercizi di Meditazione Mediterranea.* Milan: Cortina.

Derrida, J. (2008). *Adesso l'Architettura.* Milan: Scheiwiller-Motta.

Derrida, J., & Roudinesco, E. (2001). *For What Tomorrow: A Dialogue.* J. Fort (Trans.). Stanford, CA: Stanford University Press, 2004.

Di Ceglie, G. R. (2005). Symbol formation and the construction of the inner world. In: S. Budd, & R. Rusbridger (Eds.), *Introducing Psychoanalysis: Essential Themes and Topics* (pp. 95–104). London: Routledge.

Di Chiara, G. (1998). Prospettive psicoanalitiche per *Homo Sapiens. Psiche, VI, 1*: 27–33.

Di Chiara, G., Bogani, A., Bravi, G., Robutti, A., Viola, M., & Zanette, M. (1985). Preconcezione edipica e funzione psicoanalitica della mente. *Rivista di Psicoanalisi, XXXI*(3): 327–334.

Dickinson, E. (1862). The outer—from the inner. In: T. H. Johnson (Ed.), *The Complete Poems of Emily Dickinson* (pp. 216–217). Harvard, MA: Little, Brown.

Didi-Huberman, G. (2002). *L'immagine insepolta*. Turin: Bollati Boringhieri, 2006.

Domash, L. (2014). Creating "therapeutic" space: how architecture and design can inform psychoanalysis. *Psychoanalytic Perspectives, 11*: 94–111.

Donghi, P., & Preta, L. (1995). Prefazione. In: P. Donghi & L. Preta (Eds.), *In principio era la cura*. (pp. VII–XI) Rome: Laterza.

Doolittle, H. (1944). The walls do not fall. In: L. I. Martz (Ed.), *Collected Poems 1912–1944* (pp. 507–544). New York: New Directions.

Dorfles, G. (2006). *L'Intervallo Perduto*. Milan: Skira.

Eagle, M. N. (2003). The postmodern turn in psychoanalysis. A critique. *Psychoanalytic Psychology, 20*(3): 411–424.

Eckermann, J. P., & Goethe, J. W. V. (1936–1948). *Conversations of Goethe with Johann Peter Eckermann*. J. K. Moorhead (Ed.). J. Oxenford (Trans.). London: Da Capo, 1998.

Eiguer, A. (1999). Meccanismi compensatori di fronte allo sradicamento. *Quaderni di Psicoterapia Infantile. Emigrazione. Sofferenze d'identità, 40*: 105–116.

Eiguer, A. (2004). *L'Inconscio della Casa*. Rome: Borla, 2007.

Elias, N. (1987). *The Society of Individuals*. Cambridge: Blackwell, 1991.

Eliot, T. S. (1932). *Selected Essays, 1917–1932*. New York: Harcourt, Brace.

Eliot, T. S. (1943). *The Four Quartets*. New York: Harcourt, Brace.

Elliott, A. (2000). The ambivalence of identity: psychoanalytic theory in the space between modernity and postmodernity. In: A. Elliott, & C. Spezzano (Eds.), *Psychoanalysis at its Limits* (pp. 110–144). London: Free Association.

Elliott, A., & Spezzano, C. (2000). Rethinking psychoanalysis in the post-modern era. In: A. Elliott, & C. Spezzano (Eds.), *Psychoanalysis at its Limits* (pp. 1–14). London: Free Association.

Emery, N. (2007). *L'Architettura Difficile. Filosofia del Costruire*. Milan: Marinotti.

Emery, N. (2010). *Progettare, Costruire, Curare. Per una Deontologia dell'Architettura*. Bellinzona: Casagrande.

Emery, N. (2011). *Distruzione e Progetto. L'Architettura promessa*. Milan: Marinotti.

Engelmann, E. (1976). *Bergasse 19: Sigmund Freud's Home and Offices, Vienna, 1938*. New York: Basic.

Erikson, E. H. (1964). *Insight and Responsibility*. New York: Norton.

Fachinelli, E. (1974). *Il Bambino dalle Uova d'Oro*. Milan: Feltrinelli.

Fachinelli, E. (1983). *Claustrofilia*. Milan: Adelphi.

Faulkner, W. (1950). *Requiem for a Nun*. New York: Random House.

Fava, S., & Gentile, B. (1984). *La Casa e l'Abitare in Psicopatologia*. Milan: Cortina.

Ferenczi, S. (1913). Stages in the development of the sense of reality. In: *Selected Papers. Vol. 1: Sex in Psychoanalysis* (pp. 213–239). New York: Basic.

Ferrari, G. (Ed.) (2011). *Architettura e Psicoanalisi. Percorsi e Riflessioni sugli Spazi della Mente*. Milan: Ferrari Sinibaldi.

Ferraro, F., & Genovese. C. (1986). Setting. *Rivista di Psicoanalisi, XXXII*(1): 95–109.

Ferro, A. (2010). Navette per l'inconscio: rêveries, trasformazioni in sogno, sogni. *Rivista di Psicoanalisi, LVI*(3): 615–634.

Ferruta, A. (2009). Architetture della mente. In: M. Capuano (Ed.), *Miss Architect. Architetture al Femminile. Architettonicamente* (pp. 22–26). Pisa: ETS.

Filarete (c. 1460—c. 1460). *Filarete's Treatise on Architecture: Being the Treatise by Antonio di Piero Averlino, Known as Filarete*. trans. J. R. Spencer. New Haven: Yale University Press, 1965.

Filoni, M. (2014). *Lo Spazio Inquieto. La Città e la Paura*. Palermo: Passaggio.

Fiorani, E. (2012). *Geografie dell'Abitare*. Milan: Lupetti.

Flax, J. (1996). Taking multiplicity seriously: Some implications for psychoanalytic theorizing and practice. *Contemporary Psychoanalysis, 32*: 577–693.

Flax, J. (2000). Final analysis: Can psychoanalysis survive in the postmodern West? In: A. Elliott & C. Spezzano (Eds.), *Psychoanalysis at its Limits* (pp. 41–62). London: Free Association, 2000.

Fornari, E. (2011). *Linee di Confine. Filosofia e Postcolonialismo*. Turin: Bollati Boringhieri.

Foucault, M. (1975). *Discipline and Punish: The Birth of the Prison*. A. Sheridan (Trans.). New York: Pantheon, 1995.

Foucault, M. (1984). Space, knowledge, and power. In: P. Rabinow (Ed.), *Foucault Reader*. New York: Pantheon.

Freud, A. (1967). Comments on psychic trauma. In: *The Writings of Anna Freud Vol. V* (pp. 221–241). Madison: International Universities Press.

Freud, S. (1885). Letter to Minna Bernays from Paris, December 3. In: E. Jones (Ed.), *Letters of Sigmund Freud* (pp. 187–188). Mineola, NY: Dover, 1992.

Freud, S. (1895). *Studies on Hysteria*. *S. E., 2*: 1–309. London: Hogarth.

Freud, S. (1896c). The Aetiology of Hysteria. *S. E., 3*: 189. London: Hogarth.

Freud, S. (1899). Letter to Wilhelm Fliess, August 6. In: M. Bonaparte, A. Freud, & E. Kris (Eds.), *The Origins of Psychoanalysis. Letters to Wilhelm Fliess, Draft and Notes: 1887–1902 by Sigmund Freud*. (pp. 321–322) New York: Basic, 1954.

Freud, S. (1900). *The Interpretation of Dreams*. *S. E., 4–5*. London: Hogarth.

Freud, S. (1905a). Fragment of an Analysis of a Case of Hysteria. *S. E., 7*: 1–122. London: Hogarth.

Freud, S. (1905b). Postcard to the wife, September 13. In: C. Togel (Ed.), *Il Nostro Cuore Volge al Sud. Lettere di Viaggio, Soprattutto dall'Italia*. Milan: Bompiani, 2003.

Freud, S. (1907a). Delusions and Dreams in Jensen's "Gradiva". *S. E., 9*: 3. London: Hogarth.

Freud, S. (1908). Creative Writers and Day-Dreaming. *S. E., 9*: 143–153. London: Hogarth.

Freud, S. (1912–1913). *Totem and Taboo. S. E., 13*: 1–161. London: Hogarth.

Freud, S. (1913). On Beginning the Treatment (Further Recommendations on the Technique of Psycho-Analysis, I). *S. E., 12*: 123–144. London: Hogarth.

Freud, S. (1915). Papers on Metapsychology. *S. E., 14*: 105–260. London: Hogarth.

Freud, S. (1916–1917). *Introductory Lectures on Psycho-Analysis. S. E., 15–16*. London: Hogarth.

Freud, S. (1918). From the History of an Infantile Neurosis. *S. E., 17*: 1–122. London: Hogarth.

Freud, S. (1919a). Lines of Advance in Psycho-Analytic Therapy. *S. E., 17*: 159–168. London: Hogarth.

Freud, S. (1919b). The "Uncanny". *S. E., 17*: 219–256. London: Hogarth.

Freud, S. (1920). *Beyond the Pleasure Principle. S. E., 18*: 7–64. London: Hogarth.

Freud, S. (1921c). *Group Psychology and the Analysis of the Ego. S. E., 18*: 69. London: Hogarth.

Freud, S. (1922). Letter to Arthur Schnizler, May 14. In: E. Jones (Ed.), *Letters of Sigmund Freud* (pp. 282–283). Mineola, NY: Dover, 1992.

Freud, S. (1923a). Two Encyclopaedia Articles. *S. E., 18*: 235–259. London: Hogarth.

Freud, S. (1923b). *The Ego and the Id. S. E., 19*: 3. London: Hogarth.

Freud, S. (1925). *An Autobiographical Study. S. E., 20*: 3–70. London: Hogarth.

Freud, S. (1926). *Inhibitions, Symptoms and Anxiety. S. E., 20*: 77–174. London: Hogarth.

Freud, S. (1930). *Civilization and its Discontents. S. E., 21*: 59–145. London: Hogarth.

Freud, S. (1933a). New Introductory Lectures on Psycho-Analysis. *S. E., 22*: 3–182. London: Hogarth.

Freud, S. (1936a). Letter to Binswanger, October 8. In: *Lettere alla Fidanzata e ad Altri Corrispondenti, 1873–1939* (pp. 282–283). Turin: Bollati Boringhieri, 1990.

Freud, S. (1936b). A Disturbance of Memory on the Acropolis. *S. E., 22*: 237–248. London: Hogarth.

Freud, S. (1937a). Analysis terminable and interminable. *S. E., 23*: 209–254. London: Hogarth.

Freud, S. (1937b). Constructions in Analysis. *S. E., 23*: 257–269. London: Hogarth.

Freud, S. (1940). *An Outline of Psycho-Analysis. S. E., 23*: 141–207. London: Hogarth.

Freud, S. (1941f). Findings, Ideas, Problems. *S. E., 23*: 299. London: Hogarth.

Frie, R. (Ed.) (2004). *Understanding Experience. Psychotherapy and Postmodernism.* New York: Routledge.

Frigessi Castelnuovo, D., & Risso, M. (1982). *A Mezza Parete.* Turin: Einaudi.

Frosh, S. (2000). Postmodernism and the adoption of identity. In: A. Elliott & C. Spezzano (Eds.), *Psychoanalysis at its Limits* (pp. 63–78). London: Free Association.

Gabbard, G. O., & Westen, D. (2003). Rethinking therapeutic action. *International Journal of Psychoanalysis, 84*: 823–841.

Gaburri, E., & Ambrosiano, L. (2003). *Ululare con i Lupi. Conformismo e Rêverie.* Turin: Bollati Boringhieri.

Gaburri, E., & De Simone, G. (1982). L'emergenza del bello e la relazione analitica. In: G. Di Chiara (Ed.), *Itinerari della Psicoanalisi* (pp. 130–152). Turin: Loescher.

Gadamer, H. G. (1960). *Truth and Method.* New York: Continuum International, 2004.

Gadda, C. E. (1959). Our houses are changing—and the tenant must submit. In: S. Palestin (Trans.), *Texas Quarterly. A Special Issue: Image of Italy* (pp. 109–112). Austin, TX; 1961.

Gaddini, E. (1976). The invention of space in psychoanalysis. In: A. Limentani (Ed.), *A Psychoanalytic Theory of Infantile Experience* (pp. 92–105). London: Routledge, 1992.

Gamwell, L. (1989). The origins of Freud's antiquities collection. In: L. Gamwell & R. Wells (Eds.), *Freud and Art: His Personal Collection of Antiquities* (pp. 21–32). New York: Abrams.

Gardiner, M. (1972). *The Wolf-Man and Sigmund Freud.* London: Karnac.

Gautier, T. (1846). The club of assassins. In: T. Gautier & C. Baudelaire (Eds.), *Hashish, Wine, Opium* (pp. 19–54). London: Oneworld Classics.

Gibran, K. (1920). The tempest. In: *Second Treasury of Kahlil Gibran* (pp. 43–58). New York: Citadel Press, 1951.

Gibran, K. (1923). On houses. In: *The Prophet* (pp. 33–35). London: Aziloth, 2011.

Ginzburg, N. (1984). *The City and the House*. D. Davis (Trans.). New York: Arcade, 2011.

Girard, R. (1982). *The Scapegoat*. Y. Freccero (Trans.). Baltimore, MD: Johns Hopkins University Press, 1989.

Giuffrida, A. (2006). Le omosessualità nascoste. In: A. Nunziante Cesàro & P. Valerio (Eds.), *Dilemmi dell'Identità: Chi sono? Saggi Psicoanalitici sul Genere e Dintorni* (pp. 165–183). Milan: Franco Angeli.

Glass, J. M. (1993). *Shattered Selves: Multiple Personality in a Postmodern World*. Ithaca, NY: Cornell University Press.

Goretti, G. (2002). Pensieri sul tema della cura. In: G. Berti Ceroni (Ed.), *Come Cura la Psicoanalisi?* (pp. 28–42). Milan: Franco Angeli.

Gould, S. J. (2002). *The Structure of Evolutionary Theory*. Harvard, MA: Belknap.

Green, A. (1975). Le temps mort. *Nouvelle Revue de Psychanalyse, 11*: 103–109.

Green, A. (2002). *Key Ideas for a Contemporary Psychoanalysis. Misrecognition and recognition of the Unconscious*. London: Routledge, 2005.

Greenberg, J. R. (1995). Psychoanalytic technique and the interactive matrix. *Psychoanalytic Quarterly, 64*: 1–22.

Gregotti, V. (2010). *Tre Forme di Architettura Mancata*. Turin: Einaudi.

Gregotti, V. (2013, June 9). Interview with Antonio Gnoli. *La Repubblica*. Retrieved from www.repubblica.it/cultura/2013/06/09/news/vittorio_gregotti_lo_zen_e_gropius_bicocca_ed_eco_un_grande_progettista_si_racconta-60718080/ [last accessed 11 November 2013].

Grinberg, L., & Grinberg, R. (1975). *Identità e cambiamento*. Rome: Armando, 1976.

Grinberg, L., & Grinberg, R. (1984). *Psychoanalytic Perspectives on Migration and Exile*. N. Festinger (Trans.). Yale, CT: Yale University Press, 1989.

Grinker, R. R. (1940). Reminiscences of a personal contact with Freud. *American Journal of Orthopsychiatry, X*: 851–852.

Grosz, E. (2001). Architecture from the Outside: Essays on Virtual and Real Space. Cambridge, MA: MIT.

Guarnieri, R. (2006). La vertigine della distruzione: W. G. Sebald. *Psiche, 1*: 167–180.

Guderian, C. (2004). *Magie der Couch. Bilder und Gespräche über Raum und Setting in der Psychoanalyse*. Stuttgart: Kohlhammer.

Guerrini Degli Innocenti, B. (2011). Spazio onirico e spazio virtuale nel processo analitico. *Rivista di Psicoanalisi, LVII*(3): 652.

Hautmann, G. (1999). *Il Mio Debito con Bion*. Rome: Borla.

Hegel, G. W. F. (1833). *Lectures on the History of Philosophy. Volume 1: Greek Philosophy to Plato*. E. S. Haldane (Trans.). Lincoln, NE: University of Nebraska Press, 1995.

Heidegger, M. (1951). Poetically Man Dwells. In: V. Jackson, & Y. Prins (Eds.), *The Lyric Theory Reader. A Critical Anthology* (pp. 390–398). Baltimore: Johns Hopkins University Press, 2014.

Heidegger, M. (1954). Building Dwelling Thinking. In: D. F. Krell (Ed.), *Basic Writings*. (pp. 342–365). New York: Harper, 2008.

Heidegger, M. (1959). *On the Way to Language*. New York: Harper & Row.

Heidegger, M. (1966). *Introduction to Metaphysics*. G. Fried, & R. Polt (Trans.). New Haven, CT: Yale University Press, 2000.

Heller, A., & Fehér, F. (1988). *The Postmodern Political Condition*. Cambridge: Polity.

Hendrix, J. (2012). Architecture and dream construction. In: E. A. Danze & S. Sonnenberg (Eds.), *Center 17: Space & Psyche* (pp. 141–152). Austin, TX: University of Texas.

Hillman, J. (2001, April 25). Malinconia, nostra Signora dello scandalo. *Il Corriere della Sera*. Retrieved from http://archiviostorico.corriere.it/2001/aprile/25/MALINCONIA_Nostra_signora_dello_scandalo_co_0_010425497.shtml [last accessed 2 August 2015].

Hillman, J. (2006). *Il Paesaggio: Una Ricerca Psicologica*. Pavia: Cardano.

Hitchcock, H. R., & Johnson, P. (1932). *The International Style*. New York: Norton.

Hochmann, J. (1982). L'or et le cuivre. Réflexions sur quelques usages possibles de la théorie psychanalytique dans le service psychiatrique public de secteur. *Entrevues*, *4*: 3–18.

Hoffman, I. Z. (1998). *Ritual and Spontaneity in the Psychoanalytic Process. A Dialectical-Constructivistic View*. London: Routledge.

Holl, S. (1994). Questions of perception: phenomenology of architecture. In: S. Holl, J. Pallasmaa, & A. Perez-Gomez (Eds.), *Questions of Perception: Phenomenology of Architecture* (pp. 39–120). San Francisco, CA: William Stout.

Holt, R. R. (2002). Postmodernism: its origins and its threat to psychoanalysis. *International Forum of Psychoanalysis*, *11*(4): 267–274.

Homayounpour, G. (2012). *Doing Psychoanalysis in Tehran*. Cambridge, MA: MIT.

Homer (*c*.700 BC). *Odyssey*. E. V. Rieu, & D. C. H. Rieu (Trans.). London: Penguin, 1991.

Horovitz, M. (2007). Transfert et verité. In: F. Guignard & T. Bokanowski (Eds.), *Actualité de la Pensée de Bion* (pp. 45–51). Paris: In-Press.

Hugo, V. (1832). *Notre-Dame of Paris (The Hunchback of Notre Dame)*. Oxford: Oxford University Press, 2009.

Hugo, V. (1843). *Les Burgraves*. H. W. Eve (Ed.). Cambridge: Cambridge University Press, 1930.

Irigaray, L. (2011). Perhaps cultivating touch can still save us. *SubStance*, *126*(40)3: 130–140.

Israël, P. (1994). Specificité(s) de la formation analytique. *EPF Bulletin, 42*: 31–39.

Jacques, E. (1970). *Work, Creativity and Social Justice.* London: Heinemann.

Jankélevič, V. (1974). La nostalgia. In: A. Prete (Ed.), *Nostalgia. Storia di un Sentimento.* (pp. 119–176) Milan: Cortina, 1992.

Johnson, P. (1979). *Writings.* New York: Oxford University Press.

Jones, E. (1957). *Sigmund Freud: Life and Work. Vol. 3: The Last Phase 1919–1939.* London: Hogarth.

Jung, C. G. (1931). Mind and earth. In: G. Adler & R. F. C. Hull (Eds. & Trans.), *Civilization in Transition. The Collected Works of C. G. Jung, Vol. 10* (pp. 29–49). Princeton, NJ: Princeton University Press, 1970.

Jung, C. G. (1950). Man and his environment. Dialogue with Hans Carol. In: W. McGuire & R. F. C. Hull (Eds.), *Jung Speaking. Interviews and Encounters* (pp. 201–204). Princeton, NJ: Princeton University Press, 1977.

Jung, C. G. (1961). *Memories, Dreams, Reflections.* A. Jaffé (Ed.). R. Winston & C. Winston (Trans.). New York: Random, 1989.

Kafka, F. (1946). Er [He]. In: D. Frank (Trans.), *Aphorisms* (pp. 82–83). New York: Schocken.

Kahn, L. J. (1969). *Conversations with Students.* Houston, TX: Architecture at Rice.

Kant, I. (1781). *Critique of Pure Reason.* trans. M. Weigelt. London: Penguin, 2007.

Kardiner, A. (1977). *My Analysis with Freud. Reminiscences.* New York: Norton.

Kavafis, K. P. (1911). Ithaca. In: E. Sachperoglou (Trans.), *The Collected Poems* (p. 37). Oxford: Oxford University Press, 2007.

Khan, M. M. R. (1982). Du vide plein la tête. *Nouvelle Revue de Psychanalyse, 25*: 161–197.

Kingwell, M. (2002). *Practical Judgements: Essays in Culture, Politics and Interpretation.* Toronto: University of Toronto Press.

Kluzer, G. (2001). Dalla psicoterapia alla psicoanalisi (e ritorno?): Un percorso difficile per il candidato di oggi. *Rivista di Psicoanalisi, XLVII*(1): 109–128.

Kraus, K. (1909). *Dicta and Contradicta.* J. McVity (Trans.). Champaign, IL: University of Illinois Press, 2001.

Kristeva, J. (1991). *Strangers to Ourselves.* New York: Columbia University Press.

Kundera, M. (1995). *Slowness. A Novel.* L. Asher (Trans.). New York: Harper Collins.

La Cecla, F. (1993). *Mente Locale. Per un'Antropologia dell'Abitare.* Milan: Elèuthera.

La Cecla, F. (2000). *Perdersi. L'Uomo senza Ambiente.* Rome-Bari: Laterza.

La Cecla, F. (2008). *Contro l'Architettura.* Turin: Bollati Boringhieri.
La Cecla, F. (2015). *Contro l'Urbanistica.* Turin: Einaudi.
Lacan, J. (1959–1960). *The Seminar of Jacques Lacan: The Ethics of Psychoanalysis (Book VII).* D. Porter (Trans.). New York: Norton, 1992.
Lacan, J. (1966). *Écrits: The First Complete Edition in English.* B. Fink (Trans.). New York: Norton, 2006.
Lakoff, G. (1987). Image metaphors. *Metaphor and Symbolic Activity, 2/3*: 219–222.
Lanfredini, R. (2014). Essere una cosa che sente: Il sotto-categoriale in Maurice Merleau-Ponty. *Rivista di Psicoanalisi, LX*(2): 433–453.
Laplanche, J. (2002). À partir de la situation anthropologique fondamentale. In: C. Botella (Ed.), *Penser les limites* (pp. 280–287). Paris: Delachaux & Niestlé.
Lavagetto, M. (1985). *Freud, la letteratura e altro.* Turin: Einaudi.
Le Corbusier (1923). *Towards a New Architecture.* F. Etchells (Trans.). London: Butterworth Architecture.
Le Corbusier (1965). Rien n'est transmissible que la pensée. In: *Le Corbusier et Pierre Jeanneret. Œuvre complète. Vol. VIII (1965–1969)* (p. 150–181). Zürich: Les éditions d'architecture, 1995.
Leakey, R. E. (1994). *The Origin of Humankind.* New York: Basic.
Leary, K. (1994). Psychoanalytic "problems" and postmodern "solutions". *Psychoanalytic Quarterly, 63*: 433–465.
Leavitt, J. (2013). Superficie, spazio e artefatto: la presenza materiale della memoria. *Rivista di Psicoanalisi, LIX*, 3: 549–571.
Lebrun, J. P. (1997). *Un Monde sans Limite. Essai pour une Clinique Psychanalytique du Social.* Ramonville Saint-Agne: Erès.
Lefaivre, L., & Tzonis, A. (2009). Introduzione. In: L. Lefaivre & A. Tzonis (Eds.), *Santiago Calatrava. L'architettura. I protagonisti.* (pp. II–XV) Rome: L'Espresso.
Lefebvre, H. (1974). *The Production of Space.* Oxford: Blackwell, 1991.
Leopardi, G. (1817–1832). *Zibaldone: The Notebooks of Leopardi.* M. Caesar & F. D'Intino (Eds.). New York: Farrar, Straus and Giroux, 2013.
Lévinas, E. (1961). *Totality and Infinity: An Essay on Exteriority.* Pittsburgh: Duquesne University Press, 1979.
Liberman, D. (1970–1972). *Lingüistica, Interacciòn Comunicativa y Proceso Psicoanalitico, Vol. 1–3.* Buenos Aires: Galerna.
Libeskind, D. (2004). *Breaking Ground. Adventures in Life and Architecture.* New York: Riverhead.
Libeskind, D. (2014, May 31). Interview with Francesca Gugliotta. *La Repubblica.* Retrieved from http://ricerca.repubblica.it/repubblica/archivio/repubblica/2014/05/31/progetto-un-mondo-dove-vincono-le-emozioni48.html [last accessed 7 June 2015].

Libeskind, D. (2015, September 4). Interview with Marco Mathieu. *La Repubblica*. www.repubblica.it/cultura/2015/09/04/news/daniel_libeskind_l_architettura_si_occupi_di_accoglienza_-122199697/ [last accessed 10 September 2015].

Lloyd Wright, F. (1914). In the cause of architecture. Second paper. *Architectural Record, 35*: 405–413.

Lloyd Wright, F. (1927). In the cause of architecture: the architect and the machine. *Architectural Record, 61*: 394–396.

Lloyd Wright, F. (1957). *A Testament*. New York: Horizon.

Loewald, H. W. (1988). Sublimation. In: *The Essential Loewald: Collected Papers and Monographs*. (pp. 423–527) Hagerstown, MD: University Publishing Group.

Loewenberg, P. (2012). Architectural and emotional space. In: E. A. Danze & S. Sonnenberg (Eds.), *Center 17: Space & Psyche* (pp. 10–46). Austin, TX: University of Texas.

Loewenthal, D., & Snell, R. (2003). Introduction. In: D. Loewenthal & R. Snell (Eds.), *Post-Modernism for Psychotherapists. A Critical Reader* (pp. 1–7). Hove: Brunner-Routledge.

Loos, A. (1898). The interiors in the rotunda. In: M. Mitchell (Trans.), *Ornament and Crime*. (pp. 57–62). Riverside, CA: Ariadne, 1998.

Loos, A. (1903). From *Das Andere* (The Other). In: M. Mitchell (Trans.), *Ornament and Crime* (pp. 71–80). Riverside, CA: Ariadne, 1998.

Loos, A. (1910). Architecture. In: J. O. Newman & J. H. Smith (Trans.), *Spoken into the Void: Collected Essays* (pp. 73–85). Chicago, IL: Graham Foundation, 1987.

Loos, A. (1924). Ornament and education. In: J. O. Newman & J. H. Smith (Trans.), *Spoken into the Void: Collected Essays* (pp. 100–121). Chicago, IL: Graham Foundation, 1987.

Lopez, D., & Zorzi Meneguzzo, L. (2005). *Narcisismo e Amore. La Teoria della Complessità, dell' Et—Et e della Distinzione*. Vicenza: Colla.

Lyotard, J.-F. (1979). *The Postmodern Condition: A Report on Knowledge*. Minneapolis, MN: University of Minnesota Press, 1984.

Magris, C. (1992). La vita assente. In: *Itaca e Oltre*. (pp. 8–17). Milan: Garzanti.

Magris, C. (1997). *Microcosms*. New York: Random, 1999.

Magris, C. (2005). *L'Infinito Viaggiare*. Milan: Mondadori.

Malaparte, C. (1940, May 21). Un palazzo di acqua e di foglie. *Aria d'Italia*, pp. 31–39.

Mallgrave, H. F. (2013). *Architecture and Embodiment. The Implications of the New Sciences and Humanities for Design*. London: Routledge.

Malnar, J. M., & Vodvarka, F. (2004). *Sensory Design*. Minneapolis, MN: University of Minnesota Press.

Mancia, M. (1995). Spazio interno e sua rappresentazione nell'architettura primitiva Lobi e nell'opera di Antoni Gaudí. In: *Percorsi* (pp. 215–224). Turin: Bollati Boringhieri.

Mancinelli, G. (2012). Dance ce temps-là. In: VV.AA. *Antologia Proust 2012: Da Illiers a Cabourg, l'impronta di Proust nel cuore della Francia*. Retrieved from http://www.larecherche.it/testo.asp?Tabella=Narrativa&Id=2316 [last accessed 3 May 2015].

Mann, T. (1936). Freud and the future. *International Journal of Psychoanalysis, 37*(1): 106–115, 1956.

Marazzi, F. (2015). *Le Città dei Monaci. Storia degli Spazi che Avvicinano a Dio*. Milan: Jaca Book.

Marc, O. (1972). *Psychanalyse de la Maison*. Paris: Seuil.

Marchesini, R. (2001). *Bioetica e Scienze Veterinarie*. Naples: Edizioni Scientifiche Italiane.

Marchesini, R. (2002). *Post-Human. Verso Nuovi Modelli di Esistenza*. Turin: Bollati Boringhieri.

Marcuse, H. (1963). *The Obsolescence of Psychoanalysis*. New York: Black Swan, 1970.

Marx, K. (1844). *Economic and Philosophic Manuscripts of 1844*. D. J. Struik (Ed.). M. Mulligan (Trans.). Moscow: Progress, 1932.

Marx, K. (1867). *Capital, Volume I*. B. Fowkes (Trans.). London: Penguin, 1992.

Matvejevic, P. (1987). *Mediterranean: A Cultural Landscape*. M. H. Heim (Trans.). Berkeley: University of California Press, 1999.

Maura, E., & Peloso, P. F. (1999). *Lo Splendore della Ragione. Storia della Psichiatria Ligure nell'Epoca del Positivismo, Tomo 1*. Genoa: La Clessidra.

Meissner, W. W. (2004). Sdraiarsi o non sdraiarsi (lettino o non lettino): Questo è il problema. *Gli Argonauti, 102*: 213–260.

Melman, C. (2002). *L'Uomo senza Gravità. Conversazioni con J. P. Lebrun*. Milan: Bruno Mondadori, 2010.

Meltzer, D. (1973). On the apprehension of beauty. *Contemporary Psychoanalysis, 9*: 224–229.

Meltzer, D. (1992). *The Claustrum. An Investigation of Claustrophobic Phenomena*. London: Karnac.

Merleau-Ponty, M. (1945). *Phenomenology of Perception*. C. Smith (Trans.). London: Routledge, 1962.

Merleau-Ponty, M. (1995). *Nature. Course Notes from the Collège de France*. D. Séglard (Ed.). R. Vallier (Trans.). Evanston: Northwestern University Press, 2003.

Merlini, F. (2012). Schizotipie contemporanee: Essere in rete. Per una filosofia dello spazio di vita. *Quaderni de Gli Argonauti, 24*: 9–20.

Mezzadra, S., & Neilson, B. (2013). *Border as Method, or, the Multiplication of Labor.* Durham, NC: Duke University Press.

Michelucci, G. (1993). *Un Fossile Chiamato Carcere.* Florence: Angelo Pontecorboli.

Migone, P. (2004). Sulle "quattro psicologie" di Fred Pine. *Il Ruolo Terapeutico, 95*: 87–92.

Milner, M. (1952a). *On Not Being Able to Paint.* London: Heinemann.

Milner, M. (1952b). Aspects of symbolism in comprehension of the not-self. *International Journal of Psychoanalysis, 33*: 181–195.

Minkowski, E. (1968). *Lived Time: Phenomenological and Psychopathological Studies.* N. Metzel (Trans.). Evanston, IL: Northwestern University Press, 1970.

Mitchell, S. A. (1988). *Relational Concepts in Psychoanalysis. An Integration.* Harvard, MA: Harvard University Press.

Moneo, R. (2013). Gli edifici non sono solo oggetti. Bologna: Lectio magistralis. Retrieved from www.cersaie.it/evento/Lectio-Magistralis-di-Rafael-Moneo-Gli-edifici-non-sono-solo-oggetti/62304/2013 [last accessed 9 October 2015].

Money-Kyrle, R. (1956). Psycho-analysis and philosophy. In: D. Meltzer (Ed.), *The Collected Papers of Roger Money-Kyrle* (pp. 101–115). London: Karnac, 2015.

Money-Kyrle, R. E. (1931). The remote consequences of psychoanalysis on individual, social and instinctive behaviour. *British Journal of Medical Psychology, 11*: 173–193.

Monterosa, L. (2013). Lo spazio sonoro nella stanza di analisi. *Rivista di Psicoanalisi, LIX*(3): 573–590.

Moravia, A. (1937). L'architetto. In: *Racconti (1927–1951)* (pp. 1146–1203). Milan: Bompiani, 2012.

Morin, E. (2004). Migrazioni interdisciplinari. *Psiche, 2*: 13–20.

Munro, A. (2008). Munro, quella volta a Pescara per il Premio Flaiano: "Il racconto è una casa." *Il Messaggero.* Retrieved from http://spettacoliecultura.ilmessaggero.it/libri/alice_munro_nobel_letteratura_pescara_flaiano/337823.shtml [last accessed 13 November 2015].

Musarra Schrøder, U. (2012). Immagini di architettura in Italo Calvino. *Italies, 16*: 387–410.

Nancy, J.-L. (2002). *The Creation of the World or Globalization.* Albany, NY: SUNY, 2007.

Neri, C. (1999). Il calore segreto degli oggetti. *Quaderni di Psicoterapia Infantile, 40*: 129–142.

Neri, G. (2013). Introduzione. In: *Coop Himmelb(l)au. L'architettura. I protagonisti* (pp. 1–9). Rome: L'Espresso.

Nicolussi, G. (1996). Reflexiones psicoanaliticas sobre la migracion. *Revista de Psicoanalisis, 53*(1): 323–340.

Niemeyer, O. (1978). *La Forma dell'Architettura*. Milan: Mondadori.
Novalis (1802). *Henry von Ofterdingen: A Novel*. P. Hilty (Trans.). Prospect Heights, NY: Continuum, 1990.
Nunzio, D. (1976). *Paestum: Hypothesis and Reality*. Salerno: Studio P.
Obeyesekere, G. (1990). *The Work of Culture: Symbolic Transformation in Psychoanalysis and Anthropology*. Chicago, IL: University of Chicago Press.
Ogden, T. (2013). Thomas Ogden in conversation with Luca Di Donna. *Rivista di Psicoanalisi, LIX*(3): 625–641.
Ortega y Gasset, J. (1952). Il mito dell'uomo oltre la tecnica e Intorno al Colloquio di Darmstadt, 1951. In: L. Taddio, *Costruire, Abitare, Pensare* (pp. 61–79). Milan: Mimesis, 2010.
Ortigues, M. C., & Ortigues, E. (1984). *Œdipe Africain*. Paris: L'Harmattan.
Osmond, H. (1959). The relationship between architect and psychiatrist. In: C. Goshen (Ed.), *Psychiatric Architecture* (pp. 16–20). Washington, WA: American Psychiatric Association.
Oud, J. J. P. (1947, March 18). Mr. Oud replies. *Architectural Record*, p. 18.
Oudai Celso, Y. (2006). *Freud e la Filosofia Antica*. Turin: Bollati Boringhieri.
Pallasmaa, J. U. (1994). An Architecture of the Seven Senses. In: S. Holl, J. Pallasmaa, & A. Perez-Gomez (Eds.), *Questions of Perception, Phenomenology of Architecture* (pp. 27–38). San Francisco, CA: William Stout.
Pallasmaa, J. U. (2011). *The Embodied Image. Imagination and Imagery in Architecture*. Chichester: Wiley.
Pallasmaa, J. U. (2012). *The Eyes of the Skin. Architecture and the Senses*. Chichester: Wiley.
Pankow, G. (1969). *L'Uomo e la Sua Psicosi*. Milan: Feltrinelli, 1977.
Parment, U. (2000a). Introduction. *International Forum of Psychoanalysis, 9*: 3–4.
Parment, U. (2000b). What is architecture about? Interview with Jan Henriksson, Professor of Architecture. *International Forum of Psychoanalysis, 9*: 19–27.
Pasolini, P. P. (1962, October 18). Untitled article in *Nuove Vie*. In: *Saggi sulla Politica e sulla Società*. Milan: Mondadori, 1999.
Pasolini, P. P. (1964). *Poesia in Forma di Rosa*. Milan: Garzanti.
Pasolini, P. P. (1977). *Lutheran Letters*. S. Hood (Trans.). Manchester: Carcanet, 1987.
Paternostro, M. (2004). *Lezioni di Piano. Vent'Anni di Incontri con l'Architetto*. Genoa: De Ferrari.
Pavan, F. (1984). La paura di attraversare e la struttura vissuta della piazza. In: R. Rossi, & F. Petrella (Eds.), *Psicoterapia delle Fobie* (pp. 253–260). Turin: Massaza & Sinchetto.
Pélicier, Y. (1964). Aperçus généraux sur la psychologie des transplantés. *Le Concours Médical, 86*(17): 2717–2723.

Perec, G. (1974). *Species of Spaces and Other Pieces*. J. Sturrock (Ed. & Trans.). London: Penguin, 1999.

Perec, G. (1978). *Life. A User's Manual*. D. Bellos (Trans.). London: Vintage, 2003.

Pérez-Gómez, A. (2008). *Built upon Love. Architectural Longing after Ethics and Aesthetics*. Cambridge, MA: MIT.

Perniola, M. (2003). Incroci (a debate with Camilla Adami, Maurizio Balsamo, Nicoletta Bonanome, Mario Perniola, Lorena Preta, Stefano Rodotà and Tito Spini). *Psiche, 1*: 133–144.

Perrot, M. (2009). *Storia delle Camere*. Palermo: Sellerio, 2011.

Perrotti, R. (1949). La stazione di Roma. *Psiche, 3–4*: 173–175.

Pesare, M. (2007). *La Dimora dei Luoghi. Saggi sull'Abitare tra Filosofia e Scienze Sociali*. Lecce: Icaro.

Petrella, F. (1990). L'archeologia analitica nell'ultimo Freud. *Rivista di Psicoanalisi, XXXVI*(4): 956–971.

Petrella, F. (1993a). Spazio vissuto e spazio istituzionale nella schizofrenia cronica. In: *Turbamenti Affettivi e Alterazioni dell'Esperienza* (pp. 437–447). Milan: Cortina.

Petrella, F. (1993b). Interno/esterno: Spazio vissuto e ambiente terapeutico. In: *Turbamenti Affettivi e Alterazioni dell'Esperienza* (pp. 650–659). Milan: Cortina.

Petrella, F. (2010). Interpretazione psicoanalitica e interpretazione musicale. In: G. Gabbriellini (Ed.). *Psicoanalisi e musica*. (pp. 17–36) Pisa: Felici.

Petrella, F. (2014). Architetture della psiche estesa. Sullo spazio e la clinica. *Gli Argonauti, 142*: 189–200.

Petrella, F., & Berlincioni, V. (2002). La clinica e le nuove realtà tecnologiche. Una riflessione psicoanalitica. *Psiche, 1*: 171–184.

Petrella, F., & Berlincioni, V. (2004). Lavoro clinico e quadro socioculturale: Le intersezioni. *Gli Argonauti, 103*: 363–374.

Piano, R. (2000). *La Responsabilità dell'Architetto. Conversazione con Renzo Cassigoli*. Bagno a Ripoli: Passigli.

Pile, S. (2005). Building dreams space, psychoanalysis, and the city. *Annual of Psychoanalysis, 33*: 79–91.

Pine, F. (1988). The four psychologies of psychoanalysis and their place in clinical work. *Journal of the American Psychoanalytic Association, 36*(3): 571–596.

Pine, F. (1989). Motivation, personality organisation, and the four psychologies of psychoanalysis. *Journal of the American Psychoanalytic Association, 37*: 31–64.

Pine, F. (1990). *Drive, ego, Object and Self*. New York: Basic.

Pine, F. (2001). Listening and speaking ssychoanalytically—with what in mind? *International Journal of Psychoanalysis, 82*(5): 901–916.

Pinna, E. (2002). Pensieri d'architettura. Interview with Cosimo Schinaia. *Psiche, 2*: 109–114.

Pinna, E. (2013). Conversation on the House with Giordano Tironi. In: *Talking Architectures* (pp. 131–179). Genoa: Il Melangolo.

Pintor, L. (2001). *Memories from the Twentieth Century.* G. Elliot (Trans.). A. Toscano (Ed.). Chicago, IL: Seagull, 2013.

Plimpton, G. (1959). *The Paris Interviews. Vol. I.* New York: Picador, 2006.

Plutarch of Cheronea (*c.*100 AD). Concertning talkativeness. In: *Plutarch's Morals. Volume VI.* (pp. 396–467) W. C. Helmbold (Trans.), T. E. Page, E. Capps, W. H. D. Rouse, L. A. Post & E. H. Warmington (Eds.) Harvard: Harvard University Press.

Poe, E. A. (1842). *The Pit and the Pendulum.* London: Penguin, 2009.

Pohlen, M. (2006). *In Analisi con Freud. I Verbali delle Sedute di Ernst Blum del 1922.* Turin: Bollati Boringhieri, 2009.

Poincaré, H. (1902–1908). *The Foundations of Science.* G. B. Halsted (Trans.). New York: Science Press, 2014.

Ponsi, M. (2013, April 27–28). Convergenze e convivenze fra le molte psicoanalisi. II Colloquio Italo-Spagnolo, Madrid.

Pontalis, J.-B. (1988). *Perdere di Vista.* Rome: Borla, 1993.

Pope Francis (2015). *Laudato Si'. On Care for Our Common Home.* Vatican City: Libreria Editrice Vaticana.

Portoghesi, P. (1990). *La Piazza come "Luogo degli Sguardi".* Rome: Gangemi.

Preta, L. (1990). Prefazione. In: M. Ceruti, & L. Preta (Eds.), *Che Cos'è la Conoscenza* (pp. VII–XIX). Rome: Laterza.

Preta, L. (1991). La narrazione delle origini: raccontare l'inosservabile. In: L. Preta (Ed.), *La Narrazione delle Origini* (pp. XI–XXIII). Rome: Laterza.

Preta, L. (1992). Pensare immaginando. In: L. Preta (Ed.), *Immagini e Metafore della Scienza* (pp. IX–XXI). Rome: Laterza.

Preta, L. (1993). Le strategie della conoscenza. In: L. Preta (Ed.), *La Passione del Conoscere* (pp. VII–XXXIII). Rome: Laterza.

Preta, L. (1999). L'esperienza del "perturbante" nell'impatto con le biotecnologie. In: L. Preta (Ed.), *Nuove geometrie della mente* (pp. 5–20). Rome: Laterza.

Preta, L. (2002). Editoriale. *Psiche, 1*: 7–11.

Preta, L. (2004). Editoriale. *Psiche, 1*: 7–10.

Preta, L. (2006). Resti del futuro. In: M. Capuano (Ed.), *Architettonicamente. Contaminazioni tra Architettura e Psicoanalisi* [special issue of *Architetture Pisane*] *5*: 19–22.

Preta, L. (2015). *La Brutalità delle Cose. Trasformazioni Psichiche della Realtà.* Milan: Mimesis.

Proust, M. (1923). *The Captive and the Fugitive: In Search of Lost Time, Vol. V.* C. K. Scott Moncrieff, & T. Kilmartin (Trans.). New York: Random, 1993.

Puget, J., & Wender, L. (1982). Analista y paciente en mundos superpuestos. *Psicoanálisis, 4*(3): 503–536.

Puntí, J. (2012). Arqueología del futuro. In: J. Schulz-Dornburg. *Ruinas Modernas. Una Topografía de Lucro* (pp. 117–164). Barcelona: Àmbit.

Queneau, R. (1938). Strange tastes. In: J. Stump (Trans.), *Letters, Numbers, Forms. Essays, 1928–1970.* Champaign, IL: University of Illinois Press, 2007.

Quinodoz, D. (1992). The psychoanalytic setting as the instrument of the container function. *International Journal of Psychoanalysis, 73*: 627–635.

Racalbuto, A. (2005). Le parole della cura e la cura delle parole. *Rivista di Psicoanalisi, Special Issue, 1934–1954–2004, LI, 1*: 275–288.

Racamier, P.-C. (1957). Introduction à une sociopathologie des schizophrènes hospitalisés. *Évolution Psychiatrique, 1*: 47–94.

Racamier, P.-C. (1999). P.-C. Racamier risponde. In: P.-C. Racamier, & S. Taccani (Eds.) *Realtà interna Realtà esterna nell'evoluzione, nella clinica, nella cura. Seminari di Monteguidi* (pp. 77–93). Verona: CeRP.

Rank, O. (1914). *The Double: A Psychoanalytic Study.* H. Tucker Jr. (Ed. & Trans.). Chapel Hill, NC: University of North Carolina Press, 1971.

Rank, O. (1924). *The Trauma of Birth.* London: Kegan Paul, 1993.

Rasmussen, S. (1962). *Experiencing Architecture.* Cambridge, MA: MIT.

Ratti, C. (2014). *Architettura Open Source. Verso una Progettazione Aperta.* Turin: Einaudi.

Reiche, R. (1968). *Sexuality and Class Struggle.* New York: Verso, 1970.

Reik, T. (1937). *Surprise and the Psychoanalyst. On the Conjecture and Comprehension of Unconscious Processes.* New York: Dutton.

Resnik, S. (2002). Per un'estetica degli abissi. In: S. Resnik (Ed.), *L'Avventura Estetica* (pp. 25–39). Milan: FrancoAngeli.

Resnik, S. (2006). *Biografie dell'Inconscio.* Rome: Borla, 2007.

Ricci, G. (1995). *Le Città di Freud. Itinerari, Emblemi, Orizzonti di un Viaggiatore.* Milan: Jaca Books.

Ricoeur, P. (1965). *Freud and Philosophy: An Essay on Interpretation.* D. Savage (Trans.). Yale, CT: Yale University Press, 1977.

Rimbaud, A. (1873). *A Season in Hell.* P. Schmidt (Trans.). New York: Limited Editions Club, 1986.

Rinaldi, L., & Stanzione, M. (2012). Introduzione. In: L. Rinaldi, & M. Stanzione (Eds.), *Le Figure del Vuoto* (pp. 5–25). Rome: Borla.

Rodman, F. R. (2005). Architecture and the True self. *Annual of Psychoanalysis, 33*: 57–66.

Rossi, A. (1981). *A Scientific Autobiography.* L. Venuti (Trans.) Boston, MA: MIT, 2009.

Rota, I. (2010). Freud, Wittgenstein, Chareau. *Domus, 938*: 57–69.

Roux, S. (1976). *La Casa nella Storia.* Rome: Editori Riuniti, 1982.

Rykwert, J. (2012). Space and Mind. In: E. A. Danze, & S. Sonnenberg (Eds.), *Center 17: Space & Psyche* (pp. 74–88). Austin, TX: University of Texas.

Sabbadini, A. (2014). *Boundaries and Bridges. Perspectives on Time and Space in Psychoanalysis.* London: Karnac.

Samonà, C. (1978). *Brothers.* L. Lappin (Trans.). Manchester: Carcanet.

Sansot, P. (1998). *Sul Buon Senso della Lentezza. Il Ritmo Giusto della Vita.* Milan: Il Saggiatore, 2003.

Saraval, A. (1988). La tecnica classica e la sua evoluzione. In: A. A. Semi (Ed.), *Trattato di Psicoanalisi. Teoria e Tecnica. Vol. I* (pp. 533–613). Milan: Cortina.

Scapolo, B. (2011). Afterword: "Eupalinos o l'Architetto", o del fare consistente. In: P. Valery (1923), *Eupalinos o l'Architetto* (pp. 89–117). Milan: Mimesis.

Scaraffia, L. (2015). *Andare per Monasteri.* Bologna: Il Mulino.

Schinaia, C. (1997a). *Dal Manicomio alla Città. L' "Altro" Presepe di Cogoleto.* Rome-Bari: Laterza.

Schinaia, C. (1997b). Editoriale. *La Via del Sale, I*(1): 9–12.

Schinaia, C. (1997c). L'errore e l'errare. Paziente, candidato e supervisore in campo. *Rivista di Psicoanalisi, XLIII*(1): 77–88.

Schinaia, C. (1998). Il *Cantiere delle Idee. Le Feste nell'Ex Ospedale Psichiatrico di Cogoleto.* Genoa: La Clessidra.

Schinaia, C. (2000). Pedofilia, pedofilias. *Revista de Psicoanalisis, 7*: 79–101.

Schinaia, C. (2005a). Figure del transessualismo in psicoanalisi. *Rivista Italiana di Gruppoanalisi,* 2: 7–32.

Schinaia, C. (2005b). Sul numero delle sedute settimanali. Passare da tre a quattro. In: G. Berti Ceroni (Ed.), *Come Cura la Psicoanalisi?* (pp. 314–328). Milan: Franco Angeli.

Schinaia, C. (2008). Le stanze dell'analisi. *Psiche,* 2: 101–114.

Schinaia, C. (2010). *On Paedophilia.* A. Sansone (Trans.). London: Karnac, 2010.

Schinaia, C. (2012). Figures of clandestinity. Notes on a clinical case of paedophilia. *The Italian Psychoanalytic Annual, VI*: 53–72.

Schliemann, H. (1881). *Ilios: City and Country of the Trojans.* Cambridge: Cambridge University.

Schneider, M. (2002). *Big Mother. Psychopathologie de la Vie Politique.* Paris: Odile Jacob.

Schur, M. (1972). *Freud: Living and Dying.* Madison: International Universities Press.

Scott, G. (1914). *The Architecture of Humanism: A Study in the History of Taste.* New York: Norton, 1999.

Scully, V. (1966). Introduction. In: R. Venturi, *Complexity and Contradiction in Architecture* (pp. 9–12). New York: Museum of Modern Art.

Searles, H. F. (1960). *The Nonhuman Environment in Normal Development and in Schizophrenia.* Madison, WI: International Universities Press.

Sebald, W. G. (1992). *The Emigrants*. M. Hulse (Trans.). London: Vintage, 1997.

Sebald, W. G. (2001a). *On the Natural History of Destruction*. A. Bell (Trans.). New York: Random, 2004.

Sebald, W. G. (2001b). *Austerlitz*. A. Bell (Trans.). London: Penguin.

Secchi, B. (2013). *La città dei Ricchi e la Città dei Poveri*. Rome-Bari: Laterza.

Secchi, R. (2005). *Il pensiero delle forme tra architettura e scienze della vita*. Rome: Officina.

Secchi, R. (2014). Dire no esercitando il mestiere di architetto. *Psiche*, 2: 421–440.

Segal, H. (1952). A psychoanalytic approach to aesthetics. In: M. Klein, P. Heimann, & R. Money-Kyrle (Eds.), *New Directions in Psychoanalysis* (pp. 384–405). New York: Basic, 1977.

Semi, A. A. (2014). *Psicoanalisi della vita quotidiana*. Milan: Cortina.

Semper, G. (1851). *The Four Elements of Architecture*. H. F. Mallgrave & W. Herrmann (Trans.). Cambridge: Cambridge University Press, 2011.

Seneca, L. A. (49 AD). *De Brevitate Vitæ* [On the shortness of life]. London: Penguin, 2000.

Sennett, R. (2008). *The Craftsman*. Yale, CT: Yale University Press.

Serres, M. (1977). Discorso e percorso. In: C. Lévi-Strauss (Ed.), *L'Identità* (pp. 25–49). Palermo: Sellerio, 1996.

Simmel, G. (1908). *The Stranger*. Chicago: University of Chicago Press.

Simmel, G. (1909). Bridge and door. *Theory, Culture & Society, February 1994* (11): 5–10.

Simmel, G. (1989). *Diario Postumo*. Turin: Nino Aragno, 2011.

Sivadon, P. (1968). Architecture psychiatrique. Principes. Tendences actuelles. In: *Encyclopédie Médico Chirurgicale, Psychiatrie, 37925 A* (10): 1–4.

Sivadon, P. (1969). Réalisations françaises d'architecture psychiatrique. In: *Encyclopédie Médico Chirurgicale, Psychiatrie, 37925 C* (10): 1–4.

Sivadon, P., & Gantheret, F. (1969). *La Rééducation Corporelle des Fonctions Mentales*. Paris: Editions Sociales Françaises.

Skármeta, A. (1986). *The Postman (Il Postino): A Novel*. K. Silver (Trans.). New York: Norton, 2008.

Solnit, R. (2000). *Wanderlust. A History of Walking*. New York: Viking.

Solnit, R. (2005). *A Field Guide to Getting Lost*. New York: Viking.

Sonnenberg, S. M. (1990). Introducing psychiatric residents to psychoanalysis: a visiting analyst's perspective. *Journal of the American Psychoanalytic Association, 38*: 451–469.

Sonnenberg, S. M. (1991). The analyst's self-analysis and its impact on clinical work: a comment on the sources and importance of personal insights. *Journal of the American Psychoanalytic Association, 39*: 687–704.

Sonnenberg, S. M. (1993a). Self-analysis, applied analysis, and analytic fieldwork: a discussion of methodology in psychoanalytic interdisciplinary research. *Psychoanalytic Study of Society, 18*: 443–463.

Sonnenberg, S. M. (1993b). To write or not to write: a note on self-analysis and the resistance to self-analysis. In: J. W. Barron (Ed.), *Self-Analysis: Critical Inquiries, Personal Visions* (pp. 241–259). Hillsdale, NJ: Analytic.

Sonnenberg, S. M. (1995). Analytic listening and the analyst's self-analysis. *International Journal of Psychoanalysis, 76*: 335–342.

Sonnenberg, S. M. (2005). What can psychoanalysis learn from an enhanced awareness of architecture and design? *Annual of Psychoanalysis, 33*: 39–56.

Sonnenberg, S. M. (2012). A psychoanalytic reflection on Berlin, the holocaust, and interdisciplinary research. In: E. A. Danze, & S. Sonnenberg (Eds.), *Center 17: Space & Psyche* (pp. 114–138). Austin, TX: University of Texas.

Sperber, E. (2013, October). Gender and Genius. *Lilith Magazine.* Retrieved from http://lilith.org/articles/gender-and-genius/ [last accessed 13 November 2015].

Sperber, E. (2014a). Site, incite, and insight—architecture and psychoanalysis: commentary on Leanne Domash's paper. *Psychoanalytic Perspectives, 11*: 122–132.

Sperber, E. (2014b). Sublimation: building or dwelling? Loewald, Freud, and architecture. *Psychoanalytic Psychology, 31*(4): 507–524.

Sperber, E. (2015, June 9). The Architecture of Psychotherapy. *New York Times.* Retrieved from http://opinionator.blogs.nytimes.com/2015/06/09/the-architecture-of-psychotherapy/?_r=0 [last accessed 10 June 2015].

Sperry, R. W. (1965). Mind, brain and humanist values. In: J. R. Platt (Ed.), *New Views of the Nature of Man* (pp. 71–92). Chicago, IL: University of Chicago Press.

Starobinski, J. (1966). Il concetto di nostalgia. In: A. Prete (Ed.), *Nostalgia. Storia di un Sentimento* (pp. 85–117). Milan: Cortina, 1992.

Starobinski, J. (1990). Les cheminées et les clochers. *Magazine Littéraire, 280*: 26–27.

Stein, R. (1995a). Analysis of a case of transsexualism. *Psychoanalytic Dialogues, 5*: 257–289.

Stein, R. (1995b). Reply to Chodorow. *Psychoanalytic Dialogues, 5*: 301–310.

Stern, D. B. (1985). Some controversies regarding constructivism and psychoanalysis. *Contemporary Psychoanalysis, 21*: 201–208.

Stokes, A. (1963). *Painting and the Inner World.* London: Routledge.

Stoppa, F. (1984). La funzione dello spazio come metafora nell'approccio alla psicosi. *Psicoterapia e Scienze Umane, 2*: 82–87.

Stoullig, C. (1995). Symbols and forms. In: H. Bellet, C. Stoullig, & E. A. Brown (Eds.), *Brancusi* (pp. 4–10). Paris: Beaux Arts Magazine.

Szymborska, W. (1993–1997). The Silence of Plants. In: *Poems. New and Collected. 1957–2007* (pp. 269–270). London: Harcourt, 2001.

Tanizaki, J. (1933). *In Praise of Shadows*. T. J. Harper, & E. G. Seidensticker (Trans.). Sedgwick, ME: Leete's Island, 1977.

Tarantelli, L. (2013). *Il Sogno che Uccise Mio Padre. Storia di Ezio Tarantelli che Voleva Lavoro per Tutti*. Milan: Rizzoli.

Terragni, A. (2013). *Daniel Libeskind. L'Architettura. I Protagonisti*. Rome: L'Espresso.

Thoreau, H. D. (1860). *Familiar Letters of Henry David Thoreau*. F. B. Sanborn (Ed.). Boston, MA: Houghton Mifflin, 2008.

Timosci, L. (1878). Relazione di accompagnamento. In: E. Maura & P. F. Peloso (Ed.) *Lo splendore della ragione. Tomo 2* (pp. 485–488). Genoa: La Clessidra.

Tironi, G. (2007). Arti dell'architettura e corpi smembrati. *Psiche, 2*: 39–59.

Todorov, T. (2002, November 11). Quando dico libertà. *La Repubblica*. Retrieved from www.repubblica.it/la-repubblica-delle-idee/societa/2013/07/04/news/todorov_quando_il_capolavoro_nasce_in_un_clima_di_terrore-62378755/ [last accessed 25 September 2015].

Tonietti, U. (2011). *L'Arte di Abitare la Terra*. Rome: L'Asino d'Oro.

Truppi, C. (2004). Intorno a *L'Anima dei luoghi*. In: J. Hillman, *L'Anima dei Luoghi* (pp. 105–134). *Conversazione con Carlo Truppi*. Milan: Rizzoli.

Tsvetaeva, M. (1934). Homesickness. In: *Selected Poems* (pp. 101–102). E. Feinstein (Trans.). London: Penguin, 1994.

Tutter, A. (2011a). Design as dream and self-representation: Philip Johnson and the Glass House of Atreus. *Journal of the American Psychoanalytic Association, 59*: 509–548.

Tutter, A. (2011b). The path of Phocion: disgrace and disawoval at the Philip Johnson Glass House. *American Imago, 68*: 449–488.

Tutter, A. (2012). A violent atomization. Attachment versus autonomy in the Philip Johnson Glass House. In: E. A. Danze, & S. Sonnenberg (Eds.), *Center 17: Space & Psyche* (pp. 47–73). Austin, TX: University of Texas.

Tuzi, T. (1990). L'idea di piazza nella cultura classica. In: M. Pisani & P. Portoghesi, *La Piazza come "Luogo degli Sguardi"* (pp. 229–241). Rome: Gangemi.

Twombly, R. (2005). Raumplan: Adolf Loos, Frank Lloyd Wright, residential space, and modernity. *Annual of Psychoanalysis, 33*: 191–205.

Tzara, T. (1933). D'un certain automatisme du goüt. *Minotaure, 3–4*: 81–84.

Ugolini, A. (2010). Ricomporre la rovina. Conservare la rovina. In: A. Ugolini (Ed.), *Ricomporre la Rovina* (pp. 13–17). Florence: Alinea.

Valéry, P. (1921). *Eupalinos or The Architect*. W. McCausland (Trans.). Oxford: Oxford University Press, 1932.

Valéry, P. (1928). La création artistique. Conférence donnée à la Société de Philosophie. *Vues*: 285–313. Paris: La table ronde, 1948.

Vassalli, G. (2001). The birth of psychoanalysis from the spirit of technique. *International Journal of Psychoanalysis, 82*(1): 3–25.

Vattimo, G. (1989). *The Transparent Society*. D. Webb (Trans.). Baltimore, MD: Johns Hopkins University Press, 1994

Vegetti Finzi, S. (2001). Corpo-macchina e soggettività femminile. In: M. Galzigna (Ed.), *Volti dell'Identità. Le Scienze Psichiche, l'Altro e lo Straniero* (pp. 56–70). Venice: Marsilio.

Venezia, F. (2011). *Che Cosa è l'Architettura. Lezioni, Conferenze, un Intervento*. Milan: Mondadori Electa.

Venezia, F. (2012). *Divertimento. Un'Interpretazione del Guggenheim Museum di F. Ll. Wright*. Genoa: Il Melangolo.

Venturi, R. (1966). *Complexity and Contradiction in Architecture*. New York: Museum of Modern Art, 1977.

Vidler, A. (1992). *The Architectural Uncanny: Essay in the Modern Unhomely*. Boston, MA: MIT.

Vidler, A. (2007). Foreword. In: G. Bruno. *Public Intimacy: Architecture and the Visual Arts* (pp. ix–xii). Boston, MA: MIT.

Virilio, P. (1984). *The Negative Horizon: An Essay in Dromoscopy*. M. Degener (Trans.). London: Continuum, 2008.

Virilio, P. (2005). Il mondo fragile. Interview with Daniel Binswanger. *Internazionale, 12*(573): 28–32.

Visetti, G. (2013, July 5). Cina. La casa grande come una città dove nascere, vivere e morire. *La Repubblica*. Retrieved from http://ricerca.repubblica.it/repubblica/archivio/repubblica/2013/07/05/cina-la-casa-grande-come-una-citta.html [last accessed 20 September 2014].

Vittorini, E. (1975). *Le Città del Mondo*. Turin: Einaudi.

Wallerstein, R. S. (1969). Introduction to panel on psychoanalysis and psychotherapy: the relationship of psychoanalysis to psychotherapy—current issues. *International Journal of Psycho-Analysis, 50*: 117–126.

Wallerstein, R. S. (1988). One psychoanalysis or many? *International Journal of Psychoanalysis, 69*: 5–21.

Wallerstein, R. S. (1990). Psychoanalysis: the common ground. *International Journal of Psychoanalysis, 71*: 3–20.

Wallerstein, R. S. (1997). Foreword. In: J. Sandler, A. Holde, C. Dare, & A. U. Dreher, *Freud's Models of the Mind: An Introduction* (pp. xiii–xvi). London: Karnac.

Widlöcher, D. (1999). Psicoanalisi e psicoterapie. *Rivista di Psicoanalisi, XLV*(1): 71–83.

Winer, J. A., Anderson, J. W., & Danze, E. A. (2005). Introduction. *Annual of Psychoanalysis, 33*: 1–6.

Winer, J. A., Anderson J. W., & Danze, E. A. (Eds.) (2006). *Psychoanalysis and Architecture.* Catskill, NY: Mental Health Resources.

Winnicott, D. W. (1947). Hate in the countertransference. In: *Through Paediatrics to Psychoanalysis. Collected Papers* (pp. 194–204). London: Karnac, 1975.

Winnicott, D. W. (1954). Metapsychological and clinical aspects of regression within the psychoanalytic set-up. In: *Through Paediatrics to Psychoanalysis. Collected Papers* (pp. 278–294). London: Karnac, 1975.

Winnicott, D. W. (1965). *The Maturational Processes and the Facilitating Environment: Studies in the Theory of Emotional Development.* London: Hogarth.

Winnicott, D. W. (1969). Berlin walls. In: C. Winnicott, R. Shepherd, & M. Davis (Eds.), *Home Is Where We Start From: Essays by a Psychoanalyst* (pp. 221–227). London: Karnac, 1989.

Winnicott, D. W. (1971). *Playing and Reality.* London: Routledge, 2005.

Wittgenstein, L. (1953). *Philosophical Investigations.* G. E. M. Anscombe (Trans.). Oxford: Blackwell, 2001.

Wolf, C. (1976). *Patterns of Childhood.* U. Molinaro, & H. Rappolt (Trans.). New York: Farrar, Straus, & Giroux, 1988.

Wolf, C. (1983). *Cassandra. A Novel and Four Essays.* J. van Heurck (Trans.). New York: Farrar, Straus, & Giroux, 1988.

Wolfe, T. (1981). *From Bauhaus to Our House.* New York: Farrar, Straus, & Giroux.

Wolfler Calvo, M. (2007). *Archigram-Metabolism. Utopie negli Anni '60.* Naples: Clean.

Woolf, V. (1929). *A Room of One's Own.* Orlando, FL: Harcourt.

Zagrebelsky, G. (2014). *Fondata sulla Cultura.* Turin: Einaudi.

Zavoli, S. (2011). *Il Ragazzo che Io Fui.* Milan: Mondadori.

Zumthor, P. (1999). *Thinking Architecture.* Basel: Birkhäuser.

Zumthor, P. (2006). *Atmospheres: Architectural Environments—Surrounding Objects.* Basel: Birkhäuser.

INDEX

For Product Safety Concerns and Information please contact our EU
representative GPSR@taylorandfrancis.com
Taylor & Francis Verlag GmbH, Kaufingerstraße 24, 80331 München, Germany

www.ingramcontent.com/pod-product-compliance
Lightning Source LLC
LaVergne TN
LVHW021119300926
849160LV00010B/779
* 9 7 8 1 7 8 2 2 0 4 1 1 4 *